PSYCHOLOGY & YOU

An informal introduction

3rd edition

Julia C. Berryman
University of Leicester

Elizabeth M. Ockleford
University of Leicester

Kevin Howells
University of Nottingham

David J. Hargreaves
Roehampton University

Diane J. Wildbur
De Montfort University

BPS Blackwell

BLACKWELL PUBLISHING
350 Main Street, Malden, MA 02148-5020, USA
9600 Garsington Road, Oxford OX4 2DQ, UK
550 Swanston Street, Carlton, Victoria 3053, Australia

First published 1987 by BPS Books, The British Psychological Society,
in association with Routledge.
Second edition published 1997 by BPS Books.
Third edition published 2006.

1   2006

Library of Congress Cataloging-in-Publication Data

Psychology & you : an informal introduction / by Julia C. Berryman . . . [et al.]. – 3rd ed.
p.   cm.
Includes bibliographical references and index.
ISBN-13: 978-1-4051-2698-4 (pbk. : alk. paper)
ISBN-10: 1-4051-2698-1 (pbk. : alk. paper)   1. Psychology.   I. Title: Psychology and you.
II. Berryman, Julia C.

BF121.P7995 2006
150–dc22
2006001716

A catalogue record for this title is available from the British Library.

Set in 10.5/12.5pt Photina
by Graphicraft Limited, Hong Kong
Printed and bound in Singapore
by C.O.S. Printers Pte Ltd

The publisher's policy is to use permanent paper from mills that operate a sustainable forestry
policy, and which has been manufactured from pulp processed using acid-free and elementary
chlorine-free practices. Furthermore, the publisher ensures that the text paper and cover
board used have met acceptable environmental accreditation standards.

For further information on
Blackwell Publishing, visit our website:
www.blackwellpublishing.com

PSYCHOLOGY & YOU

An informal introduction

3rd edition

UNIVERSITY OF
BRADFORD

Julia C. Berryman is a Chartered Psychologist, and Senior Lecturer in Psychology at the University of Leicester.

Elizabeth M. Ockleford is at the Department of Health Sciences and is Honorary Lecturer in Psychology at the University of Leicester, and Associate Lecturer at the Open University. She is a Chartered Psychologist.

Kevin Howells is a Chartered Clinical and Forensic Psychologist, and Professor in the School of Community Health Sciences at the University of Nottingham.

David J. Hargreaves is Professor of Education at Roehampton University.

Diane J. Wildbur is a Chartered Psychologist, and Lecturer in Psychology at De Montfort University, Leicester.

The British Psychological Society's free Research Digest e-mail service rounds up the latest research and relates it to your syllabus in a user-friendly way. To subscribe go to www.researchdigest.org.uk or send a blank e-mail to subscribe-rd@lists.bps.org.uk

Contents

Start reading this book at the point, chapter or sub-heading that interests you most. Each chapter is self-contained but refers you to other related chapters as appropriate. A glossary at the end defines all the technical terms. Recommended reading is given at the end of each chapter – this may be annotated where appropriate. References are also given at the end of the book. We hope that by dipping in here and there you will soon find that you have read the whole book.

Note on References	xii
List of Exercises	xiii
List of Figures	xiv
List of Tables	xvi
Preface and Acknowledgements to the Third Edition	xvii
1: INTRODUCTION: BEGINNING TO UNDERSTAND YOU	**1**
What is psychology?	2
Psychology and common sense	4
The psychologist's approach	7
Are psychologists devious experimenters?	8
The psychological experiment	8
What we expect affects what we see	10
Experiments are not enough	10

2: BODY LANGUAGE   13

Does body language come naturally?   14

Facial expressions   14

Gestures and postures   21

Odours as body language   24

Touching   25

Lies and deceit   26

Improving body language   27

3: YOUR PERSONALITY   29

Everyone has personality   30

It depends on your point of view   30

The trait approach   31

Eysenck's theory: three critical dimensions   32

From description to explanation   33

Am I me or am I the situation? The problem of consistency   36

Cognitive perspectives: it depends on how you look at it   38

Personal construct theory   38

Attribution: answering the question 'why?'   43

Attributions and psychological distress   44

Methods for assessing personality   46

4: YOUR SEX: ON BEING MALE OR FEMALE   48

Sex or gender?   49

Biological influences   49

Hormones and behaviour   49

Sex and gender identity   51

From birth to maturity   55

Are gender differences changing?   56

Gender differences in school and afterwards   59

5: YOU AND OTHERS   **62**

Social roles   63

What we do and what we think   64

Stereotypes and prejudice   65

How do others influence us?   69

Conformity   70

Obedience and authority   73

Violence and the mass media   74

The power of social influence   77

6: YOUR EMOTIONS   **79**

Love and attachment   81

The nature of infant love   82

Adult attachment and love   83

The nature of adult love   84

Types and styles of love   87

Anger and aggression   88

Aggression hot and cold   89

The nature of anger   90

What is a provocation?   91

Features of anger   92

Can we treat anger?   95

7: YOUR BRAIN   **97**

What's in your head?   98

How do we know which bits of brain do what?   102

Cells in the central nervous system   104

Two hemispheres, one brain   108

Feeling emotional   109

Consciousness   110

Repairing damage   112

8: YOUR HEALTH — 113

Psychology, health and illness — 114

Being healthy — 115

Preventing illness — 116

Becoming ill — 119

Being treated — 123

9: YOUR DEVELOPMENT ACROSS THE LIFESPAN — 126

Studying development — 127

Development in infancy — 128

'Theory of mind': perceiving emotions in others — 132

Language development — (133)

Social cognition in schoolchildren — 137

Adolescence and adulthood — 140

10: PSYCHOLOGICAL PROBLEMS — 144

Anxiety and related problems — 145

The complex nature of fear and anxiety — 147

Sources of phobias and anxiety — 147

The treatment of fear and anxiety — 149

Social anxiety — 150

Schizophrenia — 151

Personality disorders — 152

Keeping critical about methods of classification: some limitations of diagnostic systems for personality disorder — 155

11: YOUR VIEW OF THE WORLD: PERCEPTION AND THINKING — 159

Perception is more than sensation — 160

Attention affects perception — 164

Memory mechanisms — 166

Thinking and the nature of thoughts — 169

Differences in thinking and creativity — 172

12: LEARNING ABOUT YOUR WORLD 174

Learning by linking   175

Learning by consequences   178

Learning what to expect   180

Learning from others   182

Consciousness, intelligence and learning   183

13: YOU AND OTHER ANIMALS 189

Can other animals think?   190

Intelligence, tool-use and culture   192

Is language unique to humans?   194

Sensory sensitivity in other animals   195

Awareness and consciousness   196

Human uses of other animals   198

People with other animals   199

14: WHAT PSYCHOLOGISTS CAN DO – FOR YOU? 202

Becoming a psychologist   203

Teachers and researchers   203

Clinical and counselling psychologists   204

Health psychologists   206

Educational psychologists   207

Forensic psychologists   209

Occupational psychologists   211

Sport and exercise psychologists   211

Psychologists in other areas   212

Glossary   214

References   224

Index   237

Note on References

References are included at the end of the book. For ease of reading the text, we have not always cited the author of every study to which we have referred. However, should you want to find the source material, we have annotated each reference to indicate the parts of the text to which it is relevant. Thus we recommend that readers scan the annotations to references in a chapter in which a particular study of interest to them occurs. For example, Lorenz in Chapter 6 is not referenced directly but is included in the annotation to the Sluckin reference. Similarly, a quotation cited in the text, but not directly referenced, will be referred to in an annotation. We trust that this system will enable enthusiastic readers to follow up references, without making the book too heavy to read by citing numerous authors.

List of Exercises

2.1	*Gender differences in smiling*	17
2.2	*The sense of being stared at*	21
2.3	*Can you tell when someone is lying?*	27
3.1	*Explore your own construct system*	39
3.2	*Your attributional style*	44
3.3	*A group exercise*	45
4.1	*The portrayal of women and men in the media*	57
5.1	*Saying 'No'*	76
6.1	*Measuring passionate love*	86
6.2	*Analysing your own anger*	93
7.1	*Zombie thought experiment*	109
8.1	*Test your knowledge of medical terms*	121
9.1	*False beliefs: the Sally-Anne task*	134
10.1	*Is this 'Aggressive Personality Disorder'?*	153
11.1	*Thought and language*	169
12.1	*Classical conditioning*	177
12.2	*Memory, meaning and rhyme*	184
13.1	*How unique are humans?*	191

List of Figures

1.1	Sigmund Freud (1856–1939)	3
1.2	Albert Einstein (1879–1955). Are exceptionally intelligent people healthier than others?	6
2.1	What are these people feeling? (See p. 28 for the answer.)	15
2.2	Would you be able to say what the child on the left was feeling if the snake was not visible?	16
2.3	Emotions perceived from the eyes alone	18
2.4	Pupil size variations	19
2.5	Examples of posture mimicry	23
3.1	James's view of important people	42
4.1	The weaker sex?	50
4.2	Typical male and female body shapes	52
5.1	The use of stereotyped thinking against minority groups is termed 'prejudice'	68
5.2	David and Victoria Beckham	72
5.3	Princess Diana looking very slender	73
6.1	Imprinting	81
6.2	For most people, being loved and loving someone is central to their lives	87
7.1	The main lobes of the cerebral cortex and other important features of the brain	99
7.2	A diagram to show some of the structures that can be seen when the brain is sliced down the middle	100
7.3	London taxi driver. How much bigger is his hippocampus than most people's?	101
7.4	Neurosurgeon prepares patient for brain biopsy	103
7.5	Functional magnetic resonance imaging (fMRI) image(s) showing the effects of experiencing and imagining pain	103
7.6	A diagram of a typical neuron showing the cell body, axon and dendrites	105

7.7	The synaptic gap	106
7.8	The ascending reticular activating system in the brainstem responds to input from the eyes and ears	111
8.1	From novice to expert	123
9.1	Jean Piaget (1896–1980)	129
9.2	Berkeley California baby, ten months old, participating in 'visual cliff' experiment	130
9.3	The Sally-Anne task	134
9.4	Varieties of play in children	136
9.5	Co-operative learning	138
9.6	L. Vygotsky	139
11.1	Light enters the eye and is transformed by the retina into electrical signals that are transmitted to the brain	161
11.2	Patterns of dots that illustrate the principle of good form, or *prägnanz*	162
11.3	A version of the famous Ponzo illusion	163
11.4	Is it an 'H' or is it an 'A'?	163
11.5	The label associated with a figure affects your memory of the shape you have seen	171
12.1	Pavlov explained his dogs' salivation at the sound of a bell as being a result of their linking of the two stimuli	176
12.2	Skinner explored reinforcement in his box	179
12.3	Edward Tolman suggested that animals form 'cognitive maps' of their environments	181
13.1	Does this animal have self-awareness?	198
13.2	Humans can form close associations with other animals as companions or pets	200
14.1	Psychologists at work	207

List of Tables

2.1	Eye expressions	19
2.2a	Postures, gestures and their meaning	22
2.2b	Some common forms of emotional leakage	23
3.1	The Big 5: examples of traits	36
3.2	James's personal constructs	41
6.1	Love in adults	85
10.1	DSM personality disorders	154

Preface and Acknowledgements to the Third Edition

Psychology and You has been written with you, the reader, very much in mind. The purpose of this book is to introduce psychology in a lively and accessible way – linking the subject matter to people's everyday experiences. The original idea for the book came out of my experience of teaching psychology in the Department of Adult Education (now the Institute of Lifelong Learning), at the University of Leicester, UK. I became aware of the need for a broad-based introduction to the subject that introduced topics from the viewpoint of the reader, taking into account the everyday interests of the person rather than the needs of a particular course syllabus.

Most people have a grounding in subjects such as history, geography, mathematics and the physical sciences, but psychology, a subject of immediate relevance to us all, does not form a basic part of the school curriculum and it is surprisingly difficult to find a book that introduces psychology to adults in an up-to-date manner while also starting at the point that interests them. We have tried to bring together all the topics that our teaching experience has shown are intriguing and relevant to everyday life. We hope that this book will be the beginning of a life-long interest in psychology for you, and with this in mind we have included recommended reading and references. We also hope that all those who teach psychology will find the book a readable and accessible introduction for their students, and in particular the exercises helpful in stimulating interest in each topic. Psychologists have not found all the answers in their attempts to explain human behaviour, thoughts and feelings, but we hope that you, the reader, will find that the topics which we have considered will help you to enhance your understanding of yourself and of others.

In the third edition our intention has been to add new topics, to amend the text to bring in new developments and perspectives and to update the references and recommended reading throughout the book. New chapters have been added on the brain (see Chapter 7), and on health psychology (see Chapter 8), and more information has been provided on careers in psychology in the final chapter

(Chapter 14). Research methods are briefly outlined in Chapter 1 as in the second edition and also in boxes throughout the book rather than in the final chapter as in the previous edition. The extent to which each chapter has been updated varies according to the way in which each subject area has changed since the second edition. New exercises have also been included.

The following have all played a vital part in the preparation of this book. Firstly, the students whose questions and comments were the initial stimulus for producing this book. Secondly, our families who have played an invaluable role in supporting us in various ways while we researched and wrote the book. So particular thanks are due to Philip and Tom Drew, and Eric Berryman for their help, support and love; the Ockleford family, especially Colin for his encouragement, and Kirsty Bateman for her work on the illustrations for the second edition; to Linda, Jon and Tom Hargreaves, for their patience and support; to Marguerite Howells; and to Dave Wildbur, for caring. Thirdly, to those who assisted in the production of the book by supplying information on the working lives of psychologists: these are Julian Boon, Christine Cordle, Marc Jones and Roger Westerman. And finally, to the University of Leicester for the study leave period granted to the first author, part of which was used to work on this edition. Our sincere thanks to them all.

Julia C. Berryman

1

Introduction: Beginning to Understand You

- What is psychology?

- Psychology and common sense

- The psychologist's approach

- Are psychologists devious experimenters?

- The psychological experiment

- What we expect affects what we see

- Experiments are not enough

Have you ever puzzled over someone's actions and found yourself wanting to ask:

'Why did you do it?'
'What were you thinking?'
'How did you feel?'

If so, then you are posing the questions that psychologists also seek to answer – both at the level of the individual and also for people in general. What lies behind each person's behaviour, thoughts and feelings? Psychology can be defined as the study of behaviour, thoughts and feelings and this definition is encapsulated in our three questions. If we know someone well we expect to be able to predict what they will do, think, or feel in many everyday situations.

If a member of your family is slow to wake in the morning, but is bright-eyed at midnight, you soon learn to discuss important topics with that person in the evening rather than at breakfast. You come to expect him or her to eat little at breakfast, nod rather than talk, and through the experience of many mornings together you are able to predict a whole host of other things about that person's behaviour. In a sense, we are all amateur psychologists because we observe our relatives' and friends' behaviour carefully and discover rules by which they seem to act. This ability is not unique to adults. In a family it is likely that the children and the dog have also learned to make these predictions about each other. Have you ever noticed that your dog seems to know almost as soon as you do that you are going to take him for a walk?

Perhaps, you are thinking this is all just common sense. But we hope to show that psychology goes well beyond what can be answered by common sense. It is a subject that has developed a variety of methods to assist in answering questions about human behaviour, thoughts and feelings, and these methods are illustrated by boxed examples throughout this book.

WHAT IS PSYCHOLOGY?

What does psychology mean to you? When people who have not studied the subject are asked to say what comes into their mind when the words 'psychology' or 'psychologists' are mentioned, a whole ragbag of answers is given:

'Psychologists know what you are thinking.'
'They analyse you like Freud did.'
'They measure IQ and personality.'
'Psychologists deal with problems like phobias and depression.'
'They use lie detectors.'
'They do devious experiments.'

The commonest answers deal with uncovering the hidden aspects of people and their psychological problems and, as these answers show, there is often more than a certain wariness about psychologists and their profession. Sigmund Freud's name is often mentioned in connection with psychology, and his ideas have certainly influenced psychologists. But what did he actually do?

Was Freud a psychologist?

Sigmund Freud (1856–1939), often referred to as 'the father of psychoanalysis', was not a psychologist. Freud was a Viennese physician who became interested in the role of unconscious mental processes in influencing people's behaviour and, in particular, their psychological problems. He was interested in exploring human behaviour, feelings and thoughts, but his ideas were based on his clinical work. He built up a view of what makes humans 'tick' from his deductions about the causes of the problems he saw in his patients. Thus his view of human nature was shaped by observing and trying to help those who had problems; he was not concerned with the 'normal' or average person, but just a small number of rather unhappy people.

Essentially, Freud believed that a large part of the mind is unconscious, and that our behaviour is 'driven' by instincts housed in this unconscious area of the mind. The expression of these instincts is, he suggested, shaped by our early life experiences: so, for example, a person who is deprived of adequate breast feeding, or mother love, might later show neurotic patterns of behaviour, such as a craving for comfort, food or love.

In attempting to find the causes of psychological problems, Freud's approach, in psychoanalytic therapy, was to use a variety of techniques that were intended to give insights into a person's unconscious mental processes. Two of these techniques were free association and dream analysis. In the former, a patient would lie on a couch and be asked to say freely whatever thoughts or feelings came to mind; in dream analysis the contents of the patient's dreams were explored using free association with a dream event as the initial stimulus. Freud believed that these techniques led him to the source of a patient's problems, and, by bringing that source out into the open, into conscious awareness, the emotional release (or catharsis) induced would assist in helping the patient towards a solution of the problem.

But being based on clinical evidence, which is open to a variety of interpretations, Freud's ideas cannot easily be tested or verified in the way that modern psychologists believe to be essential. So although Freud's views of the human mind and behaviour have influenced psychological thinking, they are not, as we shall see, central to it.

Figure 1.1   Sigmund Freud (1856–1939). *(Science Photo Library.)*

Three different approaches

The distinction between psychoanalysis, psychiatry and psychology needs to be clarified, because it is not a simple one. Psychiatry is a branch of medicine and, as such, psychiatrists are concerned largely with the treatment of mental illnesses and psychological problems. Any qualified medical doctor may choose to specialize and take a further qualification in psychiatry, just as he or she might select gynaecology or surgery. Psychiatrists, like medical doctors (or general practitioners), may use drugs in the treatment of mental illness, or they may use other methods such as behaviour therapy – a technique also used by psychologists.

Psychologists train by taking a degree course in psychology in which all aspects of behaviour and its underlying causes – in both humans and other animals – are studied. One distinction between psychologists, psychiatrists and psychoanalysts is that the former are concerned with all people, while the latter two are concerned solely with those who cannot cope, and who are unwell. Clinical psychologists, however, also make the patient the main focus of their work, but the treatment methods used by them involve therapies that do not rely on the prescription of drugs.

Psychoanalysts have their own training, which is quite separate from that of both psychologists and psychiatrists. This training usually involves the would-be analysts first undergoing psychoanalysis themselves in order to gain increased insight. Psychologists and psychiatrists sometimes undergo further training in order to become psychoanalysts, and thus it is perhaps not surprising that there is sometimes confusion in the minds of the public about these three professions.

In this book we are concerned with psychology, which has developed its own rigorous methods of studying humans, quite distinct from the techniques of psychoanalysis. Indeed, at the height of Freud's influence at the turn of the century, psychologists showed a marked disregard for subjective reports of mental processes (introspection) as the major source of data. Overt behaviour became the focus of attention and psychology became known as the 'science of behaviour'; thoughts and feelings were largely ignored, being intangible and unobservable. Speculations about the causes of human behaviour based on introspection were thought to be unhelpful and misleading.

PSYCHOLOGY AND COMMON SENSE

Psychologists are often said to be studying the obvious, spending years trying to find the answers to questions that common sense can tell us. We, as psychologists, believe this to be an unfair comment, and to test your common sense we should like you to answer the following questions using just your own ideas – please don't refer to books to find the answers.

Question 1

How long do dreams last? In *A Midsummer Night's Dream* (I.i), Lysander says that true love is 'brief' and 'momentary', like a dream. Do dreams really come and go in an instant as Shakespeare apparently believed? Do you think a typical dream lasts:

(a)   a fraction of a second;
(b)   a few seconds;
(c)   a minute or two;
(d)   many minutes;
(e)   a few hours?

Take a bonus point for correctly answering the following question about yourself. How often do you dream?

(f)   hardly ever or never;
(g)   about once every few nights;
(h)   about once a night;
(i)   several times every night.

Question 2

On a trip to the local supermarket with Fred, Georgina came across two brands of canned kidney beans. One of the cans was twice as wide and twice as deep as the other, but to Georgina's surprise they were similarly priced, and the labels showed that they both weighed 250 grams. 'There's probably more water in the smaller one,' she thought. She decided to play a little trick on Fred. She moved the self-adhesive price tags so as to cover the weights that were marked on the labels, and she then showed the cans to Fred. 'Fred Darling,' she said, 'I've got a problem. Are you any good at judging weights?' 'I am rather, and I can tell you've lost a bit of weight,' replied Fred, playfully lifting Georgina off the ground. 'I'm not sure which of these two cans of kidney beans is heavier,' she lied. 'What do you think? Take your time feeling them.' After lifting the cans and holding them for a while, what did Fred probably reply?

(a)   the smaller can feels slightly heavier;
(b)   the smaller can feels much heavier;
(c)   the larger can feels slightly heavier;
(d)   the larger can feels much heavier;
(e)   neither can feels noticeably heavier than the other.

Question 3

Chapter 9 of the Gospel According to St John in the Bible is devoted entirely to an episode in which Jesus restored the sight of a man 'which was blind from his birth'. More recently, surgical, rather than miraculous, methods have occasionally been used to restore the sight, late in life, of people born blind. During the first few days after the bandages are removed, do you think such people:

(a) see nothing at all;
(b) see only a blur;
(c) see only vague shapes moving about;
(d) recognize familiar objects without touching them;
(e) recognize objects by sight only after touching and looking at them simultaneously;
(f) see everything upside down?

Question 4

A group of friends decided to put some money into a kitty and spend it at the race track on Derby Day. Before each race they wrote down their private opinions about the bet that ought to be placed. Then the group assembled to discuss their individual opinions and to arrive at a group decision. On each race, the most cautious decision was not to place a bet at all, a more risky decision was to place a small bet on a horse with favourite odds of winning, and a very risky decision was to place a large bet on an outsider. Compared to the average of the individual decisions, are the group decisions likely to have been:

(a) more cautious;
(b) more risky;
(c) neither more cautious nor more risky?

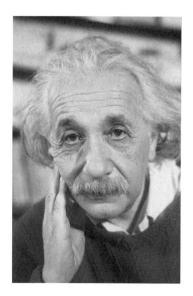

Figure 1.2 Albert Einstein (1879–1955). Are exceptionally intelligent people healthier than others?
(*Popperfoto/Alamy.*)

Question 5

The influential philosopher Friedrich Nietzsche (1844–1900) suffered from insanity and general ill-health for the last 20 years of his life. The great physicist Albert Einstein (1879–1955), on the other hand was quite sane and enjoyed good health through most of his three score years and sixteen. Are exceptionally intelligent people in general:

(a) less physically and mentally healthy than others;
(b) more physically and mentally healthy than others;
(c) similar to others in physical and mental health;
(d) less mentally healthy but similar to others in physical health;
(e) less physically healthy but similar to others in mental health?

You will find the answers on pages 11–12.

6

THE PSYCHOLOGIST'S APPROACH

Today psychologists base their conclusions about humans on both observations of the behaviour of many people, and reports from those people themselves. It is more than the 'science of behaviour', because people's own unique experiences also form part of the data.

Psychologists use a wide range of equipment to measure both easily observable and unobservable bodily changes. The well-known lie detector or polygraph is one example: this measures a variety of physiological changes, including heart rate and skin moistness, but psychologists would rarely use this to detect lies. Indeed, most psychologists are well aware of its fallibility in this respect. What is fascinating about the polygraph is that it can reveal minute changes in emotional arousal.

Read the following words:

- COMPUTER
- ROSE
- BAR
- MOTHER
- TEAPOT
- PENCIL
- SEX
- CAR
- BABY
- WINDOW

Did you detect any change in emotional level in yourself as you read them? Probably not. But a polygraph would reveal that certain words are more emotionally loaded for some people than are others. Mother, baby and sex might mean much more to you than the other words because they obviously stand for things about which many people are emotional. But if you have a friend called ROSE, or you had just bought a brand new CAR, then these words might also be emotionally loaded words for you, and this would show on the polygraph reading. Thus the polygraph can give us more information about someone's emotions than they can themselves.

The study of human behaviour, thought and emotion over many years has enabled psychologists to see how certain psychological problems may arise, and how they may be treated; by charting human behaviour, patterns emerge that enable predictions to be made about the frequency with which one event may follow on another. While there is also much to learn, there is already quite a lot that psychologists can predict about human behaviour and hence the measurement of personality and intelligence is in part, if not in total, a reality, as the contents of Chapters 3 and 12 will show.

ARE PSYCHOLOGISTS DEVIOUS EXPERIMENTERS?

Psychologists are sometimes charged with doing rather devious experiments. In the past this assertion was probably quite fair in relation to a small proportion of psychological studies and, later in this book (Chapter 5, for example), there are examples of such experiments. A certain degree of control over events under study is necessary in the initial stages of studying people, and there are good reasons for this. For example, if psychologists wish to study the effect of a substance on some aspect of human psychology or behaviour, then they must test it in such a way that the people taking part in the experiment do not know whether they are receiving the substance or not.

THE PSYCHOLOGICAL EXPERIMENT

In order to illustrate the care that psychologists must take in planning experiments, an experiment carried out by Winnifred Cutler and colleagues will be described. Research in some non-human mammals has indicated that female reproductive physiology can be affected by odours (chemical signals) from males. Cutler's research investigated this possibility in human females and this research explored the role of underarm (axillary) secretions and the menstrual cycle. See Box 1.1, which explains some technical terms that psychologists use.

Having selected a particular sample of women to act as participants, and having decided what aspects of the menstrual cycle would be measured (in this case menstrual cycle length and regularity over a number of cycles), the aim was to compare individuals who received a given dose of chemical substance (male secretions) – the experimental group – with those who received no dose – the control group. The problem was to ensure that the people did not know whether or not they were receiving the substance, despite the fact that participants had to consent to take part in the study and be aware that some substance might be used. (There are numerous regulations, or ethical guidelines, concerning these latter points that we need not consider here.)

Psychologists solve this problem by using a placebo, an inert substance that can be administered in exactly the same way as the substance under investigation. In this study, the placebo was ethanol that was given alone or with the chemical substance (the male secretions) mixed into it without being detectable. Participants in the experiment were assigned at random to the experimental (male secretions) and control (placebo) conditions, and each received identical treatment – both groups had the substance or placebo placed on the upper lip and were told not to wash the area for six hours. This treatment was carried out three times a week for about 14 weeks. The pulse and blood pressure of each participant were also recorded at each treatment to dilute the focus of the study. Details of menstrual cycles during this period were recorded.

BOX 1.1
VARIABLES IN PSYCHOLOGICAL EXPERIMENTS

The psychological experiment described in this chapter illustrates one form of a typical experiment in psychology. The experiment was designed to answer a specific question: 'Do underarm (axillary) secretions from human males influence menstrual cycle length and regularity in females?' It included an experimental group in which the chemical secretions in ethanol, the independent variable, were administered to the participants, and a control group in which the participants received a placebo, ethanol alone, instead of ethanol plus axillary secretions. The independent variable is so called because it is the variable the psychologist chooses to manipulate. The thing (behaviour, emotion, thought etc.) measured following the treatment, in this case menstrual cycle length and regularity, is called the dependent variable because it is assumed to be dependent on the treatment the experimental group receives. A comparison of the menstrual cycles of women in the experimental and control groups enables the psychologist to measure the effect of male secretions; the experiment was planned so that the only difference between the groups was the presence or absence of the male secretions, and the control group provided a baseline level of response with which the effects of the secretions can be compared. A control group of this kind is not always essential in the design of an experiment. In some cases the psychologist may simply use two or more dose levels of the independent variable (in this case male secretions), because these also enable a comparison to be made between differently dosed groups.

As we have said, the participants were unaware of, or blind, to the nature of the study (the effect of male secretions on the menstrual cycle), and the technician administering the experimental substance/placebo was also blind to the purpose of the study. Thus we say that the study was double-blind.

Participants who know the nature of a study may be sceptical about the outcome, or indeed convinced that a particular outcome may occur and be concerned to demonstrate this outcome. Sometimes the very fact of taking part in the research can have effects on participants, even in the placebo group.

To return to the experiment, the researchers did find that male secretions had an effect on female menstrual pattern by producing a reduction in the proportion of aberrant (or unusual) length cycles within the 14 weeks of treatment. This suggests that prolonged exposure to male axillary secretions may alter the female endocrine system. See Chapter 2 for more discussion.

WHAT WE EXPECT AFFECTS WHAT WE SEE

Our beliefs about things can have quite a dramatic effect on us and everyday experience can confirm this. It is generally agreed that there are no scientifically proven aphrodisiacs, for instance, and yet many people firmly believe that they know of such substances. Providing that their belief is not disturbed, it is likely that the substance will 'work' for them. The psychologist must always be aware that if he or she seeks to investigate any aspect of humans, the expectations of those humans must be taken into account and, if necessary, controlled for in a study such as the male secretions study just described.

Perhaps all this control seems ludicrously contrived, but another example may serve to show how necessary such procedures are. Parents will often assert that they always treated their children in the same way, regardless of their sex. Yet, psychological research has shown that parents' treatment, or descriptions, of babies vary greatly as a function of the sex of the infant.

In a study we carried out, a 9-month-old baby was filmed with its mother. We showed the film to groups of people who were asked to make an assessment of the baby (its behaviour, appearance, healthiness etc.), but to some groups we said, 'This baby is a little boy called John,' and to others we said, 'This baby is a little girl called Mary.' We found that on measures such as activity, fidgetiness, appearance and weight estimates, the 'boy' baby and 'girl' baby were consistently described differently. (Don't forget the baby was the same throughout.) For example, the 'boy' was seen as more active and more fidgety. Other studies show similar findings, and they reveal how easy it is for our judgements to be shaped by our preconceptions.

EXPERIMENTS ARE NOT ENOUGH

The studies described indicate just one way in which psychologists can control events in order to study human behaviour, but there are many other methods that psychologists use. Perhaps you will have realized already that the experimental method cannot be applied to just any area we want to investigate. Indeed, our discussion of the differences parents report in boy and girl babies is a case in point. We cannot assign sex to one group and not another in order to investigate how 'sex' influences behaviour. We all have a biological sex – no one is truly neutral – and thus in exploring sex differences all we can do is correlate observed behaviour with one sex or the other. If we observe that males have shorter hair than females (i.e. short hair and maleness are positively correlated), or that males cry less or fight more than females, we are not justified in saying that biological sex per se caused these differences.

Correlational studies provide useful information for the psychologist, as we shall see, but these studies outlined above are only two examples of a number of techniques psychologists have for investigating feelings, thoughts and emotions. Many more of these methods are covered in boxes throughout this book.

A lot of people find methodology difficult to understand fully until they have more idea of the questions and problems psychologists are seeking to understand. For this reason we shall discuss lots of examples of the psychologist's work first and then illustrate some of these examples, to show particular methods used in research, in boxes throughout the book.

What next?

The following chapters cover a range of topics that have been found to be of particular interest to those seeking to understand more about behaviour, emotion and cognition. The next chapter looks at a type of behaviour with which we are all very familiar – body language.

Recommended Reading

Colman, A.M. (1999). *What Is Psychology?* London: Routledge. [N.B. This book gives full details of the five questions and answers posed in this chapter and includes many more questions and answers.]

Answers to questions posed in 'Psychology and Common Sense'

1.(d,i) Score one point for realizing that a typical dream lasts many minutes (generally about 20 minutes), and take a bonus point for knowing that you dream several times every night (everyone does). You may think that you dream much less than this, because you probably only remember fragments of dreams that occur just before you wake up. Dream researchers made these discoveries while studying sleepers, recording their brain waves by sticking tiny electrodes onto their heads. The electrodes reveal characteristic patterns of electrical activity in the brain during dream sleep. Dreaming coincides with this brain activity (sleepers woken during the brain activity report dreaming), with rapid eye movements beneath closed eyelids (REM sleep), and, in men, with penile erection. Dream events appear to last about as long as the same events in waking life. Studies have demonstrated the universality of dreaming, and these answers could not have been found by introspection alone.

2.(b) Score one point. Fred is almost certain to have thought that the smaller can felt much heavier than the larger one. The illustration is reliable and startlingly powerful. Experiments have shown that when two objects are of equal weight but one is markedly larger than the other, about 98 per cent of people judge the smaller object to be much heavier than the larger one and feel certain that they are right.

3.(d) Score one point. People whose blindness is cured late in life are able to recognize familiar objects without touching them. This question has been debated since the seventeenth century, but it was not satisfactorily resolved until psychologists investigated it carefully in the 1960s and 1970s. Studies of a number of

11

individuals who were born blind, but had their sight restored late in life, confirmed this finding.

4.(b) Score one point. The group decisions are likely to have been riskier than the average of the individual decisions. This is an example of the group polarization phenomenon. Although the phenomenon is strongly counter-intuitive, it is robust and easily exhibited in classroom demonstrations. A special case of group polarization (discussed in Chapter 5), called the risky shift, was discovered by two independent researchers in the late 1950s and early 1960s. Using quite different methods both researchers showed that group decisions tend, in general, to be riskier than individual decisions. Two hypotheses have been used to explain this. One states that during group discussions most group members are likely to discover that there are others present whose decisions, individually, are riskier than their own. Because people in general admire risk, the more cautious will then change their decision. The other debate suggests that the more risky arguments are more likely to be aired in a group discussion (again because riskiness is admired), and hence others will be persuaded by these arguments.

5.(b) Score one point. Exceptionally intelligent people are in general physically and mentally healthier than others. The evidence for this comes from various sources, including a continuing study initiated by the American psychologist Lewis Terman in the early 1920s of over fifteen hundred exceptionally intelligent children.

Terman's gifted sample – the 'termites' as they came to call themselves – were selected from the Californian school system in 1921. All had IQs above 135, which put them in the top 1 per cent of the population intellectually. Their ages at the beginning of the study ranged from 3 to 19 years. They were assessed on a variety of psychological tests and were also examined physically, and the sample was retested many times again until 1982. The researchers found that the physical and mental health of the 'termites', both male and female, remained 'good' to 'very good' compared with the rest of the population throughout this time.

Comment: How did you score? If you scored six points this is exceptionally good – but we cannot think how you did it, unless you have already read quite a lot of psychology. If you truly are a beginner in psychology, we predict a score of one or two because we think you could not possibly work out these answers purely on the basis of common sense. These questions are taken from Andrew Colman's book What Is Psychology? and if you are intrigued by them, we recommend you read this book (see Recommended Reading), which is full of lots more questions of this type.

2

Body Language

- Does body language come naturally?

- Facial expressions

- Gestures and postures

- Odours as body language

- Touching

- Lies and deceit

- Improving body language

Body language, or non-verbal communication as it is also known, encompasses any cues that are 'not words'; thus tones of voice, non-verbal sounds, facial expressions, postures, odours and touch are all examples of body language. Our body language can have a very powerful influence on others. Indeed, psychologists have found that where listeners feel there is a conflict between someone's words and their body language, they are five times more likely to rely on the latter.

DOES BODY LANGUAGE COME NATURALLY?

There are both innate and learned elements in body language signals. Unlearned signals such as turning pale, or goose pimples, are involuntary responses controlled by the sympathetic part of the autonomic nervous system over which we have no conscious control. They are a result of the automatic flight or fight reaction of the body, in which blood is redirected to the muscles from the surface capillaries through the action of the hormone adrenaline.

Voluntary signals include those we learn, without being aware of it, probably very early in life, together with those we actively choose to display. An example of the first might be the use of touch in social interactions, and of the second our mode of greeting another. Edward Hall reported that Arabs touch each other much more and stand closer to friends than Americans do, and that even when Americans are made aware of this difference they find it difficult to adapt to this style of interacting. These 'rules' of social interaction appear to be learned early in life and are very resistant to change. Different modes of greeting have been discussed by Michael Argyle in his book Bodily Communication. He noted that Lapps smell each other's cheeks and rub noses, Polynesians stroke each other's faces, Arabs embrace, Japanese bow, and the British may just make a slight nod or jerk of the head. Without knowing these forms of greeting, it is clear that the scope for spoiling a potential friendship, or causing offence, is enormous.

This chapter can cover only selected areas, and concentrates on visual signals – as people tend to be most aware of these; touch and smell are discussed briefly and signs of deception are also considered.

FACIAL EXPRESSIONS

In general, we view the face as the most important part of the body for conveying information about emotions – psychologists call this facial primacy – because the face is felt to be the primary source of information about feelings and attitudes. Studies of the face indicate that, despite the enormous number of possible facial expressions we can display (for instance, one hundred different types of smile have been identified), there are only about six or seven expressions that we can identify reliably from the still face.

Six readily recognized emotions are 'happiness', 'fear', 'disgust', 'anger', 'surprise' and 'sadness'. There has been much debate over whether these facial expressions are universal, as Charles Darwin originally suggested, but this view is now generally accepted. However, as Paul Ekman points out, 'Most people manage their expressions, and these public display rules are socially learned and culturally variable.'

Context and display rules

Our interpretation of the face depends in part on the context in which the expression occurs. Often, without realizing it, we use the context to help us decode the expression (see Figures 2.1 and 2.2). Can you guess what the people in Figure 2.1 are feeling in the absence of a context, and in Figure 2.2 would you be able to say what the child on the left was feeling if the snake was not visible?

Another point to consider, as we have seen, is that different societies have different 'display rules'. Paul Ekman and Wallace Friesen in 1969 described four types of display rules: those concerned with 'de-intensifying' the emotion; 'neutralizing' the emotion, 'overintensification' of the emotion and 'masking' the emotion. Thus boys or men may be expected to mask their distress if they want to cry, having fallen

Figure 2.1   What are these people feeling? (See p. 28 for the answer.) (© *Empics.*)

Figure 2.2   Would you be able to say what the child on the left was feeling if the snake was not visible? *(Photo © Philip Jones Griffiths/Magnum Photos.)*

over in the street, but in a football match they may show 'overintensification' when hurt by an opposing player.

Facial expressions may change so rapidly that observers are unable to identify an emotion even though they have observed the face change. Research shows that facial changes that last longer than two-fifths of a second can be registered by an observer, but cannot be identified unless they last about half a second or more. Videotapes of faces show that in some cases many different emotions appear to be expressed in the face, some lasting as little as one-fifteenth of a second, but these are not seen by the observer except in slow-motion film. These 'micro expressions' generally occur when an emotion is concealed.

Facial expressions are not always of a pure or single emotion. The face can convey blends of emotions (affect blends) that also make interpretation more complex. One example might be a smile with the mouth that is not also conveyed by the eyes or other facial features.

The smile

Genuine smiles involve the muscles at the corners of the eyes, making 'crow's feet', and without these, the smile lacks authenticity and the message given may be a blend of several, possibly conflicting, emotions.

The smile is an unlearned facial expression and occurs in babies from about 6 weeks of age. Nevertheless, display rules for smiles vary across genders and

16

EXERCISE 2.1
GENDER DIFFERENCES IN SMILING

Collect a selection of newspapers and magazines that contain a reasonable number of photographs. Taking the first newspaper or magazine, look at each photo and note whether the males and/or females in each picture are smiling or not, keeping a record as you go. Do not omit any photos; simply take consecutive ones. When you have found photos of 50 males and females (you must have an equal number of each) calculate the percentage of both males and females smiling. Repeat for several other newspapers and magazines. Does smiling vary by gender? Does the type of newspaper or magazine influence this?

cultures. Women smile more than men and are more expressive than men in general (see Exercise 2.1 to explore this further). Leslie Brody notes that women are encouraged to express emotions such as warmth and cheerfulness, unlike men, who are more likely to express anger, and argues that men in more individualistic cultures tend to suppress their emotions so as not to appear weak.

It is suggested that smiling, even when someone is not inclined to do so, may be therapeutic. According to the 'facial feedback hypothesis', smiling can activate the corresponding emotion of happiness and joy. Thus putting on a happy face may actually improve your mood!

The eyes

Look into a person's pupils; he cannot hide himself.

Confucius (551–478 BC)

Eyes can give us away and reveal our innermost thoughts and we often distrust those who are shifty and won't look at us. In many cultures, eye contact is a vital element in social interaction and others are judged according to how they use their eyes. Nevertheless, there are clear cultural differences in how eye contact is used.

Cultural differences in eye behaviour

In the West, eye contact is important when people talk to each other, but it is even more important to Arabs, according to Edward Hall, who apparently do not feel comfortable talking when walking side by side. Face-to-face contact (and even breath contact) is viewed as important in a proper conversation. In contrast, the Japanese look at each other rather less than Westerners do, when in conversation. Once brief eye contact has been made, they are more likely to allow their eyes to rest on the other person's neck than to continue to look at the eyes or mouth as we do in the West.

Use of the eyes has come to be associated with particular qualities. Modesty is revealed in downward glances, interest, delight or amazement in wide eyes, craftiness in narrowed eyes, and staring is seen as an indication of aggression. But again we must be careful not to impose our own culture's norms on others.

Eye expressions

The eye itself can only reveal a small number of emotions if we separate it from the rest of the face (including the eyebrows). Paul Ekman and Wallace Friesen studied eye expressions and reported the appearance of the eyes for six common emotions. If the eyebrows were to be added to the eyes, detection of some of these emotions would be easier. In particular, anger and disgust are revealed in eyebrow movements. Other studies suggest that only pleasure, anger and surprise (or combinations of these) are accurately identified by the eyes alone (see Figure 2.3 and Table 2.1).

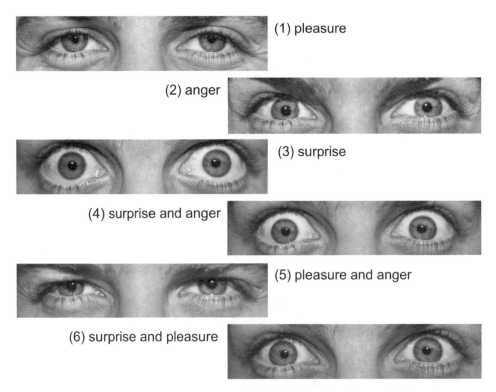

Figure 2.3 Emotions perceived from the eyes alone. *(Cordelia Molloy/Science Photo Library.)*

Table 2.1   Eye expressions (from Paul Ekman and Wallace Friesen, 1975)

1. Happiness	Wrinkles are found below the lower eye lid and crow's feet at the corners of the eye.
2. Sadness	The upper eyelids' corners may be raised due to the inner corners of the eyebrows being raised.
3. Surprise	Upper eyelids raised, white showing above and possibly below the eye.
4. Fear	Upper eyelid raised, white showing above the eye, lower eyelid drawing up and tense.
5. Disgust	Upper eyelid lowered, lines show below lower eyelid which is pushed up but not tense.
6. Anger	Eyes may appear bulging. Upper and lower eyelids are both tense, the upper lid may be lowered due to the brows being lowered and the lower lid may be raised. Eyelids may not show these patterns.

Pupil size

Psychologists have shown that we can give ourselves away, or reveal our emotions, via the change in size of our pupils. Pupils can dilate by approximately 6 millimetres, from as little as 2 millimetres up to 8 millimetres (see Figure 2.4).

Eckhard Hess was among the first to point out that pupil size reveals our emotional state and is not merely an indication of the level of illumination. In general, dilated pupils are a sign of emotional arousal, interest and attraction, a sign

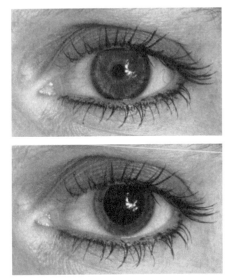

Figure 2.4   Pupil size variations. *(Eric Crichton Photos.)*

19

that we like what we are looking at. Thus, our eyes will 'dilate' when we look at someone we find attractive but, they will also dilate in response to other things that we like, such as babies, favourite foods, paintings and so on.

The change in pupil size is only momentary, and most of us are not even aware it is occurring, although Arabs seem to have been aware of this long before the research of Eckhard Hess in the 1960s. They screen their eyes when trading so as not to show too much interest in the goods they hope to purchase. Perhaps we should all keep this in mind when trying to strike a bargain!

Gaze and mutual gaze

Observe people in a café or restaurant, note who looks at whom, and for how long eye contact with another is maintained. Eye-to-eye contact, or mutual gaze, rarely lasts for long but it is continually made and broken by those who are talking or listening to each other. Gaze behaviour, the way we use our eyes, our 'looking behaviour', reveals much about the nature of the relationships between people. Returning to our café or restaurant, it is often said that married couples look at each other much less than those at an early stage in the 'pairing' process. Their lack of mutual gaze reveals their more established and settled status.

Adam Kendon suggests that gaze behaviour has four functions. The first is regulating communication: we show that we want communication to begin by trying to make visual contact, and, in the same way we avoid such contact to end, or avoid making, an interaction. Political candidates waiting hopefully at a polling station can tell whom of their usual voters are now voting for someone else because they avoid their eyes.

Monitoring feedback is also a key aspect of gaze behaviour – we find out how other people are reacting by looking at them. Cognitive activity is also revealed by gaze. Gaze aversion often occurs when we are thinking or trying to work something out. Gwyneth Doherty-Sneddon reports that children avert their gaze when thinking, and this seems to aid them with the task in hand.

Lastly, gaze behaviour is expressive; we reveal our feelings or emotions as we saw in the section on eye expressions and pupil size.

Gaze patterns

How does gaze behaviour reveal the regulatory and monitoring function described? If we observe how people use their eyes in interactions, what does it tell us about them as people?

One of the key aspects of an individual revealed through gaze is dominance: the power people feel they have in a particular context. A person who feels dominant uses less gaze, but someone trying to establish dominance is likely to use more gaze; people who feel themselves to be subordinate to those with whom they are interacting are likely to use more gaze in the interaction. It appears that the need to monitor the person is greater for the subordinate – the higher the status of an individual the less need they may feel to observe the behaviour of subordinates.

EXERCISE 2.2
THE SENSE OF BEING STARED AT

There is much scepticism about this topic and Rupert Sheldrake reports that researchers have worked on this since the 1890s with varying results. Try Sheldrake's method for assessing this experimentally. You will need at least one willing partner, but several pairs of people would be better. Designate one person in the pair as the starer and a one as the participant. Arrange two chairs one behind the other with the participant in front facing forward. The starer uses a coin and tosses it to decide whether or not to look on a given trial; for example, heads means looking at the participant's neck, while tails means looking away. The starer indicates when the trial is beginning by giving a sound signal, and care must be taken to make looking and non-looking trials identical in all but this respect. The participant should be allowed about 10 seconds to guess. The starer records the type of trial – looking or not looking – and records whether the participant was right or wrong. The participant can be told whether the guess was correct. Repeat this for at least 50 trials. If the participant is guessing at random she or he would be right on average 50 per cent of the time. Calculate the success rate. Over a very large number of trials Sheldrake found a statistically significant success rate of 55 per cent, and that some participants achieve a much better result than others.

Nancy Henley points out that gaze behaviour differs noticeably in women and men. Women tend to display behaviour like that of the subordinate, and men show dominance in their use of gaze. She argues that 'nonverbal behaviour is a major avenue of social control on a large scale, and interpersonal dominance on a smaller scale'.

In conversation, the listener generally looks at the speaker for proportionally longer (75 per cent and 40 per cent respectively), and mutual gaze (simultaneous looking) occurs for only a small part of this time. Liking and trust between those conversing gives rise to increased gaze, whereas gaze is reduced when emotionally sensitive topics are discussed.

Finally, Rupert Sheldrake suggests that the impact of being looked at is so potent that we have a sense of being stared at by those outside our visual field. He believes he has evidence that people can detect at higher than chance levels when someone is looking at them from behind (see Exercise 2.2 to try this out).

GESTURES AND POSTURES

The face is not the only part of the body to reveal emotions; other parts of the body also signal our emotions and attitudes. The term emotional leakage has been used to describe these signals found in the body below head level; as this term implies, emotions not revealed in the face may leak out elsewhere. Those in public life often have large lecterns or desks in front of them as much for protection and security as for their notes, since these barriers also conceal any 'leaked' signs of their public speaking nerves.

Showing your feelings

A number of gestures and postures have been found to accompany particular emotional states, and these are summarized in Table 2.2(a).

Maurice Krout studied the meaning of signals he felt are not intended as communication but are used instead of language, either when the person is prevented from speaking or when alone. He contrived experimentally to arouse strong emotions in his participants by putting them in rather awkward, uncomfortable or controversial situations. For example, he led each of his participants to believe that he or she was to receive a prize for an excellent performance, only then to discover 'accidentally' that through an error no prize was forthcoming. The person was at this point prevented from saying anything until given a signal to do so after his or her body language had been observed. The results of this and many other studies of posture and gesture have shown the common meanings of a variety of gestures (see Table 2.2(b)).

In general, touching of the head or face by the hand indicates negative feelings about oneself, and these signs are so common that police and customs officers watch out for them when questioning people. It should be noted however that feeling negative about oneself is not the same as being guilty of something. Indeed, there is some evidence that the more honest you are, the more uncomfortable you feel when under suspicion.

Table 2.2a Postures, gestures and their meaning

Motivation	Posture or gesture
FLIGHT	shoulder forward (one or both)
	chin in and hunch
	crouch (head to knees in seated person)
	rocking of head or body
	immobility
AGGRESSION	'beating' postures
	fist clench
	hand to neck
	expanded chest
AMBIVALENCE	fumble
	head groom/scratch
	finger sucking

Table 2.2b   Some common forms of emotional leakage

Posture or gesture	Motivation
Rubbing/stroking	self assurance
Rubbing arm of chair (when sitting)	emotional, restless
Making a fist	aggression
Foot flex and extend	aggressive/defensive
Hand to nose	fear
Fingers to lips	shame
Hand covering eyes	shame
Face picking/scratching	self blame or attack

The orientation of our bodies towards those with whom we associate can reveal our attitudes and feelings towards them. If we like a person, we orient our bodies towards them for most of the time. We lean forward, stand closer, look more, touch more and show a relaxed posture. Posture mimicry is also common between long-term friends or partners (see Figure 2.5).

Mixed feelings about a person are revealed in ambivalent postures: for example, when sitting we might have our knees pointing away, while our trunk is oriented

Figure 2.5   Examples of posture mimicry. *(Cordelia Molloy/Science Photo Library.)*

towards that person; tightly folded arms or high, tight leg crossing might reveal a withdrawal or protection of ourselves from the other. Postures of course change from moment to moment, so a snapshot glance will not necessarily reveal anything significant. It is the postures we adopt most of the time that are important and revealing.

Dominance is also shown in postures and gestures: Peter Collett describes arm 'pronation' (rotation of the arms inwards so that the back of the hand is in line with the front of the body) as an indication of power and dominance. George W. Bush often shows this typically bodybuilder-type stance when he is faced with other political leaders and this emphasizes his power and dominance.

ODOURS AS BODY LANGUAGE

In the West, people are unlikely to comment on body odours when describing someone, whereas the Arab, according to Edward Hall, appears to be comfortable in so doing and may comment on a friend's bad breath or agreeable body odour.

In fact we are quite good at distinguishing individuals by scent. Human babies show preferential responses to the smell of their own mother's milk within a few days after birth. Other relatives have been shown to be able to identify their 'family' baby by odour too; sometimes with an accuracy of over 90 per cent. This research has led to the idea that we have an 'olfactory signature' that has our own unique olfactory characteristics.

Another intriguing aspect of body odour is its capacity to have profound effects on the physiology of another's body. Michael Russell showed that a human female exposed regularly for several months to the odour of a small amount of underarm secretion from another female will synchronize her menstrual cycle with that of the donor, even though the females have never met. Other research (described in Chapter 1) has shown that women, when exposed to male underarm secretions, show reduced variability in menstrual cycle length when compared to women in the control group. It seems likely that odours are the salient stimuli here, but it is also possible that absorption of these secretions could also play a part. Of course most women are exposed to a daily bouquet of male and female body odours but the effects between females have been noted in girls and women living in close proximity, in places such as boarding schools or college dormitories.

Breath and face odour

Feeling another's breath on one's face is the stuff of romantic novels, but is generally not something many in the West allow to happen in day-to-day interactions. However, Arabs do not avoid such contact and just as they appear to enjoy body smells, withholding one's breath in conversation is interpreted as being evasive or ashamed. Breath contact is as important to them as is eye contact to British people. Similarly, in the Eskimo culture, rubbing noses is not just about physical contact – smelling the face of someone you meet is also an important part of greeting.

Perfumes as sexual attractants

In addition to natural odours from scent glands around the body – the feet, armpits, anal and genital region, chest and face – many adults add a variety of perfumes in the shape of soap, deodorant, creams, scents and so on. We wash off our natural smell and replace it with a socially acceptable one. But many expensive perfumes include secretions used as sexual attractants for other mammals; the musk deer produces a substance that evidently adds potency to our perfumes. In non-human animals, certain odours have a potent effect in sexual behaviour. Odours from the male pig (boar) elicit the mating stance in females; this substance is now available in spray form and, in the absence of the boar, can induce the female pig to stand for artificial insemination. Human bodily odours may also be sexually arousing. Iranaus Eibl-Eiberfeldt, in his study of people in some Mediterranean areas, observed villagers using odours to stimulate women in a courtship dance. A man waves a handkerchief, which he has carried in his armpit, in front of the woman of his choice. The smelly cloth is then supposed to arouse the passions of the woman he has selected.

TOUCHING

Being touched, or touching others, varies with our age, our sex, the context and the culture. To take the last first, some psychologists talk of 'contact' and 'non-contact' cultures, and this is exemplified in a study by Marc Jourard in which the frequency of contact between couples per hour was counted in various cities worldwide. He found such contacts to be 180 in San Juan, Puerto Rico, 110 in Paris, France, but only two in Gainesville, Florida, and zero in London, UK.

Our use of touch may be linked to our early experience of it. Japanese babies are carried on their mothers' backs and are physically closer to their mothers for longer periods than are babies in parts of the Western world who are often wheeled around in pushchairs. In the latter situation, eye contact may be more important for mother and baby than it is in Japan, where, in adult life, eye contact is used less in social situations than it is in the West.

In adulthood, being touched, whether or not we are aware of it, appears to alter our perception of a situation, and touching the arm, particularly the elbow, is the most appropriate place to touch someone without being misunderstood.

A number of studies reveal the power of touching – see Box 2.1 for an experiment on touching. Touching others may be useful in getting favours, getting signatures on petitions, getting bigger tips if you are a waitress or greater compliance from your students if you are a psychology tutor.

Nancy Henley argued that touch is an indication of power. She observed that men are more likely to initiate touch with women, than women are with men, and suggested this is not merely a reflection of interest or affection. Observers viewing others who touch seem to regard the initiator of the touching as the person with the greater power if the touch is not reciprocated. Other studies indicate that the toucher is also seen as showing more assertiveness and warmth.

BOX 2.1
AN EXPERIMENT ON TOUCHING

In 1976, a Purdue University experiment revealed what happened when a woman at the library desk 'accidentally' touched some students (male or female) when handing back their library cards (this was the experimental group). The woman was described more positively – as warm, sensitive and trustful – by those who were touched (whether or not they recalled being touched) and as distant, formal and insensitive by those who had not been touched (the control group), but had otherwise been treated in the same way. (See the reference by J. Fisher and others for further details.)

LIES AND DECEIT

there is no typical non-verbal behaviour which is associated with deception.

However, some behaviours are more likely to occur when people are lying than others.

Vrij, 2000

Before starting to read this section you may like to try out Exercise 2.3. How is lying studied? Research on lying has some obvious ethical difficulties – but one study by American researchers Paul Ekman and Wallace Friesen overcame this problem to a great extent by using a simulated real-life situation. They reasoned that nurses may sometimes find themselves in a situation where they must conceal from their patients the true facts of their illness, and they used this approach in comparing nurses' honest and dishonest accounts.

Another study by Aldert Vrij and Samantha Mann investigated a murderer's behaviour in a videotaped interview when he was telling truthful accounts (other evidence corroborated his words) and dishonest accounts (other evidence showed them to be untrue). Detailed analysis of the taped interview plus a subsequent confession revealed differences in body language associated with lying.

Gaze aversion, slower speech, speech pauses and errors all occurred more in the dishonest parts of the interview. But in the confession, which also included some dishonest elements, this pattern was not wholly consistent. Here there was less gaze aversion. This study reveals that we must be cautious in assuming certain patterns are likely, even in the same individual. A guilty suspect, when interviewed by police, is generally planning to lie, but not all lies are so calculated. We can be caught out lying when we thought we were not suspected and we can tell white lies while feeling no guilt at all; indeed we may feel more guilty telling the truth (your new dress is hideous!).

EXERCISE 2.3
CAN YOU TELL WHEN SOMEONE IS LYING?

Do you think any of the following are changed when someone is lying? If so, circle the direction of change (i.e. are they reduced or increased in frequency of occurrence when someone is lying, compared with when the person is speaking truthfully) for each type of behaviour.

Eye contact	reduced/increased
Body shifts	reduced/increased
Hand and finger movements	reduced/increased
Arm movements	reduced/increased
Leg movements	reduced/increased
Speech rate	reduced/increased
Pauses during speech	reduced/increased
Speech errors	reduced/increased
Perspiration	reduced/increased
Blushing	reduced/increased
Blink rate	reduced/increased
Smiling	reduced/increased
Twitching	reduced/increased
Head or neck scratching	reduced/increased

Now read the text to find out our current knowledge concerning which of the above are likely to change when someone is lying.

In general, Aldert Vrij reports that liars do not show gaze aversion, are less likely to fidget, show fewer illustrators (hand and arm movements associated with speech), display fewer leg movements and subtle hand and finger movements, and also slower speech with less fluency. Faces, surprisingly perhaps, do not give liars away, but microfacial expressions do differ between honest and dishonest accounts. These patterns are most evident when liars feel guilty and when lying takes some mental effort. So, be warned: detecting everyday lies is not a straightforward business.

IMPROVING BODY LANGUAGE

The clinician Joseph Wolpe wanted to assist excessively anxious and passive individuals to improve their social skills. Using methods such as role-play, the anxious person enacted a situation that caused him or her difficulty, and a therapist offered comments and advice. Gradually, the anxiety caused by the difficult situation reduced as the patient recognized that the role-play situation helped improve his or her social skills.

Michael Argyle and colleagues were also internationally known for their work on this topic, and argued that social behaviour is acquired in the same way as any other behaviour: we have to learn it the same way we learn the skills of word processing, driving or swimming. Today, courses on social skills and life skills are widely available and many people find them extremely helpful.

Recommended Reading

Bull, P. (2001). Nonverbal communication. *Psychologist, 14(12),* 644–647.

Furnham, A. (1999). *Body Language at Work.* London: Institute of Personnel and Development.

Guerrero, L.K., DeVito, J.A. and Hecht, M.L. (eds.) (1999). *The Nonverbal Communication Reader: Classic and contemporary readings.* Prospect Heights, Ill.: Waveland.

Knapp, M.L. (1992). *Non-verbal Communication in Human Interaction.* New York: Harcourt Brace Jovanovich.

Morris, D. (2002). *Peoplewatching.* London: Vintage.

Pease, A. and Pease, B. (2004). *The Definitive Book of Body Language: The secret meaning behind people's gestures.* London: Orion.

Answer to Figure 2.1

Figure 2.1 (p. 15) They are staff at the Fokker Space Company in the Netherlands looking at a television monitor as the unmanned Ariana 5 explodes 66 seconds after take-off from its launch pad. It seems likely they are feeling surprise and shock.

3

Your Personality

- Everyone has personality

- It depends on your point of view

- The trait approach

- Eysenck's theory: three critical dimensions

- From description to explanation

- Am I me or am I the situation? The problem of consistency

- Cognitive perspectives: it depends on how you look at it

- Personal construct theory

- Attribution: answering the question 'why?'

- Attributions and psychological distress

- Methods for assessing personality

Many of us first take an interest in psychology because we have become intrigued by some characteristic or behaviour of our own or of another person and become curious about it. Jack, a colleague at work, may often act in an aggressive way, but Anna is quiet and withdrawn, while Amy is sociable, friendly and outgoing.

Curiosity is increased when two people differ markedly despite the fact that they have been exposed to apparently similar circumstances. Vince and Louis have both been exposed to the stress and turmoil of suddenly being made redundant. Their financial, domestic and general life circumstances are much the same, and yet they react in different ways. Vince becomes increasingly anxious, dejected and apathetic, while Louis recovers quickly from his initial disappointment and remains undented by the blow, maintaining a steadfast, if unrealistic, cheerfulness. In trying to understand these differences between people we are concerned with the study of personality.

EVERYONE HAS PERSONALITY

Beyond the assertion that personality concerns individual differences it is very difficult to give a more detailed definition of personality with which psychologists of different persuasions will agree. In general, psychologists see personality as concerned with the stable, consistent internal aspects of the person's functioning. It must also be borne in mind that the man or woman in the street may use the term 'personality' in a different way. They might, for example, refer to someone as having 'lots of personality' or 'not much personality'. Personality, here, refers to the possession of attractive or salient social qualities. For the psychologist, everyone has a personality and the person of low social attractiveness is of as much interest, as much in need of explanation, as the opposite type.

IT DEPENDS ON YOUR POINT OF VIEW

The field of personality is one of the most perplexing to the reader new to psychology. In psychology evening classes, for example, students starting to learn about the psychology of personality are alarmed to discover that what appear to be simple human behaviours can be viewed in radically different ways, depending on the theoretical orientation of the person studying the behaviour. For example, in discussing 'difficult', uncontrollable behaviour in a child (refusing to comply with parents, tantrums, aggression) they would be surprised and even disappointed to find that the typical psychology textbook might give four or five different explanations. One might emphasize the child's general temperament and its biological foundations (the biological perspective), another might suggest that difficult behaviour is learned and conditioned because the parents rewarded (reinforced) the child's problem behaviour by giving in to his or her wishes (the conditioning or behavioural perspective, see Chapter 12), yet another that the unacceptable behaviour was merely a symptom of underlying unconscious conflict stemming from the child's relationships in infancy (the psychodynamic perspective).

Not only is there a range of explanatory theories, but they suggest radically different ways in which the child and family should be assessed and treated, ranging from treating the child with drugs to behaviour modification and family therapy. A common reaction to this quandary is to ask, 'Which theory is correct?' But this proves to be a question without a clear-cut answer. In this chapter we sketch a few contemporary approaches to personality and personality problems and some of their strengths and limitations. We also go on to discuss how these different approaches give rise to different methods for measuring and assessing personality.

THE TRAIT APPROACH

We are all trait theorists to some degree. In describing a person we like, we might describe them as 'friendly', 'interested in people', 'intelligent' or 'perceptive'; and conversely, the villains in our lives are 'distant', 'uninterested in people', 'stupid' and 'unperceptive'. Individuals may be idiosyncratic in terms of the relative importance of particular traits in their judgements of themselves and others, as we shall see when we discuss Personal Construct Theory, but we all have a vast number of terms available to us to describe the attributes and dispositions of people. It has been estimated that there are 18,000 or more 'trait' descriptions of this sort in the dictionary.

Naming is not the same as explaining

A trait description is no more than a summary of some consistencies in the behaviour of the person we are judging, but it is easy for people to believe that, in attributing a trait to someone, we have somehow explained their behaviour. They act in an unfriendly way because they are unfriendly people. The evidence for their being unfriendly is that they act in an unfriendly way! This is, of course, entirely circular. It is important to bear in mind, therefore, that traits are no more than summary descriptions of people's behaviour.

Some traits are limited in scope – Caitlin is 'respectful of her teachers'. While others summarize broad aspects of the person – Marguerite is 'empathic towards others'. The former, more specific, traits are sometimes referred to as secondary traits, the latter, more general characteristics, as central traits that may apply in a wide range of contexts. A cardinal trait has a very wide range of applicability – it influences behaviour in just about every aspect of the person's life. People described as 'lacking in self-awareness', for example, might be expected to show this characteristic at home, in friendships, in academic or work settings and the trait might apply to their thinking, their emotions, their social behaviour and their everyday activities.

It's all a matter of degree

There have been many studies in psychology of single traits. The most common approach is to view a trait as a dimension in terms of which people vary. Thus on

31

a dimension of 'dominance' there will be individuals who obtain extremely high scores, others who obtain very low scores because of their submissive behaviour, with the majority of the population near the middle of the range.

Most trait researchers attempt to create reliable, objective tests of the particular dimension they are interested in, and then use such tests to discover how other aspects of behaviour can be predicted from test scores. For example, the researcher might speculate that 'dominance' is an important requirement for being an effective leader and go on to compare successful and unsuccessful leaders on a measure of dominance to see if this particular prediction is upheld. A vast number of single trait tests of this sort now exist and are widely used in work, educational and medical settings (see further discussion of personality tests below).

Just how many traits are required to account for differences between people is a matter of some debate. Some of the best known and most influential personality theorists have brought a particular statistical technique, factor analysis, to bear on this question. Perhaps the most famous and enthusiastic exponent of the factor analytic approach has been the British psychologist, Hans Eysenck.

EYSENCK'S THEORY: THREE CRITICAL DIMENSIONS

Factor analysis is a mathematical method for investigating the degree of association ('correlation') between different behaviours or between different traits. It reduces the complex patterns of association found to a small number of underlying clusters or 'factors'. It is a way, then, of revealing the underlying structure; a structure not likely to be easily visible to anyone who simply scans the scores of a large number of people on a whole range of tests or observations.

Eysenck used and advocated the factor analytic method for more than 40 years, studying very diverse groups of people and using a wide range of measures – scores from questionnaires, ratings of the person by others, scores on psychological tests or even biographical information (e.g. whether or not the person ever received psychiatric treatment). He claimed that throughout this work three underlying factors were revealed with considerable consistency. The two long-standing factors he described are Extraversion–Introversion and Neuroticism–Stability. To these he subsequently added a third: the dimension of Psychoticism–Impulse control. Eysenck called these 'types', each type being composed of a cluster of traits that together define the type.

Extraversion–Introversion

The associated traits that make up Extraversion include sociability, liveliness, activity, assertiveness, the tendency to be sensation-seeking, carefreeness and dominance. The implication is that individuals high on any one of these traits will tend to be high on the others. Introversion is defined by the opposite traits; for example, low sociability and low activity.

Neuroticism–Stability

Neuroticism, on the other hand, comprises traits of anxiety-proneness, depression-proneness, guilt feelings, low self-esteem, tension, moodiness and emotionality. The implication is that individuals high on any one of the traits will be high on the others. Stability is defined by the opposite traits; for example, low anxiety and calmness.

Psychoticism–Impulse control

Psychoticism, in turn, includes aggressiveness, coldness, lack of empathy and a divergent kind of creativity. Impulse Control is defined by the opposite traits; for example, good control and interpersonal warmth.

   The distribution of each of Eysenck's types in the general population is a 'normal' one, meaning that both extremes of each dimension are relatively rare, with most people scoring near the mid-point of the continuum, showing, for example, a balance of introverted and extraverted tendencies.

FROM DESCRIPTION TO EXPLANATION

What distinguished Eysenck from a number of other trait and factor analysis researchers was his attempt to move beyond a simple description of how traits and behaviours can cluster together (the taxonomy of behaviour) to the 'dynamics' of behaviour: the attempt to explain why humans differ on these three dimensions. The specifics of his explanatory theory changed over the years as it was reformulated to accommodate new findings. We shall look here, however, at some of the more enduring aspects of Eysenck's theory, concentrating particularly on the Extraversion–Introversion dimension.

It's mainly in the genes

Eysenck sees individual differences as firmly rooted in biology. For him, the cause of extraverted patterns of behaviour is firmly located within differences in the nervous system, and the type of nervous system a person has is genetically determined. This is not to say that Eysenck rules out environmental factors. Social factors also contribute to whether a person is extraverted or introverted in behaviour, but Eysenck clearly saw himself as a crusader against overenthusiastic environmentalists who have entirely ruled out biological predispositions.

The extravert is inhibited?

The Extraversion–Introversion dimension is identified with differences in the level of arousal in the cerebral cortex (see Chapter 7, on the brain). The level of arousal is, in turn, a product of the activity of a 'cortico-reticular loop' involving a part of the mid-brain called the ascending reticular activation system, one of whose functions is to alert and activate the parts of the brain responsible for 'higher' psychological functions. In simple terms, the introvert's cortex is more aroused and more arousable than the cortex of the extravert, which is more prone to 'inhibition'. The cortex is responsible for many of the higher level 'control' functions of the brain and thus, paradoxically, a high level of arousal in this structure is associated with controlled, rather than excited, behaviour. Similarly alcohol, which generally has an 'inhibiting' effect on brain functions, will reduce arousal in the cortex and produce less controlled, more extraverted, social behaviour.

From explanation to practical prediction

One of the great strengths of theorists such as Eysenck was that his theorizing led to clear predictions that were eminently testable. Among the predictions of the theory are that extraverts (E's) and Introverts (I's) will differ in their 'vigilance'. Vigilance refers to a state of readiness to detect and respond to small or infrequent changes occurring in the environment, as in scanning a radar screen to detect a 'blip'. Eysenck predicts poor vigilance in extraverts because, in everyday language, they have poor concentration and become easily bored.

Another important prediction was that E's and I's differ in their conditionability, I's being more easily conditioned and hence more likely to be socially conforming. In his early work Eysenck made this idea the basis of a theory of criminality, and it has, therefore, attracted much attention. In general, there has been little evidence to support the idea that a general factor of conditionability exists. There may also be important differences between 'aversive' conditioning (e.g. learning to associate fear with a neutral stimulus) and 'appetitive' conditioning (learning to associate gratification or pleasure with a neutral stimulus). Eysenck went on to reformulate the theory to suggest that it is the impulsivity component of extraversion, rather than the sociability aspect, that is related to low conditionability.

Are introverts more sensitive?

One of the many interesting predictions from the theory is that E's and I's differ in the sensory thresholds; the introvert's aroused cortex is more alert and hence efficient at detecting low levels of stimulation. As introverts are more aroused by stimulation so they will react more to stimuli.

It is not difficult to see how differences in sensitivity to stimulation might have consequences for medicine and related areas. One of the authors can recall having had some painful dental treatment, in the middle of which the dentist asked why individuals vary in their pain sensitivity. He was able to suggest that 'Git gall gepends gone gehter gou gare gan gintrovert gor gextravert.' At least, according to Eysenck's theory, if introverts are more sensitive to stimulation, we would expect them to feel pain more acutely. Eysenck sees pain as part of a continuum of sensory stimulation. Both very low levels (sitting in the dark in a quiet house) and high levels of stimulation (a crowded, noisy party) may be perceived as unpleasant, while stimulation in the intermediate range is pleasant or neutral. If introverts generally 'amplify' stimulation because of the nature of their nervous system, we would expect them to be less troubled by low levels of stimulation but to be made uncomfortable by high levels of stimulation sooner (at a lower point on the continuum). Extraverts, conversely, will find low levels of stimulation more unpleasant but will be more tolerant of high levels of stimulation. Eysenck labels the introvert as stimulus aversive and the extravert as stimulus hungry. So at a noisy party we might expect the introverts to be the first to complain about the music being played too loudly, though this assumes that they will be bold enough to voice their irritation and also that they would have attended the party in the first place.

Criticisms of the factor-analytic approach

The factor-analytic method has not been without its critics, some saying that the apparent objectivity of these statistical methods is illusory. There is certainly a subjective element in that what is derived from factor analysis depends in part on the nature of the items included in the first place, and the mathematical patterns derived need to be labelled and interpreted by the researcher. Moreover, a number of different factor analytic methods exist, making it possible to derive quite different factors from the same test results.

Cattell's 16 dimensions

One check on the validity of any assertion that core personality dimensions have been isolated (as claimed by Eysenck) is to compare the findings with those of other researchers who use different methods. One such, Raymond Cattell, concluded that there are 16 major personality factors, rather than 3. Closer inspection of Cattell's work, however, reveals many similarities with the conclusions of Eysenck. Cattell was not concerned to establish independent factors and his 16 dimensions are correlated with each other. If an attempt is made to derive 'second order' or more general factors from Cattell's work, the two major factors produced are strikingly similar to Eysenck's Extraversion–Introversion and Neuroticism–Stability. There does, therefore, seem to be an emerging consistency of findings.

Or is it five?

There have been many subsequent reanalyses of Cattell's data which have suggested that the correlations can be reduced to five underlying factors. In recent years a degree of consensus has emerged that these five factors recur again and again: extraversion, warmth, conscientiousness, stability and openness. Some of the typical characteristics making up the 'Big 5' are shown in Table 3.1.

Again, it can be seen that a substantial degree of overlap exists with Eysenck's dimensions.

It would appear that some progress has been made in mapping the broad temperamental dimensions on which individuals vary. Few would claim that

Table 3.1   The Big 5: examples of traits

(1)	Extraversion	High:	talkative, assertive, outgoing
		Low:	quiet, retiring, withdrawn
(2)	Warmth	High:	kind, affectionate, warm
		Low:	cruel, cold, unfriendly
(3)	Conscientiousness	High:	organized, efficient, reliable
		Low:	disorderly, careless, irresponsible
(4)	Stability	High:	calm, unemotional, stable
		Low:	tense, emotional, anxious
(5)	Openness	High:	wide interests, imaginative, original
		Low:	narrow interests, restricted views, conventional

knowledge of a person's position on two or three dimensions would tell the complete story about their personality. But controversial though Eysenck's theory has been, few theories can have generated so many testable hypotheses across so many areas of psychological enquiry.

AM I ME OR AM I THE SITUATION? THE PROBLEM OF CONSISTENCY

The American psychologist, Lawrence Pervin, encapsulated in this question a debate that has rumbled on for about 20 years among personality researchers. What is at issue is easily demonstrated. Ask a person who knows you well to name one of your most undesirable personality traits.

One of the authors of this book was bold enough to try this experiment and was told he was 'obsessionally tidy' by a colleague who had clearly found this characteristic to be rather tiresome. The immediate response to this label was to become aware of how unfair and overgeneralized it was. Admittedly he kept his office very tidy and was fussy about clearing his desk before leaving but, on the other hand, his wife complained he was appallingly messy when working in the kitchen. His daughter suggested he was the scruffiest dad in the playground when picking her up from school!

It all depends?

How can we maintain the notion of a trait of tidiness, with the implications of consistency over time and across situations, in the light of such apparent inconsistencies? Does the concept of a fixed personality not collapse and need to be replaced by the notion that particular responses have been learned for particular situations?

These questions and a range of related ones were raised by Walter Mischel in a book in 1968. Mischel produced evidence which, he suggested, demonstrated that intellectual skills apart, traits and dispositions showed little evidence of stability over time or across situations. Where consistency was present, he argued, it was because of similarities in the situation. According to Mischel, although the attribution of trait characteristics ('sociability', 'aggression', 'shyness') appears to be a useful way of organizing our perceptions of other people, traits do not reflect the actual patterning of behaviour in the real world. Perceived consistency may be simply a matter of the 'halo' or stereotyping effect, whereby the perception of a characteristic in one setting leads one to expect and perceive it in other settings.

Mischel's criticisms had some major implications for the assessment of personality. If Mischel was correct, it would be expected that any test of a trait or disposition would be poor at predicting actual behaviour in a specific real-life setting. To return to the earlier example, our author's score on a test of 'obsessional tidiness' would not be very useful in predicting how neat and clipped he kept the edge of his garden lawn. Mischel found that correlations between trait scores and actual behaviour were indeed very low. Given that the whole purpose of personality testing is often to make specific predictions (e.g. using personality tests to predict who will not be a good salesperson, or who will or will not be readmitted after discharge from a psychiatric hospital), Mischel's conclusions were of considerable practical importance.

Assessing the person or the situation

It is not difficult to see how 'situationism' of this sort suggests very different techniques for assessing a person's suitability for a job, for instance, or for assessing the problems of a patient on discharge from a psychiatric hospital. The situationist would try to define the specific tasks the person might meet in the job (or living outside the hospital), and then assess how the person would behave or has behaved in situations of this sort. It might even be desirable to devise a similar situation for the person to respond to at interview. The traditional trait approach to assessment would be to assess dispositions of a very general sort through personality tests or interview assessment. As we shall see, there is something to be said for combining both person and situation factors in assessment.

Kenneth Bowers and Jack Block in the United Stated are among those who have written in defence of the trait approach. Bowers has concentrated on some of the logical inconsistencies of the extreme situationist position. Block argues that many of the studies reported by Mischel were badly carried out, and that many were done with children, who would be expected to be less consistent than adults. Block's own work, studying individuals long term over a period of 20 years, found evidence of considerable consistency over time in personality ratings. Individuals rated as 'dependable' and 'responsible' at school tended to be rated in the same way some 20 years later.

The effect of Mischel's early work was to produce some shift towards an appreciation of the external situation. Contemporary thinking about personality tends to be increasingly interactionist, accommodating both internal and external factors.

The world is largely what we make it

The word 'interaction' signifies not only that both person and situation are important but also that the effect of situations will vary depending on the nature of the persons exposed to them and, conversely, that the effect of personality traits will vary with the situation. Life changes – changing job, moving house – may overall be associated with stress and anxiety, but there will be some individuals who thrive on such changes, while others suffer. It may not be possible to separate personality and situation. Particular personalities may create life changes, while others minimize them. In this sense, the environments to which we are exposed are, in part, an expression of our personality.

COGNITIVE PERSPECTIVES: IT DEPENDS ON HOW YOU LOOK AT IT

Views about personality have always reflected accepted general psychological theories and methods of a particular era. There have been times when psychodynamic, humanistic, behavioural and other perspectives have dominated. Since the 1980s cognitive perspectives have been dominant in general psychology and cognitive perspectives on personality have been very influential. The meanings of 'cognitive' and 'cognition' are various, but the terms usually refer to mental representations of events: to the processes of interpreting, predicting and evaluating the environment, as well as to beliefs, thoughts and expectations. What the cognitive theorist brings to the study of individual difference in behaviour is summed up in the often-quoted maxim of the philosopher Epictetus: 'Men are not moved by things, but the views which they take of them.' Cognitive theory, then, leads us to try to understand, assess and, in a clinical context, change mental representations of the world, including the self and the external environment.

There is no one cognitive approach to personality. We describe here two areas of research that share a cognitive perspective.

PERSONAL CONSTRUCT THEORY

The American psychologist George Kelly proposed an elaborate theory of personal constructs in the 1950s, which was some 20 years or more ahead of its time, anticipating many later developments in cognitive theorizing, though Kelly himself would reject the term 'cognitive' as being too narrow to characterize the theory. Kelly's starting point is a view of the person as a scientist engaged in the task of interpreting and theorizing about the world and using these theories to predict the future. Kelly's theory is rooted in the philosophical position of constructive alternativism, which states that the world can be construed in infinitely varied ways. Individuals construe the world in terms of personal constructs which are bipolar descriptions, these personal constructs being organized into systems. Thus a person may view his or her relationships with other people in terms of the bipolar construct 'a relationship in which I am dominant' versus 'a relationship in which I am submissive'. Any one important construct will have implications for other constructs in the system. A relationship in which 'I am submissive', for example, might imply for that person 'an uncomfortable relationship'. The importance of constructs will vary for different individuals (constructs are personal), as will the implications of the construct within the system. For some people submissiveness may be associated with comfort and relaxation.

The nature of the personal construct approach to personality is best shown by exploring your own construct system. Kelly devised a method for doing this – the 'repertory grid' – which has been widely used in a range of applied settings including hospitals, prisons and education. Instructions for completing a grid on yourself are given in Exercise 3.1 [see below]. You may wish to try this exercise before reading the next section, which describes the use of the repertory grid with a psychiatric patient seen by one of the authors.

EXERCISE 3.1
EXPLORE YOUR OWN CONSTRUCT SYSTEM

In recent years some very complex ways of analysing repertory grids have been developed, most of them requiring the assistance of a microcomputer. Nevertheless, it is not difficult to evaluate your own grid in a very simple way. You will need to allow about one hour to complete this exercise.

1. Prepare 10 pieces of blank card, each about the size of a filing card. Mark each card in the top left-hand corner from 'a' to 'j'.
2. On card 'a' write 'Mother', on 'b' 'Father', on 'c' the name of your spouse/girl/boyfriend, on 'd' the name of someone you dislike, on 'e' the name of someone you consider successful, on 'f' the name of a friend, on 'g' the name of your immediate 'boss' or employer, on 'h' the name of any other family member. On 'i' write 'Myself as I am', on 'j' write 'Myself as I would like to be.
3. Put card 'i' on the table in front of you. Shuffle the other cards and randomly select two cards from the pack and put them on the table with 'i'.
4. Think about the three people whose cards are in front of you. Try to identify some important way in which two of these people are similar and different from the third. For example, both my father and I are 'sympathetic', while my boss is 'unsympathetic'. Record this 'construct' on a separate sheet of paper.
5. Keep card 'i' on the table. Put the other two cards back in the pack and shuffle. Randomly select two others.

6. Repeat 4 above.
7. Continue doing this until you have a list of 8 constructs.
8. On a separate sheet of paper construct a repertory grid like that shown, using your own eight constructs across the top. The 'people' whom we have used are termed 'elements' in the repertory grid.
9. Think about Construct 1. Think about each person from 'a' to 'j' in turn, and apply the construct to them. If they are like the first end of the construct ('sympathetic'), put a '1' opposite their name. If they are like the other end of the construct 'unsympathetic', put a '0'.
10. Repeat 9 for constructs 2 to 8.

People (Elements)	Personal constructs			
	1. Sympathetic– Unsympathetic	2. Clever– Stupid	3. Assertive– Shy	4. Etc.
a	1	1	1	
b	1	0	1	
c	0	1	0	
d	0	0	0	
e	1	1	0	
f	0	0	1	
g	1	0	1	
h	0	0	0	
i	0	1	0	
j	0	0	0	

Things to ponder:

•   Reflect on the fact that these are your personal constructs. Another individual would provide a very different list. Are/were you aware that these are the dimensions you used to structure your world?
•   How do your constructs associate with each other? Check this by comparing any column of 1's and 0's with the other columns. If the pattern of vertical '1' columns and 0's matches (or nearly matches) this suggests overlapping meaning between the two constructs. Does it surprise you that any particular constructs match? What does a match reveal about your way of thinking? Remember that a reversed match (all 1's match with 0's) is equally significant.

- How do the people compare with each other? Do any people have identical or similar patterns of 1's and 0's in the horizontal rows? Are the similarities suprising? What do they suggest?
- Who is most like 'Myself as I am'? Would you have guessed this?
- How similar is 'Myself as I am' to 'Myself as I would like to be'? On what constructs is there a gap between your actual and ideal self?

James was a man in his early 30s who worked for an insurance company doing what most people would consider 'a good job'. He had applied for promotion some months previously but had been unsuccessful. He was upset by this for a few weeks but eventually regained his equilibrium. Shortly afterwards an important relationship with a girlfriend broke up. He reported good relationships with his parents and his two brothers. In the period before he went to see a psychologist he had been moody, irritable and prone to bouts of depression. He was pessimistic about his future and about the world in general.

The repertory grid technique was used to explore his view of significant people in his life and of himself and to elicit the constructs actually important to James. An interview estabished that the major people in his life at the time were his father, his mother, a brother whom he saw frequently, a friend at work, his boss at work and his recent girlfriend. Constructs elicited from James are shown in Table 3.2. James was asked to think about each of his important people and to decide where he would place them on each construct.

There are a number of mathematical methods for assessing which constructs were the most important for James. These suggested, and he was able to confirm this himself, that the construct relating to 'respect' (1) was a vital one. There was an association between this construct and constructs (2) 'educated' and (6) 'successful'. A second important construct was that relating to 'confidence' (7) which was also associated with constructs (3) and (5). These two groups of constructs cluster together, then, suggesting they reflect two important dimensions for James in judging himself and others. Another way to demonstrate this is to plot the location of significant people on important dimensions. This is illustrated in Figure 3.1.

Table 3.2 James's personal constructs

1.	'respected by others'	versus	'looked down on by others'
2.	'educated'	versus	'poor education'
3.	'warm, open people'	versus	'cold'
4.	'overemotional'	versus	'stable'
5.	'relates easily to others'	versus	'has difficulties in relating'
6.	'successful at work'	versus	'a failure'
7.	'confident with other people'	versus	'unsure of themselves'
8.	'did well at school'	versus	'did poorly at school'

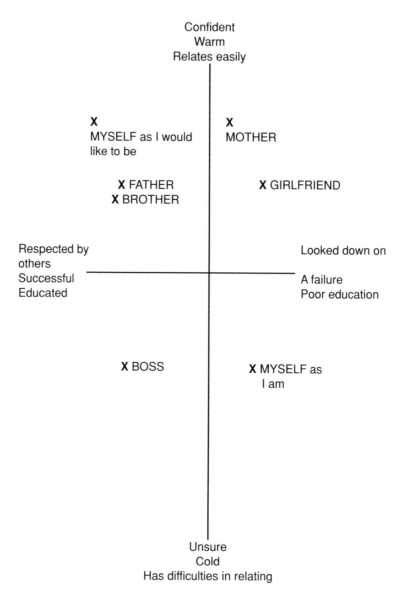

Figure 3.1 James's view of important people.

Perhaps the most striking thing about this map of James's world is the great distance between himself as he is and how he would like to be. He falls short on both the 'respect' and 'confidence' dimensions. Despite his good job, he clearly has major doubts about his achievements and his status in relation to other people. The other males in his family, his father and brother, approximate to his ideal. It is not difficult to see how many lines of further enquiry a repertory grid of this sort opens up and we shall leave it to you to think further about what sort of help James might need, given his view of the world.

ATTRIBUTION: ANSWERING THE QUESTION 'WHY?'

George Kelly has not been the only psychologist to stress that people create the-ories about themselves, others and the world in general, and that understanding personal theories is crucial to understanding their behaviour. Over the same period that Kelly's theory was beginning to influence the thinking of many clinical psychologists a line of research was gathering pace within experimental social psychology, which has become known as 'attribution theory'. Attribution theory concerns itself with one particular form of construing the world; namely, with the perception of causality. From an attributional perspective, people are viewed as engaged in the task of explaining why events happen.

Laying the blame

Arriving at an attribution for a particular action involves the use of complex information about the context of the action. If you see, for example, a stranger A assault another person B in the street, in order to arrive at an attribution for why this has happened, you would need to consider: Is A violent in general or is his or her violence specific to B? This is called 'distinctiveness' information.

You might also need to consider whether B is often the victim of assaults by other people ('consensus' information).

Finally, has A hit B before or is this the only occasion? ('consistency' information).

Contextual information of this sort will play a part in determining whether we isolate A, B, or some temporary factor in the situation as the cause of what happened. It is obvious that on many occasions in everyday life we fail to make rational use of such information. If a stranger acts in an unfriendly way towards you, you might assume that you have offended him or her in some way without attempting to find out whether he or she acts in this way towards everyone (fail-ing to use 'distinctiveness' information). Similarly, you might explain some pro-blems you have in terms of your 'inadequacy' without stopping to consider that many other people have an identical problem ('consensus' information). If you would like to find out a bit more about your own attributional style, try out Exercise 3.2.

Psychologists have asked whether, when we try to explain behaviour, we evalu-ate the situation rationally or whether we are biased towards arriving at particu-lar sorts of attribution. One particular form of bias has been suggested in studies. People in general often show a 'positivity' bias; that is, a tendency to explain things in such a way as to maintain self-esteem. Many of us tend to explain successes in terms of our own qualities, and failures in terms of factors outside ourselves. As we shall see later, people vary markedly in this. People with psychological diffi-culties often show a reversed positivity bias, habitually explaining bad events in ways that are highly damaging to their self-esteem.

EXERCISE 3.2
YOUR ATTRIBUTIONAL STYLE

1. Think about the two worst things that have happened to you in the past year. Write 200–300 words describing each event.
2. Consider the two events again. For each event write a few sentences explaining why the event happened.
3. Complete 1 and 2 before turning over the page. (Seeing the point of the exercise might bias how you carry it out.)
4. Attribution theory would suggest that you would spontaneously try to explain the two events. Look through your two original accounts. Are there any phrases that suggest an explanation ('because', 'therefore', 'as a result', 'since' etc.).
5. Look through both your spontaneous accounts and the explanations asked for under 2, and try to classify your explanations in terms of Peterson and Seligman's depressive attributional style (see text).
6. How similar were the explanations for the event in terms of (a) internal, (b) stable and (c) global factors?
7. What might be your own attributional style for bad events?

ATTRIBUTIONS AND PSYCHOLOGICAL DISTRESS

One of the most important applications of attributional ideas has been to depression. Christopher Peterson and Martin Seligman have argued, and amassed much evidence to support their view that there is a habitual way of construing causality (an attributional style), which predisposes people to become depressed, should they experience unpleasant and stressful life events.

People prone to depression explain 'bad' events that happen in particular ways. First, they attribute the event 'internally' rather than 'externally'; and second, the internal case is 'stable' rather than 'unstable'. Finally, the internal cause is 'global' rather than 'specific'. Let us illustrate this by an example quoted by Seligman himself.

If the event you are trying to explain is a rejection by a girlfriend, and you are predisposed to depression, you explain this occurrence in terms of something about you rather than something about her ('I am unattractive' rather than 'she was cruel'). You may make depression even more likely if your explanation is stable and unlikely to change ('I am unattractive' rather than 'I had been acting strangely'). Finally, you may explain the rejection in terms of a very general quality of yourself that extends beyond the particular situation ('I am useless as a person' rather than 'I have difficulty in sexual relationships'). Depressed people have been shown in some studies to think in this way, but the question must then be asked whether the attributional style is a consequence of the depression rather than a cause of it. Ideally, to prove Seligman's theory, it needs to be demonstrated that bad attributional styles precede depression. To assess people's attributional style prior to their meeting stressful life events and becoming depressed is no easy task. We must also bear in mind that depressives' apparently biased ways of thinking may sometimes be valid and more realistic than those who do not get depressed.

Try out Exercise 3.3 below.

EXERCISE 3.3
A GROUP EXERCISE

Consider the following event that might happen. Sean (aged 18) has had a regular girlfriend (Sandy) for the past year. She fails to turn up for a night out they have planned. When he gets home, Sean finds a telephone message from her on the voicemail telling him the relationship is over and she does not want to see him again. How might Sean attribute the cause for this event? Write down possible explanations Sean might come up with. Now categorize the explanation in terms of the following dimensions:

- Is the cause internal to Sean (e.g. something about me caused the break-up) or external (something about Sandy or the situation)?
- Is the cause something stable (something that will not change) or unstable (could change)?
- Is the cause global (a wide-ranging cause such as being a lousy boyfriend) or specific (a narrow cause such as drinking too much on nights out)?
- Is the cause controllable or uncontrollable by Sean?

What would the different effects be on Sean for these different types of attribution? Identify a cause that is internal, stable, global and uncontrollable for Sean. What would the emotional and behavioural consequences be for this attribution? What might he feel? Identify a cause that is external, unstable, specific and controllable. How might Seam feel and act?

Some discussion questions:

1. What sorts of attributions might generally be found in people who are prone to feeling depressed? Prone to anger?
2. Do some people have a bias towards particular patterns of attributions for things that happen to them?
3. What would be the consequences for their personality?

45

BOX 3.1
A CORRELATIONAL PREDICTION STUDY OF OFFENDERS

Many applied psychologists work in prison settings. One important task is to assess the personality of offenders in prison in an attempt to predict the likelihood of them reoffending on release from prison.

Two Canadian psychologists – Wagdy Loza and Amel Loza-Fanous – gave a 'Self-Appraisal Questionnaire' (SAQ) to 305 Canadian sentenced offenders prior to their release to the community. They were followed up for 60 months at 4-month intervals. The outcomes measured were violent recidivism, committing a new offence of any sort, and violation of parole conditions. The SAQ scores were predictive of all these outcomes. The average correlation between the total SAQ score and reoffending was +0.4. In particular, having criminal/antisocial beliefs and having antisocial personality problems were both predictive of recidivism in the community. Thus personality measures of this sort are useful in prediction assessments.

For further details see:

Loza, W. and Loza-Fanous, A. (2003) More evidence for the validity of the Self-Appraisal Questionnaire (SAQ) for predicting violent and non-violent recidivism: A five-year follow-up study. *Criminal Justice and Behavior, 30*, 709–721.

METHODS FOR ASSESSING PERSONALITY

A person may undertake a personality assessment for a variety of reasons. These range from curiosity about his or her 'make-up' to the need to assess suitability for particular forms of employment or type of psychological therapy. The form of psychological assessments will be strongly influenced by the theoretical orientation of the assessor (e.g. a psychodynamic versus a behavioural or cognitive perspective). Many personality assessments may be conducted by persons who are not trained psychologists, who are trying to determine whether, for example, the individual 'is sufficiently outgoing for the position' or 'conscientious enough for the meticulous work involved'. In general, personality assessments by psychologists differ from everyday or lay assessments in several respects:

- The assessment is more likely to be based on a theory of personality that has some scientific and empirical support.
- The assessment techniques will have been validated in a scientific manner.
- Multiple sources of information will be used in making the assessment.

Typically, a comprehensive assessment would incorporate psychometric tests, behavioural observations and interviews.

Psychometric tests of personality are manifold. Unfortunately, it appears to be the case that the tests most widely recognized by the general public are those least favoured by scientifically oriented psychologists. The Rorschach Inkblot Test and the Thematic Apperception Test (TAT) probably fall in this category. The Minnesota Multiphasic Personality Inventory (MMPI) is one of the most widely administered psychological tests in the world, particularly in psychiatric settings, though, strictly speaking, it is an assessment of psychological and psychiatric abnormality rather than of personality per se. The NEO (Neuroticism, Extraversion, Openness) Personality Inventory is a modern, well validated personality inventory designed to measure the Big 5 personality dimensions (see discussion above).

Exclusive reliance on self-report inventories (such as the MMPI and the NEO) has many pitfalls. Despite safeguard scales built into the tests, people can still misrepresent their personality (faking-good or faking-bad). The social desirability bias (faking-good) is particularly problematic in job-related assessments, where it is clearly in the testee's interest to deny negative traits. For these and other reasons, it is essential that direct behavioural observation is a component of personality assessments. The act frequency approach attempts to list specific behaviours that make up a particular trait (e.g. shyness)and then gets the person (plus, preferably, other observers) to record the frequency of the behaviours. In a clinical setting, reduction of such behaviours may be a more sensitive measure of change than conventional psychometric inventories. Cognitive behavioural therapies also require the assessment of particular damaging thoughts or cognitions (e.g. the frequency of the thought that 'I am useless') in addition to overt behaviour.

Interviewing undoubtedly has an important place in the toolbox of the personality assessor. The same caveats exist for interviewing, however, as exist for psychological inventories or questionnaires. Interviewing data needs to be compared with information gleaned from other sources and particularly with direct behavioural observations and with known facts from the life history of the individual.

Recommended Reading

Boeree, C.G. (current). *Personality Theories*.
http://www.ship.edu/~cgboeree/perscontents.html.
http://www.socialpsychology.org/person.html.
Engler, B. (1999). *Personality Theories*, *5th edn*. Boston: Houghton Mifflin.

4

Your Sex: On Being Male or Female

- Sex or gender?

- Biological influences

- Hormones and behaviour

- Sex and gender identity

- From birth to maturity

- Are gender differences changing?

- Gender differences in school and afterwards

Our sex is something we just take for granted. 'Is it a girl or a boy?' is the question expectant parents all ask, sometimes at the scanning stage in pregnancy, or more typically after the birth of a baby. However, once answered, a whole host of expectations follow about what being a girl or a boy means. Ask anyone to describe a typically masculine male or typically feminine female, and they can easily tell you: the stereotype of the 'masculine' individual is someone who is tough, ambitious and dominant, and that of the 'feminine' individual is seen as gentle, non-assertive, and caring. But do these stereotypes reflect biological differences between sexes?

SEX OR GENDER?

We shall use sex differences to refer to biological differences, inborn characteristics related to sex chromosomes, sex organs and reproduction, whereas gender differences refer to psychological characteristics and social categories. The relationship between sex and gender is not a straightforward one, as gender differences may have their origins in biology, or be created by environmental influences, or an interaction of these two. There continues to be much debate and research surrounding these issues.

In this chapter we shall explore gender differences from the beginning: from conception. We shall examine the impact of sex chromosomes and hormones on the individual, and in particular their feelings about themselves as males or females. We shall also consider some of the areas where males and females are said to differ: in particular, intelligence and abilities.

BIOLOGICAL INFLUENCES

Maleness is determined by the presence of the Y chromosome and thus by definition a male's sex is determined by his father. England's King Henry VIII was quite wrong in blaming his wives for not having sons – it was his fault if it was anybody's – but of course it was not under his control.

In the absence of the Y chromosome, an individual develops as a female, and even if only one X chromosome is present (as in Turner's syndrome) the resulting individual is female (although she does differ in some respects from an XX female). The presence of the Y chromosome speeds up the growth and division of cells that form the male gonads (or testes), and by about 16 weeks after conception the male is fully differentiated, sexually. The differentiation of the gonads (ovaries) in the female starts and ends later and is achieved by about 20 weeks' gestation. Once formed, the testes and ovaries begin to secrete sex hormones and the rest of the process of sexual differentiation is under hormonal control.

HORMONES AND BEHAVIOUR

Male hormones are collectively called androgens, and the chief one of these is testosterone. Androgens have a masculinizing action on the developing body, and are

Figure 4.1 The weaker sex? *(David Reed/Alamy.)*

responsible for the growth of the extra muscle and bone that characterize the body of the adult male.

The female is hormonally more complicated than the male. She has oestrogens, which, in early development, are concerned with sexual differentiation, and later are concerned with the growth of the eggs (or ova) in the ovaries, with the maturation of her genitals and breasts, and with the increased deposition of fat during adolescence. Also present in the female is progesterone. Its role is to prepare the womb (or uterus) for pregnancy, maintaining the pregnancy after conception, and nourishing the developing embryo. In adult females of childbearing age, the secretion of oestrogens and progesterone is cyclic, and, on average, the cycle, known as the menstrual cycle, is repeated every 28 days.

In both sexes, hormones more usually associated with the opposite sex are to be found.

The expression of various types of sexual and non-sexual behaviour is affected by sex hormones. Indeed, almost all forms of behaviour can be displayed by both males and females. Examples from non-human animals illustrate this point, although of course we cannot assume that humans function in exactly the same way. Mounting in mammals is a pattern of behaviour we associate with male sexual behaviour – because it is a typical pattern in copulation. However, a female may also show this response around ovulation. Indeed a cow, when ready for the bull, will often mount other cows, and the farmer observing this knows she is ready to mate (or ready for artificial insemination). Thus 'male' sexual behaviour of this type is shown by both sexes and is not uniquely male.

Physiological studies of rodents have shown the impact of sex hormones on development and behaviour. If a male rat is castrated at birth before full sexual differentiation has occurred, and then primed with female hormones, in adulthood, its behaviour is like that of a female, although it cannot reproduce. Similarly, the removal of ovaries from the infant female rat makes her behaviour more masculine in adulthood and she behaves as a male in the presence of a receptive female. In both these cases, genetic sex does not determine the behaviour; it is the presence or absence of hormones that plays the crucial role.

SEX AND GENDER IDENTITY

Does having male hormones, and developing physically along male lines make an individual feel like a male? Gender identity is the individual's private experience of himself/herself as male or female, and psychologists do not, as yet, have a full understanding of how gender identity develops. There are several approaches or theories concerning how it might develop. The first approach that we shall look at is the biological one.

Biology and gender identity

Parents often express concern when their children show an excessive interest in the toys of children of the opposite sex. They feel it is not 'right', and may actually lead them to express behaviour and feelings inappropriate to their sex. All cultures have views about what characteristics, behaviour patterns, dress and occupations are appropriate for a given sex, and the acquisition of these is called sex-typing. A concern over a deviation from sex-appropriate patterns suggests that, deep down, we believe this might lead to something undesirable.

If biology determines gender identity, then presumably 'boys will be boys' and 'girls will be girls', whatever happens to them during development. What evidence have we that this might be so?

Studies of rare individuals who are not clearly one sex or the other throw some light on this problem.

Julianne Imperato-McGinley and colleagues studied a community from the city of Santa Domingo in the Dominican Republic. Here some people in the community had a rare genetic disorder (5 ∝-reductase deficiency) in which males, as babies, often appeared to be female, but subsequently, at puberty, developed male genitals and secondary sexual characteristics. Such female-like males appeared to be able to change to males, in terms of behaviour and gender identity, even though they were reared as females initially. The researchers argued that biology shaped their gender identity, and not their female upbringing.

51

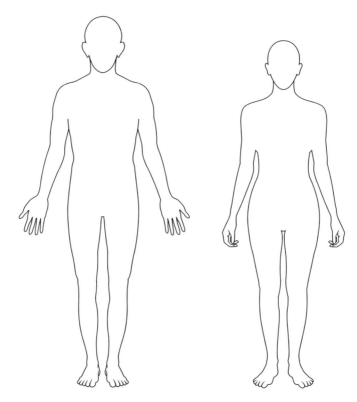

Figure 4.2   Typical male and female body shapes.

However, a rather different view was shown by John and Joan Hampson, who carried out research on over 100 pseudohermaphrodites (people showing incongruities between the appearance of their genitals at birth and various internal structures such as gonads, chromosomes and hormones). Their research suggested that pseudohermaphrodites who were assigned a sex at birth, which was subsequently found to be inappropriate, grew up well adjusted to their assigned sex even when later evidence showed they were predominantly the opposite sex to the one assigned to them. This led the Hampsons to argue that at birth the infant is psychosexually neutral, and that gender identity is learned. Box 4.1 highlights the issue of whether gender identity can be learned.

What sense can we make of these apparently contradictory findings?

We cannot overlook the fact that both studies are concerned with individuals who are quite different from the norm; in such people the pressures to be normal are presumably greater than they are for most individuals. The Santa Domingo study would seem to indicate that gender identity can be shaped by rearing early on, but hormonal influences can play a role in changing the initial gender identity. But did the masculinization at puberty serve as a pressure for them to change over to males? Perhaps the only conclusion can be that there is no single answer to the establishment of gender identity and the relative contribution of nature or nurture,

BOX 4.1
CAN A BOY LEARN TO BECOME A GIRL:
A 'NATURAL' EXPERIMENT

A 'natural' experiment is one where the researcher does not manipulate the independent variable, but takes advantage of a naturally occurring event. This 'natural' experiment throws some light on the question of whether gender identity can be learned, as John Hampson suggested. It is not possible, or indeed ethical, to investigate differences between the sexes in humans in the way it has been in rats. But, as the result of a surgical accident a natural experiment occurred.

In 1965, Bruce Reimer, one of twin boys, lost his penis following a botched circumcision at 7 months. At 22 months, after seeking advice, his parents were advised to bring up the damaged twin as a girl, Brenda, after he had had surgery to remove the remaining male genitals and gonads. Reconstructive surgery was not possible at this time. Would this boy develop a female gender identity and appropriate feminine behaviour? His twin Brian developed normally as a boy. Although initially thought to be a success, Brenda had many problems, was very masculine in her behaviour, and on learning about her early history when aged 15, reverted to living as a boy, David, and eventually had reconstructive surgery. He later married and became a stepfather.

This 'natural' experiment has been used to support the notion that biology shapes gender identity rather than early learning experiences. Nevertheless, David did have some early experience as a boy, and thus biology and early experiences cannot be easily disentangled. Sadly, David's life came to an unhappy end: at the age of 38 he committed suicide. His brother had died of a drug overdose two years earlier. See John Colapinto for further details of this case.

and the interaction between the two varies depending on the circumstances of a given individual's biology and rearing. However, we do know that another condition – transsexualism – adds a further strand to this debate.

A transsexual believes he or she has been trapped in the wrong body. Gender identity and biology are opposed. Because this condition has not been linked with a physical cause, although research has been carried out to see if there are any differences in, for example, hormone levels, no clear differences have been identified. This indicates that biology does not automatically determine gender identity and suggests that experience may play a role. There does seem to be evidence that the parents of transsexuals may have permitted them, or even encouraged them, to dress as the opposite sex in childhood.

Transsexualism lends some support to the notion that early life experiences, or learning, rather than biology, may play a role in gender identity development, but there are other theories about gender identity development we should also consider.

Psychoanalytic theory

Sigmund Freud's views of the development of gender identity centre on the occurrence, at 3- to 5-years-old, of the Oedipus and Electra complexes during the phallic stage of psychosexual development. At this stage, Freud believed, children become aware of the differences between boys' and girls' genitals and notice that boys have a penis unlike girls. The boy develops a desire to replace his father in his mother's affections and feels rivalry towards him. But, fearing his father will castrate him for his illicit desires he resolves this problem by trying to become like his father (and thus also appeal more to his mother) and he identifies with him, resolving the Oedipus complex. Hence gender identity is achieved through identification with the father.

For girls, the Electra complex concerns the girl's feeling of penis envy, whereas for boys the Oedipus complex concerns the fear of losing the penis. The Electra complex was less well worked out by Freud, but for both boys and girls in the normal course of events, Freud argued that the phallic stage ends in identification with the same-sex parent.

To psychologists, Freud's theory, despite being highly influential over the last century or so, is not viewed as a useful explanation. The evidence that exists does not support Freud's views, and many parts of the theory are simply inaccessible to empirical investigation. Other approaches have been viewed as more fruitful.

Cognitive developmental theory

Lawrence Kohlberg put forward a rather different way of looking at gender identity development; he was influenced by Piaget's stages of cognitive development (discussed in Chapter 9). His theory looks at the child's thinking in relation to her or his awareness of gender differences and discusses how the child makes sense of the self as male or female. Initially, the child focuses on superficial differences between the sexes but once the child understands that she or he is female/male the child will want to do things consistent with her/his category. Kohlberg thinks it is natural to value things consistent with or like the self. Thus the child will imitate those like herself/himself – typically mothers for girls and fathers for boys.

Kohlberg sees biology and the environment as both having a role in shaping the development of gender identity. The important aspect of this theory concerns the child's thinking about gender, and how the boy or girl comes to make sense of this knowledge.

Social learning theory

A further theory put forward in the 1960s by David Lynn and Walter Mischel explains gender identity development in terms of social learning. This theory suggests that gender identity occurs through the internalization of characteristics of a person or role through observation, imitation and reinforcement (discussed further in Chapter 12). Initially, children of both sexes are likely to identify with the mother, but through encouragement and reinforcement little boys soon learn to model themselves on males such as the father, since 'male-appropriate' behaviour is reinforced. Little girls are encouraged to be feminine and model themselves on females. Social learning theory predicts, unlike psychoanalytic and cognitive developmental theories, that as children are primarily cared for by females, the process of learning to be feminine is easier for girls than is the process of learning to be masculine for boys.

It may never be possible to test which of these explanations is correct, but there can be no doubt that imitation and identification are powerful forces in forming our unique personalities.

FROM BIRTH TO MATURITY

A glance at a tiny baby in a nappy will not tell us whether it is male or female, but once we know the child is male or female the effect on a us is profound. There is no doubt that some of the differences that exist between women and men can be traced back to influences in childhood and adolescence. Soon after birth, studies of parents and their young babies have clearly shown that boys and girls are often treated differently. One investigation found that fathers rated their newborn sons as more alert, well-coordinated and strong, and their newborn daughters as more inattentive, soft and delicate. This was from having only looked at them – they had not yet even picked them up. From this we can see that it seems quite likely that some form of stereotyping affects parent's attitudes to their baby sons and daughters.

Once out in the world the influence of gender stereotypes becomes increasingly powerful and children soon learn what are 'male-appropriate' and 'female-appropriate' forms of behaviour. Research shows that from around the age of two, children begin to make verbal distinctions between 'mummy' and 'daddy' and maybe between 'boy' and 'girl', although these distinctions are merely labels initially. As children get older, they begin to grasp the fundamental differences between the sexes. But at what age children come to recognize the unchanging nature of their sex is still debated, as we saw in our discussion of the development of gender identity.

The pace of development

Boys lag behind girls in most areas of early physical development, such as standing, walking and talking, and this lead carries on into the early school years when girls are generally ahead of boys in most areas of infant school work. Girls mature physically more quickly than boys, which in turn affects their intellectual development, and it is suggested that the female-dominated world of childhood that is usually centred on the mother and female teachers may also enhance female development.

However, girls typically lose their early advantage after the age of 6 or so when boys seem to catch up in many areas of school work.

For girls puberty typically occurs a year or so earlier than in boys, and the 'growth spurt' occurs approximately between the ages of 11 and 13, and 13 and 15 years respectively. But while girls reach their maximum height around puberty, boys continue to grow for several years afterwards. Adolescence is a crucial period in the formation of the identity of the emerging adult, and gender is a central part of this. John Archer has suggested that different 'developmental pathways' exist for boys and girls, partly as a result of cultural expectations.

For example, he suggested that boys seem to be more rigid and inflexible than girls with respect to opposite-sex behaviour: 'tomboys' are much more socially acceptable than 'cissies', for example, and girls can take part in boys' games more readily than vice versa. However, this flexibility differs over the lifespan for boys and girls, as girls' interests are more flexible in childhood, but narrow down in the teenage years, centring on physical and sexual attractiveness and personal relationships. Whereas boys' interests typically widen, rather than narrow, in the teenage years.

ARE GENDER DIFFERENCES CHANGING?

In 1974, Eleanor Maccoby and Carol Jacklin published their famous book The Psychology of Sex Differences. These authors carried out a comprehensive review of all the published research literature at the time, and their conclusions received a great deal of attention and discussion. Research has continued in the intervening years, and more recent reviews suggest that some of the originally identified differences seem to be disappearing, and some new gender differences have been found that were not originally identified by Maccoby and Jacklin, and so the debate continues. See Exercise 4.1, which looks at the portrayal of men and women in the media. Let us now look at the differences between the sexes in personality, behaviour and intelligence.

Personality and behaviour

Many suggestions have been made about how the personalities of the sexes differ. Qualities such as ambition, drive and competitiveness are regarded as typically masculine, whereas passivity, nurturance and emotionality are seen as typically feminine. It is extremely difficult for researchers to get any clear answers as to whether or not these views have any foundation. Aggression, for example, has frequently been studied and there is no doubt that boys engage in more physical fighting and rough-and-tumble play than girls. However, when verbal aggression such as taunts and insults are taken into account, it is by no means clear that girls are any less aggressive than boys. Other studies in this vein have suggested that boys tend to be more adventurous, independent and competitive, and that girls are correspondingly more affectionate, socially sensitive and emotional.

Do these differences between boys and girls carry on into adult life?

EXERCISE 4.1
THE PORTRAYAL OF WOMEN AND MEN
IN THE MEDIA

Instructions

For this exercise select a range of magazines from Sunday newspapers. Taking each magazine, cut out the first 10 pictures of males and the first 10 pictures of females. Write down for each picture how the male or female is dressed, what she or he is doing (including whether active or passive) and what task she or he appears to be engaged in. Also note any relationship to others in the picture. Record this for all pictures. For example, you might write, 'Female wearing party dress, sitting down drinking wine and looking at a male,' or 'Male in smart suit, driving expensive car fast through Manhattan.'

When you have completed the task, compare your records for males and for females.

Results

What do your records tell you about the portrayal of males and females? Which sex is portrayed more actively, in positions of greater power or in activities or jobs of higher status?

You may like to repeat this exercise, but this time videotape 10 TV adverts and then note how the women and men in these are portrayed.

It is often claimed that females are more interested in people, whereas males may be more interested in objects, or things. This is certainly true in children's play. Many studies have shown that girls' games tend to revolve around other people, such as playing with dolls, and acting out school, home or hospital scenes, whereas boys tend to have mechanical and 'scientific' play interests – in machines, construction games and computers, for example. In adulthood we can see a similar trend: popular reading material and magazines would suggest that men focus on hobbies and pastimes with things – cars, trains, and do-it-yourself, whereas women are much more concerned with people and relationships.

In his widely read book *Men Are from Mars, Women Are from Venus*, first published in the 1990s, John Gray argues that men and women adopt very different styles in relationships. He believes for example that 'a woman's sense of self is defined through her feelings and the quality of her relationships', whereas 'a man's sense of self is defined through his ability to achieve results'.

He goes on to suggest that although they speak the same language, what they mean by their words is very different. These views seem to support the notion that women are much more people-orientated than men, with the implication that these are the fundamental differences. Gray's ideas are not based on psychological research, but some have partial support from such research.

Other differences between women and men include, for example, that women conform more than men in situations involving group pressure; that they are more susceptible to persuasion than men; and that they are more sensitive to non-verbal cues than men. It also seems that men and women have different styles of communication: analyses of conversations show that men are more assertive, and tend to control the interaction to a greater extent than women. We might say that there are important differences in the power strategies typically used by men and women.

Gender differences in intelligence and abilities

For centuries males have accepted without question the idea that not only are women and men different, but also that women are inferior to men. This is captured in Charles Darwin's summary of the differences:

> The chief distinction in the intellectual powers of the two sexes is shown by man's attaining to a higher eminence, in whatever he takes up, than can woman – whether requiring deep thought, reason, or imagination, or merely the use of the senses and hands.

Today, while most of us would not accept Darwin's ideas, there is still much research and discussion about gender differences in intelligence and abilities. It is widely accepted that women and men do not differ in general intelligence, but the overall spread of scores on intelligence tests does differ between the sexes. The psychologist Alice Heim, in 1970, discussed 'the mediocrity of women', by which she meant that more females gained intelligence tests scores around the average, while more males gained scores at the extremes of the range. In other words, there may be greater variability, or scatter, among the males.

When we look at ability differences, Eleanor Maccoby and Carol Jacklin concluded that females tend to do relatively better on tests involving words (verbal skills), and males tend to be correspondingly better on spatial and mathematical tests – at working with shapes and numbers.

In verbal abilities, recent analyses by Janet Hyde and Marcia Lynn suggest that girls do slightly better than boys on most aspects of verbal abilities, with the largest difference in speech production. Michael Rutter and others have shown that throughout the English-speaking world reading disability is substantially more common in boys.

In mathematics, when three different areas are examined, computation, concepts and problem-solving, it has been found that the main difference is in problem-solving, where males outperform females from about the age of 14, although females are initially superior at computation at 6–10 years old. Similarly, as far as spatial abilities are concerned, the main difference favouring males is in mental rotation (the ability to imagine how objects will appear when rotated in two- or three-dimensional space).

However, recent studies suggest that these differences may be diminishing: for example, there are many studies of mathematical abilities that have not found gender differences.

What are the causes of these observed differences, and why is the degree of difference changing? Some suggest that sex differences in the lateralization of function in the cerebral cortex (i.e. the extent to which each hemisphere is specialized for particular jobs), or the degree to which each hemisphere is linked by fibres in the corpus callosum, may partially explain these gender differences. Simon Baron-Cohen argues that prenatal testosterone accelerates the growth of the right hemisphere in males, and as this hemisphere is more involved in spatial abilities, this explains in part male superiority in spatial/mathematical ability tests. On the other hand, in the female it is suggested there is less lateralization of function, and it is thought that bilateral representation for language may be a factor in females' superior performance. There is some evidence to support these views when the after effects of stroke are observed in males and females. The connections between the two hemispheres via the corpus callosum, which is bigger in women, has also been linked to better verbal fluency.

Nevertheless, we should not underestimate the extent to which differences between the sexes in their treatment and upbringing enhance what may be relatively minor biological differences. Stereotypical views about what is appropriate for males and females foster greater gender divergence. As equal opportunities continue to be encouraged in the developed world, we may find that ability differences continue to decline.

GENDER DIFFERENCES IN SCHOOL AND AFTERWARDS

In schools today, we still find that boys and girls tend to have different interests. For example, right from kindergarten onwards, boys use computers more than girls, both in school as well as at home. However, several factors other than pure biology, may account for this gender difference. Research shows that parents are more likely to buy boys computers, and computer games generally have predominantly male characters. Thus, one impact of the stereotypical notion that 'computers are for boys' is that opportunities for girls to participate, and feel equally involved in the games, are reduced.

How do differences in abilities influence the performance of males and females in school examinations. Statistics on GCSE exams in England in 2004 revealed that 'girls continue to outperform boys, particularly at the higher grades'. A similar pattern is shown for A-level results, where again girls did better than boys, both in the pass rate and in achieving higher grades. However, when we look at the numbers taking these exams we again find gender preferences. For example, there are higher numbers of girls taking subjects like psychology (three times more) and English (two times more), whereas more boys take physics (nearly four times more) and computer studies (eight times more).

BOX 4.2
WHISKERS AND PROFESSORS

Many differences between males and females are simply correlations that may or may not have a causal link to biological differences. Such correlations may be genuinely linked to biological differences, for example adult height, while others are purely cultural differences – such as a correlation between hair length and gender: with females generally having longer hair. A recent piece of research by Sarah Carter and Kristina Åström showed that while 10.5 per cent of university lecturers were bewhiskered, this rose to 21.4 per cent for professors. Intermediate levels of staff had intermediate percentages of whiskers. Does this tell us that high levels of testosterone influence likelihood of becoming professor or could it be discrimination? You may like to discuss the possible reasons for this finding with friends and family.

These school exam results certainly do not confirm the old idea that boys are cleverer than girls, even though gender preferences for particular subjects are evident – overall girls now outperform boys.

With such success in school, do we find that women are equally successful in the workplace? Today, although many more women are in paid work than in previous decades (including the majority of women with young children), males still predominate in positions of greater power, and in jobs thought be more intellectually demanding – such as universities, for example. Is this due to ability differences or discrimination? In 2005, Larry Summers, President of Harvard University, asserted that the small numbers of women on maths and engineering faculties in the most elite research universities were due to 'differing availability of aptitude at the high end'. Is there a biological explanation for this lack of women or do cultural factors, especially negative sexist stereotypes, play a far greater role in influencing who is appointed at such universities, as Alan Dershowitz, Professor of Law at Harvard, believes? Evidence of discrimination at this level is clearly shown in a study of Swedish academics, which found that women had to be two and a half times better (have published two and a half times more material) to be awarded a research grant when compared to men applying for such grants. (Also see Box 4.2 on another example of the predominance of males at professorial levels in universities.)

In English law, equal opportunities have been enshrined for more than three decades, but, according to 2004 statistics, males earn 19.5 per cent more than females. In the UK in 2004, the government led a drive to close this pay gap and Patricia Hewitt, the Trade and Industry Secretary, commented that 'Career sexism limits opportunities for women of all ages and prevents them from achieving their full potential.' Although women now make up 49 per cent of the workforce, they are concentrated chiefly in just a few occupations such as administration, childcare, sales and nursing. 'There are many women who want to get into science or manufacturing jobs, but are put off by the misconception that a woman simply cannot do the job,' Hewitt claims. No matter how many opportunities women and men are given to enter jobs that are non-traditional, it is still likely that there will not be an even distribution of males and females in specific areas. Even if women and men still show preferences for particular types of work, providing that males and females are equally valued, then this should not matter.

A dilemma for women is that although most now participate in the workforce, there is not a proportional reduction in their domestic duties. Statistics for the UK show that women still do the majority of these tasks (see the National Statistics Online 2004). It is not possible for women's roles to change without this also affecting men's. With the rise of divorce and one-parent families, chiefly headed by females, it seems likely that childcare and housework will continue to remain the province of females rather than males.

Greater equality of opportunity for the sexes is evident in Britain and also in other parts of the Western world, nevertheless there are many areas where sexism is entrenched and shows no sign of disappearing. For instance, the male-first rule of succession is still part of the British monarchy, and precedence of male heirs over female ones is also the case in many aristocratic families. While sexual discrimination is still part of the fabric of our society it is hard to see how we can truly achieve equality of opportunity. It may be an ideal for some, but of course many people are resistant to the arguments in favour of such equality and, in the twenty-first century, if our goal is equal opportunities, then there is still much to achieve.

Recommended Reading

Archer, J. (1995). Sex differences. In A.S.R. Manstead and M. Hewstone (eds.), *The Blackwell Encyclopaedia of Social Psychology*. Oxford: Blackwell.

Archer, J. and Lloyd, B. (1985). *Sex and Gender, rev. edn*. Cambridge: Cambridge University Press.

Basow, S.A. (1992). *Gender Stereotypes and Roles, 3rd edn*. Belmont, Calif.: Brooks/Cole.

Nicholson, J. (1995). *Men and Women: How different are they?* Oxford: Oxford University Press.

Matlin, M. (2000). *The Psychology of Women*. London: Harcourt College Publishers.

Trew, K. and Kremer, J. (1998). *Gender and Psychology*. London: Arnold.

5

You and Others

- Social roles

- What we do and what we think

- Stereotypes and prejudice

- How do others influence us?

- Conformity

- Obedience and authority

- Violence and the mass media

- The power of social influence

- A 10-year-old schoolboy wears his Real Madrid replica football shirt day in, day out, changes his hairstyle frequently to follow the current style of his idol David Beckham and dreams of scoring penalty goals in international matches.
- A group of teenage schoolgirls follow their favourite singer Robbie Williams to concerts around the country, buy all his records and plaster their bedrooms with his pictures.

SOCIAL ROLES

One theory of personality development – of how we grow up to be the way we are – is that our selves are partly formed by our imitating or *taking on the role of* other people, who can be thought of as *models*. The two examples illustrate two models, from the worlds of sport and entertainment, that commonly influence older children and teenagers. Whereas younger children may be powerfully influenced by models present in the home (their parents or other relatives, for example), the models become more and more varied as they get older. They might include friends, teachers or neighbours, and this broadens out in later life to include sports stars, media personalities, social reformers or politicians. This shows very clearly that people are essentially *social beings*: we constantly act, talk and think in relation to other people.

This process is known as *role taking*, and it shows how we think and act to fit in with patterns of behaviour laid down by society. Each person is at the centre of a complex web of interrelated roles, so you might, at different times of the day, 'act out' the part of parent, motorist, churchgoer, gardener, secretary and so on: different roles are demanded by different situations. These roles can be taken on at three different levels. The most superficial is *role enactment*: a person who carries out a disliked job purely for the pay, or a stage actor in an unsympathetic part, is merely 'going through the motions' with no personal commitment to that particular behaviour.

In contrast to this are those people whose commitment to a certain role is so strong that it becomes an essential part of their personality: most doctors would adopt a responsible, caring attitude towards others, for example, whether or not these doctors were on duty. We could say that they have *internalized* the role behaviour, and perform it automatically and unconsciously.

In between these two is the level of *role taking*, at which certain parts of the role are identified with and others are not. A schoolteacher, for example, may have completely internalized educational ideals concerning the welfare of her pupils, but, faced with classroom disruption, she may be forced to resort to punishments of which she disapproves. She experiences *role conflict* when this occurs. Some jobs have 'built in' role conflict: prison officers are expected to be both punitive and rehabilitative with respect to their charges, for example, and this can lead to many moral dilemmas. How do we deal with these matches and mismatches at the level of the individual?

WHAT WE DO AND WHAT WE THINK

- Have you ever gossiped or complained about another person behind their back? Have you ever expressed one view to your boss at work and then expressed a different view to your workmates when the boss was not there?
- You are very sympathetic to the needs of substance abusers and ex-offenders, and believe that the best way to cope with their rehabilitation is through care in the community. Your local city council decides to open a drop-in centre for the homeless just two streets away from the school your children attend, and the parents' association passes a resolution to oppose the opening of the centre, because of fear that the children may be in danger on their way home from school. How should you vote at the school meeting at which this resolution is debated?

Almost all of us must truthfully answer 'yes' to the first set of questions. We all hold different attitudes in public and in private, and many modern-day politicians seem to have made this into something of an art! It is not quite so obvious how different people might respond to the drop-in centre problem, however. Some would stick to their social principles, and vote in favour of the centre: others would put their private interests above their publicly held beliefs, and vote against it.

These dilemmas make it clear that what we say and think are often at variance with what we do: our *attitudes* and our *behaviour* are often inconsistent with each other. The reason for this, once again, is that most of our behaviour is social: it has to take account of decisions that must be taken in relation to other people. The result is that people sometimes do what seem to be illogical or irrational things, as a result of *social influence*. As social psychologist Elliot Aronson puts it, 'People who do crazy things are not necessarily crazy.'

Social comparison

This idea has been expressed more formally by Aronson's mentor, Leon Festinger, in his theory of social comparison. The basis of this is that people have a constant need to validate their opinions by comparing them with those of others.

Suppose Colin, a successful publishing executive, meets up with his old university friend Mark, who stayed on to do a doctorate and is now lecturing at another university, ten years after their graduation. Both were heavily involved in student peace campaigning, and took part in active protests against military regimes while at university, though only Mark remains involved.

Mark is now organizing a coach trip to a national demonstration against the US involvement in Iraq, and invites his old student friend to come. However, Colin feels he has grown out of protest marching, and does not want to attend: but is unsure how to reply to Mark. He considers making the (dishonest) response that he now has some sympathy with the British Government's position, in view of the 'special relationship' between Bush and Blair: or he may even say he would like to attend the march, but has another engagement on that day. What he will not do is express the opinion he would if he were discussing this with his partner or his publishing colleagues. Festinger's theory suggests that our opinions and beliefs are constantly being shaped by this kind of process.

Saving face

In this fictitious story, there is a fundamental inconsistency in Colin's attitudes. He has a negative attitude towards the march, and a positive attitude towards (and indeed admiration for) his friend Mark, but this is incompatible with Mark's positive attitude towards the march. Colin may resolve the problem by using the 'special relationship' argument (thereby 'saving face'), or by ignoring it (the 'other engagement' excuse). These different ways of resolving the problem form part of *cognitive consistency theories* in social psychology, and probably the best known of these is Leon Festinger's *cognitive dissonance theory*, published in 1957. Festinger proposed that a state of dissonance exists when there is inconsistency between the different beliefs and attitudes people hold, or between those attitudes and their behaviour. The theory suggests that individuals experiencing dissonance are motivated to reduce it, and that there are three main ways of doing this.

The first is to *change attitudes and/or behaviour* so as to make them more consistent: Colin should either go on the march, even change his attitude towards Mark, arguing perhaps that they have 'grown apart' over the last decade. The second is to *get new information* that supports your attitude or behaviour: Colin might seek information from the Internet which shows that the people of Iraq are receiving many benefits from the US involvement, such as food supplies, which are not widely reported in the press. The third is to *minimize the importance of the conflict*: Colin could 'agree to disagree' with Mark, and maintain friendly contact. These three strategies are used to change our behaviour and/or attitudes in order to save face.

STEREOTYPES AND PREJUDICE

- Are the Japanese industrious, polite and formal?
- Are Americans materialistic, pleasure-loving and loud?
- Are women more nurturing, caring and submissive than men?
- Are professors eccentric and absent-minded?

Some people would answer 'yes' to these questions, and would therefore have certain expectations about the behaviour of any new Japanese, American, female or professorial person they might encounter. There can be no doubt that these expectations are faulty. Some Japanese are sloppy and imprecise: some Americans are quiet and reserved; some women are dominant and assertive; some professors are dynamic and business-like; and so on.

Such *stereotypes* about distinguishable groups of people persist, nevertheless. They involve overgeneralization: people erroneously attribute all the characteristics of the stereotype to individual members of the group, even though only some (if any) of those characteristics are truly applicable. Stereotypes can be based on a number of different group characteristics: in the examples above, we have chosen nationality, gender and occupation as the basis for them, but they might also be based on other sources of difference such as race, age, social class or even attitudes and preferences.

Are stereotypes always wrong?

The eminent social psychologist Roger Brown has suggested that views about ethnic and racial stereotypes have changed over time, pointing out that the term 'stereotype' was first introduced in 1922 by the political commentator Walter Lippman in his book *Public Opinion*. Lippman's view was that national and racial stereotypes were erroneous – that it was not only irrational but also potentially dangerous to propagate oversimplified stereotypes about why Jews, Hispanics or other groups had particular personality types.

Some further empirical evidence about ethnic stereotypes was provided in a classic study carried out by David Katz and Kenneth Braly in 1933, who asked 100 Princeton University students to assign 'typical' personality traits (e.g. industrious, intelligent, materialistic, sly, progressive, treacherous) to each of 10 ethnic groups (such as Germans, Italians, Jews). The researchers found clear evidence of stereotyping, and argued that because there were such wide variations in what was considered to be 'typical' of each group, the stereotyping displayed by their subjects was indeed irrational and divisive. Although a further study of a group of Princeton students in 1951 found that the level of stereotyping had declined, a third study in 1967 by Marvin Karlins, Thomas Coffman and Gary Walters showed that it had 'rebounded' once again to 1933 levels, which suggests that the beliefs expressed may not have been so irrational after all.

The problem lies in the relationship between scientific evidence and the social and political context in which it is expressed: in the 'politically correct' 2000s, it is increasingly difficult to express what could be seen as any kind of prejudiced opinion about members of minority groups. Roger Brown's perhaps wiser and more mature view is that it is naive to suggest that there is no basis whatsoever for ethnic or other group stereotypes. Although it may still often be wrong to try to describe what is *typical* of a given group, it may nevertheless be possible to define what is partly characteristic of them. The tendency to categorize is a basic aspect of human cognition, and it seems odd that stereotypes persist so strongly if they have no basis in reality whatever.

One recent and newsworthy area of research is on the effects of so-called 'problem music' styles such as hip hop, rap, punk, and heavy rock: there are moves in North America to restrict or censor these, and it has been argued that the lyrics can inflame prejudice and cause acts of violence, criminal behaviour, and even suicide. Some research reviews indicate that fans of this music tend to commit more criminal acts, such as shoplifting, and are more likely to use illegal drugs than are non-fans. A recent study by Adrian North and Lorraine Sheridan of Leicester University, using two Internet surveys of 1,376 and 696 respondents from North America and Europe, found that fans of problem music did indeed score higher than non-fans on both the Eysenck Criminality Scale and the Eysenck Addiction Scale.

BOX 5.1
A SURVEY OF POP MUSIC FANS AND THEIR
ATTITUDES

Adrian North and Lorraine Sheridan, using two separate Internet question-naires, carried out a large-scale survey of the relationship between pop music preferences and attitudes towards criminality and addiction. This enabled them to reach a much larger and more geographically widespread sample than would otherwise have been possible. The questionnaires were public-ized via the host university's website and supplemented by press releases targeted at both the European and North American pop music press. Both questionnaires first asked respondents to rate their liking for each of 22 musical styles by clicking one of 11 choice buttons.

The rest of the first questionnaire, which attracted 1,376 respondents, involved completing the Eysenck Criminality Scale (see Eysenck, 1996), which measures the tendency toward criminal behaviour. The rest of the second questionnaire, which attracted 696 respondents, involved completing the Eysenck Addiction Scale (see Eysenck, 1997). The website access was arranged so that respondents who had completed Questionnaire 1 could not also complete Questionnaire 2. The results of the study suggest a link between a liking for 'problem music' and high scores on these two scales.

They conclude that these relationships may be rooted in fundamental personality variables, rather than in American cultural stereotyping. If this is true, we may need to reassess the evidence for the existence of stereotypes. (See Box 5.1.)

Prejudice

Even if stereotypes do have some basis in reality, they can be very damaging when they are used to convey generalized negative or hostile attitudes towards groups of people. The use of stereotyped thinking against minority groups is what we might call *prejudice*. A very visible, offensive example of this is of course racial prejudice: some people really believe that blacks are stupid and lazy, and the recent beha-viour of some European soccer fans in making animal noises at black players and throwing bananas on to the field is a horrific reminder of uncivilized attitudes that should have died out long ago. Prejudice can be defined as 'an attitude (usually negative) toward the members of some group based solely on their membership of that group'. These attitudes have nothing to do with the actual behaviour of those individuals, but are based instead on their membership of particular groups.

Figure 5.1   The use of stereotyped thinking against minority groups is termed 'prejudice'. *(Janine Wiedel Photolibrary/Alamy.)*

It's only a joke

Prejudice is at the heart of a good deal of racist humour: the basis of 'Irish jokes' in Britain is that the Irish are stupid, and there are similar Polish equivalents in the USA, for example. Do these jokes simply serve to 'let off steam'? Do we express prejudiced attitudes to other members of the group in a harmless, joking context (such as the revue in the social club) because we do not really hold them? Or is it that the humour itself creates prejudice: that sharing jokes about Irish or Polish stupidity, Scottish meanness or about mothers-in-law actually reinforces our stereotypes of these groups?

This latter idea is the first of four possible explanations of prejudice: that once we have acquired a stereotype or *negative schema* about a particular group, we tend to take much more notice of information that fits in with it than of that which does not. The idea is that we form systematically biased ways of thinking about that group that become self-confirming. The second explanation is that prejudice arises from *competition* between different social groups: that when jobs, good schooling or housing are in short supply, prejudiced attitudes can be fuelled. In Great Britain, for example, there is ill-feeling among some unemployed indigenous whites towards immigrant groups who have jobs, such as the Asian communities in cities like Leicester and Birmingham, and this might fuel prejudice against individual Asians.

The third explanation is based on *social categorization*; that is, people's natural tendency to divide those around them into two basic groups, 'us' (who are valued) and 'them' (who are devalued). A good example of this is in present-day Northern Ireland: the divisions between Catholic and Protestant members of the population are powerful and long-standing, and strangers are quickly categorized as members of one group or the other, so that certain attitudes and behaviour are attributed to them. The fourth, *social learning* explanation is that prejudiced attitudes are learnt from parents, peers and others, from early childhood onwards. In Northern Ireland, generation after generation of children are taught within the family to despise the members of the opposing group. When such attitudes are implanted at an early age, it is easy to see that they are likely to be particularly strong and also very hard to change.

HOW DO OTHERS INFLUENCE US?

Consider the following questions:

- Do you think that you would perform an everyday task in exactly the same way when on your own as you would in the company of others?
- If you were to collapse in a crowded street, would you assume you had more chance of getting help than if there were very few people nearby?
- If you found yourself in a group in which others were saying something contrary to the evidence of your own eyes, would you speak out and tell them so?

The answers to these questions may seem an obvious 'yes'. In fact, research by social psychologists has shown that in each of these situations the answer is quite likely to be 'no'. People's behaviour and decision making is influenced by the presence of others, and this may apply even if there is no direct interaction between them.

Social loafing and bystander apathy

The presence of others can actually inhibit our likelihood of responding. For example, in a tug-of-war team it was found that the more team members there were the less hard each pulled on the rope. This reduction in action has been called *social loafing*. Another example of inhibited behaviour was also shown by bystanders in a particularly dreadful murder case in America. In 1964, Kitty Genovese was murdered but 'For more than half an hour 38 respectable, law-abiding citizens . . . watched a killer stalk and stab a woman in three separate attacks . . .' None came to her aid or called the police during that time. This case, and other research, led psychologists to conclude that 'The larger the number of onlookers, the smaller the individual probability of helping, and the longer the delay.' It seems that witnesses look to others to define the situation, and thus action is delayed or none is taken. This is called *pluralistic ignorance*. It is also suggested that the larger the group the greater the *diffusion of responsibility* because no one takes personal responsibility for initiating action.

There are other studies, however, that do not find this inhibitory effect of the presence of others – indeed, they demonstrate quite the reverse.

Social facilitation

Robert Zajonc and many others have reported that individuals perform better when others are around than when they are alone. In a number of tasks it was found that people working together, or in the presence of others, perform at a faster rate. These effects have been termed *coaction* and *audience effects*. However, the presence of others works best on simple or well-learned tasks; if the task is new or difficult, then the presence of others impairs performance. (Have you ever tried to find something in the presence of someone who is eager for you to find it? Why is it you can never find it while they are there, but find it as soon as they've left the room?)

Mary Brickner and co-workers have suggested that the importance of the task and the cultural context are factors that may explain both the inhibitory and enhancing effects of others on us. They argued that loafing was more likely to occur in relation to unimportant tasks. Studies of different cultures indicate that a situation producing social loafing in the West may actually produce an enhancing effect in China and Japan. Perhaps it depends on whether a culture stresses the importance of the individual or the group in its ideology.

Social influences on decision making

A number of researchers have shown that it's not just what you do but what you *think* that can be influenced by others.

As we saw in the first chapter, group decisions can often be more extreme than an individual's decision made alone. This is known as the *group polarization phenomenon*, and the example we cited in Chapter 1 (see Question 4) was the *risky shift*, a particular form of the phenomenon discovered by James Stoner. Stoner was surprised to find this, because people generally think that decisions made by boards and committees are likely to be safer decisions because an extreme view will be stifled.

Other research indicates that the presence of others may result in pressure to conform, and this is exemplified in a classic study by Solomon Asch.

CONFORMITY

In 1951, Solomon Asch published an experiment on visual perception in which participants were asked to match a standard line with one of three alternatives. (This is a task that all people with normal vision can do quite accurately.) Tests were run using groups of seven to nine people who were asked to answer aloud. However, the experiment was rigged. Asch used only one true participant – all the others were confederates whose answers had been predetermined. Each naive participant was placed towards the end of the row so that the majority of the confederates' responses were given first.

Asch determined in advance that on two-thirds of the tests confederates would unanimously respond with one of the wrong alternatives. How would the naive participant react when confronted by this? On testing over 100 naive participants, he found that only 25 per cent of them remained independent. Across the whole sample the error rate was 36.8 per cent of judgements, whereas in normal circumstances it would have been less than 1 per cent. Why did the participants 'give in' or conform to the majority judgement, despite the indisputable evidence before their eyes?

Why does conformity occur?

The high level of conformity found in the Asch study prompted a number of further experiments. Asch found that the size of the group, providing that it was of at least three confederates, did not affect the degree to which a single naive participant conformed. (Later research indicated that conformity increases up to a group size of seven confederates, and thereafter does not rise. A larger crowd does not appear to enhance the effect.) The attractiveness of the group and the confidence of the naive subject in his or her ability also influence conforming behaviour. Participants who perceive the group as desirable, and who feel that they are less competent than average will, experiments show, be more likely to follow the lead of the group rather than stick to their own view.

In addition to this, other research suggests that there is also a physiological pressure to conform. Measures of the fatty acid levels in the blood of participants in an experiment of this type show an increased level of blood fatty acids when they held out against the confederates' wrong responses, but this was lower for participants who conformed. Evidently not conforming is an uncomfortable experience.

How did participants explain their conformity? Asch found that many participants complied, while privately rejecting the majority view that was voiced. But they still underestimated the extent to which they conformed and voiced wrong answers. This suggests that their judgement was partly distorted by group pressure.

More recent reviews have argued that Asch's findings have been misinterpreted, and it has been pointed out that participants managed to resist conformity pressures on about two-thirds of the judgements. Thus conformity was the exception, rather than the rule.

Resisting the pressure to conform

Having an ally is one important way that can enable a participant to resist group pressure. If two naive participants were present in an Asch-type experiment, conformity dropped to 5.5 per cent of the judgements given. The support of someone else agreeing with the participant's view clearly enabled her or him to resist strong group pressures.

Other research indicates that conformity varies depending on the consistency of the confederate's judgements – the greater the consistency shown, the greater the conformity from the naive participant and vice versa. Cultural factors also play a

Figure 5.2 David and Victoria Beckham. (© *Empics.*)

part and research on conformity in different countries has found some variations. But in general there are still quite high levels of conformity wherever research is carried out. Finally, conformity tends to lessen with age.

The research on conformity is shocking in some respects. Most of us would hope we could resist pressure of this kind, but even though some resistance was occurring, it is still a matter of concern that group pressure can be so potent. Let us now look at an everyday example of the desire to conform.

Conformity and body image

Since the 1950s or so in Western culture the ideal body shape for women has changed to one that is very thin compared to earlier decades. In the media, models, film stars and singers, for example, are admired for their slender dimensions, and the desire to conform to this image by girls and women seems to have led to an epidemic of eating disorders such as anorexia nervosa and bulimia. Well-known figures such as Princess Diana and Geri Halliwell succumbed to problems of this type. Research shows that women tend to perceive themselves as heavier than they actually are and many are continually striving to reduce their weight. When the ideal image is too thin for good health, then the problems of trying to conform are obvious.

Figure 5.3 Princess Diana looking very slender. *(Anwar Hussein/All Action.)*

OBEDIENCE AND AUTHORITY

Having considered fairly subtle forms of pressure, let us now explore how people react to being given quite specific instructions on what to do. Would you obey instructions when you felt what you were being asked to do was harmful?

Some controversial experiments on obedience were carried out by Stanley Milgram at Yale University. His 'teacher' participants, who thought they were taking part in an experiment on the effects of punishment on memory, were told to deliver electric shocks of increasing intensity when a 'learner' subject, out of sight in an adjacent room, made an error in a task. Shocks ranged from 15 to 450 volts, and shock buttons were labelled from 'Slight shock' to 'Danger: severe shock' at the top of the scale. The learner, who was actually an actor confederate of the experimenter, behaved as if he actually received the shocks (in fact, he did not) and could be heard crying out as they were apparently given. The true aim of the study was to explore the extent of the 'teacher' participants' obedience to the instructions they had been given.

Estimates of the level of obedience in this situation both by psychiatrists and later by college students predicted that no more than 1 per cent would obey instructions to this degree (i.e. up to the severe shock level).

All the participants in Milgram's experiment were men of above-average intelligence, and yet *two-thirds* of them obeyed the instructions, delivering shocks up to the danger zone, while showing great distress in doing so and even pleading with the experimenter to stop the study. The power of the experimenter was extraordinary, and obeying instructions appeared to override humane considerations.

Milgram's experiment and the subsequent variations that have been carried out have been severely criticized. Many believe that trust in psychologists and the health and dignity of the participants were greatly at risk. The fact that the participants were debriefed only goes part of the way towards allaying these ethical objections. Nevertheless, the results clearly show that authority is very powerful. It is of some comfort to report that studies of the Milgram type carried out in Australia, Germany and the Netherlands have shown that obedience, in certain conditions, can be minimal. The main factor that enabled the individual to resist was having an experimental accomplice who refused to obey instructions. Just as we saw in the Asch study, so too in the Milgram situation, support from one other individual makes a crucial difference. Perhaps what we can learn from this is that standing alone in our views is a very difficult thing for most people; if we have no support, we need to look for it, and this seems to provide the strength to resist those seen as being in authority. For another example of the way in which authority can change people see Box 5.2.

Being independent is not easy, as we have seen, and the increasing number of books and courses on 'assertiveness training' (mentioned in Chapter 2) are an aid to those who feel they are 'Yes-people' – people who cannot, or dare not, say 'no'. Exercise 5.1 (page 76) helps you to say 'no' more effectively.

VIOLENCE AND THE MASS MEDIA

The growth of the mass media has led to a great increase in the size of the group that can influence us. Today there are films, radio, television, newspapers, magazines, computer games and the myriad of information available worldwide on the Internet. Research investigating the effects of TV violence on people's behaviour and attitudes has burgeoned in recent decades, but estimates of the amount of violence seen on TV vary. One American survey, for example, identified an amazing 1,846 violent scenes on broadcast and cable TV screened between 6.00 a.m. and midnight in Washington, D.C. In contrast, other reviewers suggest that media violence in the UK and the US forms only about 1 per cent of programme content. Whichever is the more accurate assessment, violence on TV has a much greater frequency than it has in real life and its impact on all of us is a matter of serious concern.

Researchers of this topic must look not only at the incidence of aggression but also at the way in which it is portrayed. A violent cartoon is unlikely to have the same impact as violence in news footage. Because of the ethical difficulties of using very violent images in such research, one problem of this type of research is that it may be in a rather contrived setting, or involve acts of aggression that

BOX 5.2
POWER AND TYRANNY: A FIELD STUDY

A famous study, designed to explore the social psychology of power, called the *Stanford Prison Experiment* was conducted by Philip Zimbardo and colleagues in the early 1970s. In this research, Zimbardo set up a simulated prison environment in which participants – who were stable, healthy, normal people – were each randomly assigned to either a prisoner or guard role. Participants who took the role of guards became so tyrannical and brutal in their behaviour that the study had to be halted after six days for the safety and welfare of the prisoners. Zimbardo concluded that powerful roles lead inevitably to tyranny. Both prisoners and guards were similar sorts of people yet the power of the guards changed them, even though they knew it was a make-believe situation.

In 2002, a BBC Prison Experiment led to questioning of Zimbardo's conclusions. Although set up like the Stanford study, with both prisoners and guards, other manipulations were also introduced; this study provided opportunities for prisoners to improve their situation, and to question the legitimacy of various features of the study. In this research the conclusion was that tyranny is not an inevitable and automatic expression of role (in this case guards), although the authors noted that the participants were close to forming a new and more draconian structure in an attempt to create order out of the failure of the group to work together and establish their own social roles.

may be perceived as relatively minor ones. See Box 5.3 for a classic experiment on the effects of TV violence.

Nevertheless, in their review of the research on the impact of media violence, Edward Donnerstein and Stacey Smith indicate that viewers may not only learn to be more aggressive as a result of such viewing, but there is also likely to be engendered an increased callousness towards violence among others (the *desensitization effect*), and viewing violence may also lead to apprehension about being the victim of such acts (the *fear effect*). These authors report on a review by the American Psychological Association noting 'the almost universal exposure of American children to high levels of media violence' and 'there is absolutely no doubt that those who are heavy viewers of this violence demonstrate increased acceptance of aggressive attitudes and increased aggressive behaviour'.

Such comments leave us in very little doubt about the negative impact of TV violence, but this view is not universally accepted. Guy Cumberbach is cautious in his assessment of the evidence, and cites a range of examples from different countries where results of research are conflicting.

EXERCISE 5.1
SAYING 'NO'

Saying 'no' can be difficult because we often associate saying 'no' with being nasty, selfish, hurtful and rejecting. But, by saying 'no' we are merely *refusing a request*; we are *not rejecting the person* who made the request.

How to do it?

When we become more confident in saying 'no', we may be able to say it quite simply: 'No I'm not prepared to do it.' (Use extended eye contact, don't smile, and if possible, leave the situation.)

But most people find this difficult – so use the technique below to clarify what is being asked, and then say 'no.'

Use:

1. Reflective listening – repeat back to the questioner what was said to you.
2. Say 'no' without excuses or apologies.

Role-play with a friend

Choose one of the following situations in which you want to say 'no', or take a situation that occurred to you recently in which you could not say 'no' but wanted to.

1. The persistent salesperson is trying to sell you a vacuum cleaner, which you stopped to look at in a shop.
2. A friend phones and assumes that she or he can come round because she or he is bored, but you had planned a relaxing evening with the family.

First, get your friend to act out either one or two above and answer it as you normally would. Did you find it difficult and make lots of excuses? Now keep it simple and use reflective listening before you say 'no'. For example: 'I can see you are eager to sell the vacuum cleaner but, no, I don't want to buy one.'

Or 'I can see you are bored and would like to come round, but no, I can't do it tonight.' [You can always arrange another time if *you* want to.]

Keep practising this until your friend tells you your reply is firm and effective. Most people are surprised at how well it works; making excuses tends to encourage others to keep trying to persuade you.

It would seem that in spite of the conflicting evidence, the current mood among psychologists is to be inclined to the view that if there is any positive evidence linking the viewing of violence with adverse changes in behaviour and attitudes, then steps should be taken to protect people, especially children, from exposure to such material.

BOX 5.3
AN EXPERIMENT ON THE EFFECTS OF TV VIOLENCE

Stanley Milgram carried out research in America on this topic. He contrived that a TV programme shown in some areas would contain two antisocial acts: breaking a charity box, and making an abusive phone call (the viewers in these areas comprised his experimental group). The 'control group' consisted of viewers of a programme that did not contain these acts, and was shown in parallel broadcasts in other viewing areas. Many people watched the shows in viewing studios containing charity boxes and telephones, but no significant differences in subsequent antisocial acts were found between the two viewing areas. This result provides no immediate evidence for the large-scale imitation of TV violence, and tells us nothing about the possible long-term effects of such viewing.

As a footnote to this topic, Sarah Coyne warns that indirect aggression (e.g. spreading rumours and manipulative behaviour) portrayed on TV should not be overlooked in this debate. She cites evidence that shows it is more common than physical violence on popular TV programmes and can also have harmful effects on viewers.

THE POWER OF SOCIAL INFLUENCE

This chapter has illustrated the immense power of other people upon our behaviour. Social influence shapes what we do, what we think, and indeed, many aspects of our personalities. It determines our impressions of other people and our attitudes and behaviour towards them. The mere presence of others can alter and distort our judgements, even when we disagree violently with them. Under certain circumstances, social pressures may force us to do things we would not otherwise have contemplated. The study of football hooliganism, in Great Britain at least, seems to suggest that some of the worst offenders are law-abiding, unexceptional citizens who hold down respectable jobs in everyday life. It is only when they are in certain social situations, notably crowds, that they become antisocial and potentially harmful to others.

Social influence can be used for the good of humankind as well as for its ill, however, and the increasing power of the mass media and the Internet have immense potential in this respect. This is shown by the success of charity relief appeals such as 'Band Aid' and 'Comic Relief' in raising very large sums of money to relieve the suffering of famine-stricken inhabitants of the Third World, and in mobilizing huge levels of support for the victims of the South East Asian tsunami disaster in December 2004. Many affluent Westerners who would otherwise have ignored charity appeals have in this case made generous donations to the cause, partly because they are responding to the actions of their friends, neighbours and colleagues.

The power of social influence in the twenty-first century is becoming ever greater as electronic communication and information storage becomes increasingly efficient. The potential effects of the Internet in creating a 'global village', and its effects on people's personal, local and national identities, for example, are only just beginning to be explored. The insights of social psychological knowledge will become increasingly important in evaluating the effects of the tremendous changes in human communication that are currently taking place.

Recommended Reading

Aronson E. (2004). *The Social Animal, 9th edn.* New York: W.H. Freeman.
Aronson, E., Wilson, T.D. and Akert, R.M. (2002). *Social Psychology.* Upper Saddle River, N.J.: Prentice Hall.
Brown, R. (1986). *Social Psychology: The second edition.* New York: Free.
Milgram, S. (2005). *Obedience to Authority: An experimental view.* London: Pinter and Martin.

6

Your Emotions

- Love and attachment
- The nature of infant love
- Adult attachment and love
- The nature of adult love
- Types and styles of love
- Anger and aggression
- Aggression hot and cold
- The nature of anger
- What is a provocation?
- Features of anger
- Can we treat anger?

What are emotions? In Chapter 1 we considered the question 'How did you feel?' and identified it as one focusing on the *emotion* someone might have experienced. Indeed, we often talk of emotions and feelings as being one and the same, but in fact emotions are more than just feelings. It is true that a key element in emotion is a bodily change – a physiological response such as a beating heart, sweating, flushed or pale face, weakness at the knees, or butterflies in the stomach – accompanied by a particular strong feeling, such as love, terror, anger or fear, but emotions are not separate from the rational, thinking part of our minds, as we shall see.

In general, emotion and cognition are bound up together, and although we can identify an emotion as 'a state of agitation' that has measurable physiological changes, emotional experience is linked with an attribution process. (For a fuller explanation of 'attribution process' see Chapter 3.) We seek an explanation for our feelings; the physiological changes are not a sufficient condition for the occurrence of an emotional experience. A rapidly beating heart may be due to love, anger or even vigorous exercise; the emotional experience depends on various cognitions that enable us to determine which. However, the interpretation of our feelings or bodily changes is not always as simple as we might believe and may depend on a variety of factors, as the following example shows.

Donald Dutton and Arthur Aron showed that men made anxious by crossing a swaying bridge were judged to be more attracted to a woman whom they met on the other side (a confederate of the experimenter), when compared with a control group who crossed a more sturdy bridge. The men in the experimental, swaying bridge group, it was argued, attributed their feelings of high arousal, at least in part, to the attractions of the woman, rather than to the anxiety caused by their nerve-wracking bridge crossing. Although this study has been criticized, subsequent work has confirmed that it is possible for us to attribute bodily sensations to the incorrect source, as was suggested here (for further discussion of the relationship between physiological changes and emotional experience see the section 'Anger and Aggression' later in this chapter).

There has been much discussion about what the basic human emotions are. At one time the Chinese believed there were four basic emotions: anger, happiness, sorrow and fear. As we saw in Chapter 2, Ekman discussed six: happiness, surprise, sadness, anger, fear and disgust.

Psychologists used to believe that some emotions were an instinctive drive, and some arose through a learned association with such a drive. Thus a drive to satisfy a basic physiological need such as hunger was seen as a fundamental drive or motive, unlike love, which was viewed as a secondary drive. A baby was said to come to love its mother, because the mother by feeding her baby satisfied the primary drive of hunger and thus a need or love for mother was derived *by association*. We now know that love for the mother is not dependent on this association with food. Nevertheless, there are certainly both inborn and acquired aspects to emotions.

Humans are capable of experiencing very many different emotions, but in his book we cannot hope to do justice to all of them. We have therefore decided to concentrate on just two areas of emotional experience: 'love and attachment' and 'anger and aggression'.

LOVE AND ATTACHMENT

We use the word 'love' in many different ways to describe our feelings for people, for other animals, for food and drink, inanimate objects (home, work) and much more. We shall confine ourselves in this chapter to animate objects.

Psychologists have suggested that love or attachment is 'an affectional tie that binds one individual to another', and that such an emotion is likely to be manifest in certain types of behaviour, such as that designed to promote proximity and physical contact with the object of the attachment. This definition makes it possible to identify patterns of behaviour that are signs of an attachment, and thus to measure the emotion.

First love

When does a baby first feel love? Does love develop rapidly after birth or is it a gradual process? Studies of non-human animals, such as those by Konrad Lorenz, have been influential in shaping our ideas. Lorenz was an ethologist who observed that goslings form a strong attachment to their mother, or, if they were separated from her at hatching, would follow, and become attached to, almost any reasonably large animal, or object, to which they were exposed. Their attachment was so strong that Lorenz likened it to a pathological fixation and termed it 'imprinting'. Imprinting was found to have long-term effects on social and sexual behaviour.

Although the physical features of their mother (her voice and smell) are learned rapidly by human babies, love for her does not develop quickly: it takes months. Rudolph Schaffer found that by studying babies in the home and during short and longer separations from the mother, specific attachments are formed between 6 and 9 months of age, and this has been described as the *sensitive period* for attachment in human babies.

Have you ever held a friend's 8- or 9-month-old baby and found it was very upset when you did so – even though it was happily held by you several months earlier? Typically, babies of this age will smile only at specific individuals, and will

Figure 6.1 Imprinting.

be comforted only by those same individuals. If a stranger smiles at them, or tries to comfort them when they are upset, they will become even more upset. At 7 or 8 months a baby is likely to be described as 'clingy' by the parents, and at this time babies find both short- and long-term separations from those to whom they are attached very distressing.

THE NATURE OF INFANT LOVE

Do all babies show love for their mother or carer in the same way? Mary Ainsworth has studied the nature of the relationships between a baby and his or her carers and has shown that there are qualitative differences in the types of attachment shown by babies. Their love is expressed in different ways, and she described this in terms of the *level of security* shown in the infant's attachment. Because babies begin to show preferences for particular individuals around six to nine months Mary Ainsworth used this knowledge to develop her standardized method of assessing infant attachment.

She designed the *Strange Situation*, a procedure in which the infant and caregiver undergo a short series of seven episodes, each lasting about three minutes. The infant, the caregiver (such as mother or father) and a stranger take part in these. The idea is that the baby experiences a series of situations with the caregiver and/or a stranger or alone. Signs of attachment measured include proximity and contact seeking, contact maintaining, resistance, avoidance, search, interaction at a distance and the infant's response when reunited with its caregiver.

The attachment or love shown by the infant leads to classification in one of three categories following assessment in the 'strange situation'. These are *securely attached* infants (Type B), and two categories of *anxiously attached* infants: those showing avoidance (Type A) and those showing *resistance* or *ambivalence* in their relationship to the caregiver (Type C). Later on a further category was added, which we need not consider here. The category given applies to the *one* relationship measured and not to all the baby's relationships; thus a baby could be securely attached to the mother but anxiously attached to the father, or vice versa – it is not possible to generalize.

The *Strange Situation* has been widely used and is generally thought to be a reliable indicator of the nature of a particular relationship, not merely a measure of the infant's temperament. Initially, it was used for infants aged between 12 and 24 months but a similar form of assessment has been used with children up to the age of six, and with older children and adolescents questionnaire forms about separation anxiety have been devised to measure attachment between children and parents.

We must be cautious in assuming that this classification is appropriate universally, because in different cultures the styles of interaction between caregiver and baby can be so different. For example, in cultures where babies are never away from their mothers, but carried with them constantly, any form of separation may be extremely distressing, which could lead to a distorted assessment of the relationship if the *Strange Situation* is used.

Love unlimited?

The importance of the first love or loves in the infant life has been stressed by John Bowlby; before him Sigmund Freud had emphasized the damaging long-term effects on the individual of not having a satisfactory early loving relationship. Similarly, in non-human animals Lorenz reported on the later severe social and sexual problems that can arise in the absence of an appropriate early attachment figure. Bowlby believed that a warm, intimate and continuous relationship with a mother (or mother substitute) was essential for mental health. He also said that a baby is unable to form attachments to more than one person (known as 'monotropism'). Subsequent research by Rudolf Schaffer and Peggy Emerson showed that babies *can* have several attachment figures, and providing that these caregivers are a regular part of the child's life, and do not number more than four or five, the child can become attached to each of them.

Occasionally, there are people who have been without *any* opportunity to become attached to someone in infancy or childhood, and the evidence available suggests that, for those who have not loved or been loved, the long-term effects are marked. Such a person develops into the so-called 'affectionless character', unable to feel any attachment for others in later life and unable to form loving relationships with other people. For children who have been orphaned, or have been separated from those they love, the long-term effects are much less serious. Loving in adult life appears to be built on early experiences of loving in childhood, and it is undoubtedly better for babies and children to have loved and lost than never to have loved, in terms of the long-term effects on adult relationships. See Box 6.1 for a 'natural experiment' on children deprived of parental love.

ADULT ATTACHMENT AND LOVE

The long-term consequences of the early mother/child bond are reflected in the adult's thoughts and feelings about attachment relationships and the *Adult Attachment Interview*, AAI, has been developed to explore the latter. In this interview, questions are asked about memories for, and current evaluations of, past experiences of attachment related distress. The AAI responses enable the adult to be classified in one of four patterns: *autonomous* (well loved and supported by parents), *dismissing* (rejected or neglected in childhood but having an unrealistically positive image of parents and tending to dismiss the significance of early attachment relationships), *preoccupied* (had many caring duties towards parents and are angry and confused about childhood relationships with caregivers), *unresolved* (having suffered loss and trauma in childhood or later and are still grieving).

Most adults (65%) in the non-clinical population are in the first category and are secure. In clinical psychiatric populations, the other categories predominate; for example, in one study, 50 per cent were found to be in the preoccupied pattern in one study.

Why do adults love each other? Erik Erikson sees the adult's ability to love and form an intimate close relationship as a sign of adequacy and normality in an

BOX 6.1
CHILDREN WITHOUT PARENTAL LOVE:
A NATURAL EXPERIMENT

Psychologists would never conduct experiments to find out what happens to children who do not have parental love, but it is sometimes possible to find children who have been without parental love for some period in early life and compare their progress with family reared children.

This was the case for six German-Jewish orphans, studied by Anna Freud and Sophie Dann, who survived the Holocaust and spent several years in a concentration camp. The children had been orphaned when only a few months old, but were kept together in the camp and were released at the age of three, and sent to Bulldog's Bank in England. Although severely mal-nourished the children were intensely attached to each other, but were fear-ful and hostile towards adults. Despite being difficult, hypersensitive and aggressive, the children made surprisingly good progress and all but one were adopted within the next few years. At a follow-up many years later it was clear that they had not been irreparably damaged, but had made impres-sive and even inspiring progress. It seems that the attachment they formed for each other as orphans went some way towards ameliorating the effects of their early parental deprivation.

individual. Some believe that the role of love is to motivate people to be parents and take on the tasks of parenthood.

Love between adults can take several forms: we may love those of the same sex as us, or of the opposite sex, and sexual attraction may or may not be included in our feelings. The definition of attachment given earlier (on page 81) makes no distinction between sexual love or love without this component.

THE NATURE OF ADULT LOVE

Love is the triumph of imagination over intelligence.

H.L. Mencken

Signs of love

Bernard Murstein suggests that signs of love come in three forms or charac-teristics, as we see in Table 6.1(i). We *feel* it, but this is not a reliable index of love, because a person may love his or her partner, but at a given moment feel

Table 6.1 Love in adults

(i) The characteristics of love: within the individual
Behaviour – responding to the other's needs
Feelings – physiological correlates, such as palpitations
Judgement – a cognitive decision

(ii) The development of love
Passionate – the initial stages, intense arousal
Romantic – the idealization of the loved one
Conjugal/companionate – occurs later in the relationship, involves liking and trust,
knowledge replaces fantasy

(iii) Sternberg's triangular theory of love: three components within a relationship
Intimacy – feelings of closeness and being bonded
Passion – the drive to satisfy the love physically
Decision/commitment – the decision to love and then maintain that love

(iv) Lee's colours of love: love styles
Primary colours
Eros – powerful physical love
Ludus – playful love
Storge – companionate love

Secondary Colours
Mania – desperate and mad love
Pragma – pragmatic love
Agape – selfless, altruistic love

---

angry with him or her. Yet most of us would not say this temporary state overrides the love felt. A similar problem can occur when we consider an individual's *behaviour*, as loving behaviour is not always exhibited in those who claim to love. So finally we are left with love as a judgement, a 'cognitive decision by the individuals that they love one another'. This decision may of course be reversed, but it seems that this is the key to adult love; be it based on feelings or behaviour, it is a conscious decision.

The development of love

Three stages of love have been identified (see Table 6.1(ii)): *passionate*, *romantic* and *conjugal*, but the sequence of these stages has not been studied. Passionate love involves intense arousal, and romantic love involves idealization of the loved person. If you would like to find out the strength of your passionate love for your loved one, then fill in the *Passionate Love Scale* in Exercise 6.1. The least intense form of love is conjugal because it occurs after marriage (or a full partnership) is established and the couple habituate to each other and live their day-to-day existence together; passion may well be there, but liking and trust are the key elements in any relationship of this kind.

EXERCISE 6.1
MEASURING PASSIONATE LOVE

These items ask you to describe how you feel when you are passionately in love. Think of the person whom you love most passionately right now. If you are not in love right now, think of the last person you loved passionately. If you have never been in love, think of the person whom you came closest to caring for in this way. Choose your answer remembering how you felt at the time when your feelings were the most intense.

For each of the 15 items, choose the number between 1 and 9 that most accurately describes your feelings. The scale ranges from 1, not at all true, to 9, definitely true. Write the number you choose next to each item.

1	2	3	4	5	6	7	8	9
Not at all true				Moderately true				Definitely true

The passionate love scale

1. I would feel deep despair if ____ left me.
2. Sometimes I feel I can't control my thoughts: they are obsessively on ____.
3. I feel happy when I am doing something to make ____ happy.
4. I would rather be with ____ than anyone else.
5. I'd get jealous if I thought ____ were falling in love with someone else.
6. I yearn to know all about ____.
7. I want ____ physically, emotionally, mentally.
8. I have an endless appetite for affection from ____.
9. For me, ____ is the perfect romantic partner.
10. I sense my body responding when ____ touches me.
11. ____ always seems to be on my mind.
12. I want ____ to know me – my thoughts, my fears, and my hopes.
13. I eagerly look for signs indicating ____'s desire for me.
14. I possess a powerful attraction for ____.
15. I get extremely depressed when things don't go right in my relationship with ____.

SCORING: add up your scores for the 15 items. The total score can range from a minimum of 15 to a maximum of 135. The higher your score, the more your feelings for the person reflect passionate love; items to which you gave a particularly high score reflect those components of passionate love that you experience most strongly.

For further details see:

Hatfield, E., and Rapson, R.L. (1995). *Love and Sex: Cross-cultural perspectives.* New York: Allyn and Bacon.

Figure 6.2 For most people, being loved and loving someone is central to their lives. *(PCL/Alamy.)*

TYPES AND STYLES OF LOVE

Is there just one type of love, or is love made up of a number of dimensions, as is personality (see Chapter 3) or intelligence (Chapter 12)? We shall consider two theories – those of Robert Sternberg and John Alan Lee.

Robert Sternberg identifies three components of love in his triangular theory (see Table 6.1(iii)). These are intimacy, passion and commitment. Each of these is said to vary in different love relationships; thus love at first sight will be higher on passion and lower on the other two components. This approach provides a good foundation, but needs further refinement to deal with all the complexities and subtleties.

Another approach to love has been John Alan Lee's analysis of the styles of love. Lee is less concerned with the definition of love, but more in enabling those who love to define the 'different colours' of love, as represented in Table 6.1(iv). Lee investigated Canadian and British people's loving relationships by asking them to complete lengthy questionnaires on their relationship. Lee sees love as arising from blends of three 'primary' colours; these are *Eros*, *Ludus* and *Storge*.

Primary and secondary colours of love

The first colour of love is *Eros*. This is a love based on physical attraction and a quest for the lover's ideal beauty. *Ludus*, the second colour, is a playful love, unconcerned with commitment and skilled at the tactics of the game. The final primary colour is *Storge*, a love that is compassionate rather than passionate. Lee found that few love affairs are pure examples of one type, and the 'primary colours' of love blend to give new types with their own unique properties: the 'secondary colours'. For example, a blend of Eros and Ludus produces Mania. The manic lover swings from ecstasy to despair, unlike erotic lovers who do not suffer pains with their pleasure. Some people describe Mania as a neurotic type of love (see Table 6.1(iv) for more details).

John Lee believes that a lasting relationship is more likely if a couple share the same style of loving, but of the various types, the storgic lovers are most likely to survive together longest.

The conception of love in Western culture is that it *precedes* a long-term commitment and is something that is not under full rational control; thus it is common to hear people worrying over whether they love enough to make such a commitment as marriage. In other cultures, love is expected to *follow*, rather than precede, marriage; this shows us how entirely different are these two views of love, for clearly here it is what is *thought* that influences and shapes the loving that follows.

Lee studied people of all ages, classes and educational backgrounds and found that his classification of loving styles fitted all his groups. He also studied homosexual males, and again the typology fitted their styles of loving. It should be emphasized, however, that this analysis has not been applied to other cultures, so we do not know whether it accurately reflects women's and men's love universally.

Let us now turn to entirely different emotional experiences: anger and aggression.

ANGER AND AGGRESSION

Psychologists are often accused of having little to say about what the man or woman in the street regards as the 'real' issues and concerns of everyday life. This certainly applies to our topic of 'love between adults', but happily there are many areas of psychological research that do not support this generalization, and few more so than human anger and aggression.

Aggression, anger and hostility feature prominently on many people's lists of important concerns and have been widely researched. Most of the major schools of thought in psychology have had something to say about this form of experience and behaviour, and some of these ideas have sprung directly from personal concern about the extent of human suffering caused by aggressive behaviour and from fears for the future of the species.

Once again, the first major difficulty lies in defining terms. A useful starting point is to *distinguish aggression from the related concepts of anger and hostility*. Anger refers to a state of emotional arousal typically accompanied by activation of the autonomic nervous system and by characteristic patterns of facial expression (described in Chapter 2). It is clear that a person may be angry without being physically destructive. Equally, aggressive behaviour might occur without the aggressor feeling angry prior to the action. Hostility refers to negative appraisals or evaluations of people or events. Psychologists frequently use the term 'cognitive' to describe this aspect of aggression. It would, of course, be possible to appraise a particular group in society (capitalists or communists, for instance) in very negative, hostile terms without feeling anger or behaving aggressively, though, as we noted earlier, as a rule cognitive and emotional processes are intricately linked.

Aggression refers to overt or observable behaviour, though precisely what sort of behaviour may be deemed to be aggressive is controversial. It has been suggested that the term 'aggression' is restricted to acts resulting in personal injury or destruction of property, while accepting that injury may be psychological as well as physical. Even this apparently simple definition meets some difficulties. Are we to class as aggressive an injurious act that was 'accidental' (e.g. shooting a person unintentionally) or an act that was intended to injure but 'failed' (attempting to shoot another, but missing)? In general, the definition of an act as aggressive involves a value judgement on the part of the observer. Injurious acts may not be labelled as aggressive when they are socially prescribed or approved – thus capital punishment or beating a child to improve its character are often not construed as acts of aggression. In this sense, labelling a behaviour as aggressive always has a social and political dimension to it.

AGGRESSION HOT AND COLD

It is useful to make a distinction between two kinds of aggression – *angry* and *instrumental*, or what some have called *annoyance-motivated* and *incentive-motivated aggression*. The former is preceded by strong feelings. The person is in an aroused, physiologically activated state, often induced by environmental frustration of some sort. This is *hot* aggression. In instrumental aggression, on the other hand, the aggressive act is used as a way of obtaining some environmental reward, and heightened emotion may not be present, as in the case of someone using violence to rob a bank. There is a clear difference between a *cold* act of this sort and someone assaulting a neighbour following an angry argument. The two classes are, of course, not entirely independent, in that aggression is also intended to some extent to secure a 'reward' from the environment, though in this case the reward obtained is likely to be that of inflicting pain or injury itself.

Learning to survive

The many sources of instrumental aggression have been well documented in psychological research. That some *aggressive behaviour is indeed learned socially* because it is effective in securing environmental rewards or because aggressive models for imitation exist is now widely accepted. The rewards for aggression are many and powerful. Young children may learn to become physically aggressive because initial attempts at fighting off a bully by 'hitting back' prove to be effective. The reward in this case is the alleviation of pain. Similarly, the marked differences between societies in the levels of violent crime are probably attributable in part to the differing extent to which violent behaviour is rewarded and punished. There exist cultures, and also subcultures within societies, in which violence is so strongly reinforced that it is pervasive. In such circumstances aggression may be necessary for success and even essential for survival.

Anger in society

Of late there has been increased interest in the study of angry forms of aggression, and it is on this emotion that we shall focus for the rest of this chapter. It is striking that *anger is an important feature of much of the violence that causes social concern.* Studies of homicide, for example, suggest that this violent act is often a response to intense anger. The violent person is often described as in a 'fury' or a 'rage' directed in many cases at a person with whom they have an intimate relationship (a wife or husband). In a recent critical review of research into antecedents for sexual offences such as rape and child molesting, one of the present authors and his colleagues found that anger as well as other emotional states such as depression and anxiety were common occurrences in the period leading up to the offence.

High anger is not only associated with harm to others. In recent years, psychologists such as Charles Spielberger in Florida have shown in research studies that high trait anger (i.e. the person becomes angry frequently and intensely) is *associated with physical disease*, in particular with cardiovascular disease such as high blood pressure and heart attacks. Correlations of this sort are sometimes hard to interpret. Is it that anger causes disease, or does the disease cause high anger, or is it that both the anger and the disease are caused by some third factor such as constitutional or temperamental factors? We can probably rule out the notion that the correlation is due to disease causing anger, in that people who develop such disorders are higher in anger prior to the disease developing. The third interpretation cannot be ruled out, however. It may be, for example, that anger and disease are both caused by some form of heightened psychophysiological reactivity within the nervous system.

THE NATURE OF ANGER

Most people have experienced intense anger at some time, yet it is an emotion we rarely analyse in any rational and objective way. We asked a group of students to recall and write in detail about a recent experience of anger in their everyday lives. Here are two representative incidents recalled.

'The house we had just moved into was promised to be ready for the start of term by the landlady. But the downstairs was still undecorated and this was causing us a lot of inconvenience. What made me angry was the fact that the things we had been promised had not occurred. The landlady always had some poor excuse as to why things were going wrong. I got fed up with her excuses. I felt my blood boiling. It didn't last long because I started to laugh and then I calmed down. I thought to myself, it's no use getting annoyed over the situation because that wouldn't help matters and I cooled down.'

'I was sitting in a bus, while the bus driver was collecting the tickets. When he came to the back seat there were three black guys and one white sitting there. They couldn't find their tickets straight away, and fooled around a bit while looking for them. Suddenly the bus driver stated that he had had enough of their fooling around and ordered them off the coach, threatening them with the police if they refused. I couldn't believe my ears at first. Then I started getting really upset – I was almost on the point of physically showing my anger.'

What does psychology have to say about experiences of this sort? It is possible to identify various components in the experience of anger: the *environmental trigger*, *cognition/appraisal*, *emotional/psychological arousal*, the *impulse to aggress* (labelled as an action-tendency by psychologists) and *aggressive behaviour* itself. That these components have very complex interrelationships is now clear. All these components are likely to be involved in the incidents just described. The first two of these elements, in particular, have been the focus for recent experimental investigation.

WHAT IS A PROVOCATION?

Anger and angry aggression are generally preceded by a *triggering environmental event*. In the incidents above, for example, they are the landlady's failure to carry out her promises and the unjust treatment of the passengers. There are a number of theories concerning the nature of the event that is likely to be important. The *frustration-aggression* theory, for example, suggests that the blocking of activities directed towards an important goal for the person is likely to be crucial. This is more obvious in the first incident than in the second. The famous American psychologist Leonard Berkowitz has argued persuasively that environmental events elicit aggression to the extent that they are 'aversive' for the person or animal. The absence of an expected reward (as in the first incident) or the blocking of goal-directed activity produce aggression because they are unpleasant. Experiencing failure, being insulted, unjustly treated or attacked, share the property of aversiveness and are capable, therefore, of producing anger and aggression. Leonard Berkowitz suggests that humans and other animals are born with a readiness to flee or to fight when confronted by an aversive stimulus. Which response will occur depends on previous learning experiences (fight, for example, may have been found previously to be more effective) and on the nature of the particular situation (a situation where the person has a sense of being 'in control' may make fight more likely).

A number of laboratory and naturalistic studies give support to this theory, showing, for example, that pain is a powerful elicitor of angry aggression. Unpleasant smells, 'disgusting' visual stimuli (e.g. pictures of diseased and suffering animals) and high temperatures have also been found to lower the threshold for aggression, though in the latter case the effect is curvilinear: that is, fairly high temperatures make us more irritable, but very high temperatures may actually reduce aggression, perhaps because of their tendency to make us sleepy and lethargic.

It is important to recognize that when we become angry we are not reacting just to an immediate trigger. That trigger is 'embedded' (as Raymond Novaco describes it) in a broader social context that often involves stress for the individual. A mother may lose her temper one afternoon while trying to control her 'naughty' 3-year-old, but her reaction is likely to be affected by prior exposure to frustration and stress earlier in the day. Somehow, she transfers her anger and frustration from the earlier situation to the later one. It has been suggested that 'residual excitation' (at a physiological level) may account for this transfer. This raises the question whether an individual's exposure to unpleasant and aversive social conditions (unemployment, poor housing conditions, financial problems) may contribute directly to anger, and even violence, in response to the familiar frustrations of everyday life.

FEATURES OF ANGER

Psychologists such as James Averill have conducted diary studies of anger and aggression with a view to finding out what we report as making us angry in everyday life, rather than relying on rather unnatural laboratory studies. If you would like to keep an 'Anger Diary', see Exercise 6.2 at the end of the chapter.

Diaries tend to confirm the importance of aversive/frustrating events for anger, but also suggest a feature of anger not always apparent in the laboratory – that it is *predominantly elicited by interpersonal events*. Other *people*, rather than things or impersonal occurrences, make us angry. James Averill reports that people become mildly to moderately angry in the range of several times a day to several times a week, and that only 6 per cent of incidents are elicited by a non-animate object. The frustrating person in over half the episodes was someone known and liked – friends and loved ones are common sources of aversive experiences.

The second component of anger, the cognitive aspect, is *concerned with the way in which we appraise, interpret and construct the social environment* (see Chapter 3 on Personality). Attribution theory has been a major force in cognitive theorizing, and attributions are now widely believed by psychologists to be relevant to anger and aggression. Attributions are best viewed as the person's attempt to explain why an aversive or frustrating event has happened. The nature of the explanation people arrive at determines in part how they will feel and what they will do. An everyday example may make this clearer.

Suppose you are knocked off your bicycle by a car while travelling home from work. This painful and aversive event may be attributed by you to your own inadequacies ('I failed to look where I was going') or to chance ('given the number of cars and bicycles on the road, it is inevitable that accidents occur'). Neither of these attributions is likely to produce anger or aggression. If you made the attribution, however, that the car driver deliberately intended to knock you off your bicycle, or was driving carelessly, your threshold for anger and aggression is likely to be

EXERCISE 6.2
ANALYSING YOUR OWN ANGER

Your own experience may be a rich source of ideas about the nature of anger and aggression. An 'Anger Diary' is simple to keep and often revealing. Keep a diary over a period of two weeks. This should be filled in at the same time every evening. Write an account of the experiences of anger that have arisen in the course of the day. For each experience try to answer the following questions:

1. What was the precise event that elicited my anger? What irritated me most?
2. Was the source of my anger another person? Myself? An object or thing?
3. What interpretations did I put on the frustrating event? Are there other interpretations I did not consider? What sorts of things did I say to myself following the frustration that made me more angry?
4. What physical sensations accompanied the anger experience?
5. What behavioural reaction did I show? Was my response verbal aggression? Physical aggression? Withdrawal from the situation?

Comment
A series of incidents analysed in this way will reveal the patterns of your own experience of anger and may encourage you to formulate your own ideas and to compare them with those discussed in this chapter and in the further reading recommended at the end.

considerably lowered. Attributions of 'malevolent intent' of this sort have been shown to be important in understanding human aggression.

Psychologists have tried to tease out the factors that determine whether hostile attributions are made. Social judgements of this sort prove to have complex origins. Studies suggest that to assess the actor's responsibility for the harmful event the perceiver attempts first to establish whether the act was intended or unintended. If unintended, a decision is made as to whether the harmful consequences were foreseeable or unforeseeable. If intended, the action may be construed as malevolently or non-malevolently motivated. It may be the case, of course, that particular individuals are biased in their appraisals. The person who is generally more angry and aggressive than others may habitually see the worst in other people's intentions and motivations and fail to undertake a rational evaluation of what caused a particular event to occur.

Psychological studies strongly suggest that *cognitive processes of appraisal and attribution are crucial determinants of anger* and of our emotions in general. One of the exciting developments of the 1990s and 2000s has been the increasing interest shown in the emotions by cognitive scientists. Gerald Clore and his colleagues have tried to specify the cognitive conditions giving rise to anger and a range of related emotions. It appears that the appraisals underlying anger are complex, with subtle differences being found between anger and emotions such as resentment, reproach and frustration. You might find it useful to try to specify the conditions and appraisals giving rise to the emotions of anger and, say, sadness, based on your own experiences of these emotions. You might then compare your account with the theories put forward by cognitive scientists such as Gerald Clore and Andrew Ortony.

See Box 6.2 on the correlates of trait anger.

BOX 6.2
AN EXPERIMENTAL METHODOLOGY FOR INVESTIGATING TRAIT ANGER

One of the authors of this book was recently involved in a research project with a student researcher into high trait anger (see Personality, Chapter 3) in a student population. This is an example of an experimental study in which an independent variable was manipulated. The main focus of the study was to investigate how high trait anger individuals might differ from low trait anger individuals in their cognitive appraisals of a provoking event.

High and low trait anger students were recruited using a psychometric test to define the two groups. They were then shown brief videotaped stories showing social events. For example, one situation involved a person sunbathing on a beach (this research was conducted in Australia!). Someone walks past with the result that sand is kicked over the sunbather. Two versions of the story are presented, one in which what is going on is ambiguous (not clear the person kicks the sand deliberately). In the other version, there is greater evidence to suggest that the kicking is deliberate.

How did the research participants react to and interpret this situation? Some findings:

1. High trait anger (HTA) participants rated themselves as more angry than low trait anger participants (LTAs) if this incident were happening to them.
2. HTAs blamed the protagonist (the kicker) more.
3. HTAs were more likely to think the protagonist was being antagonistic.
4. HTAs were more upset by what happened.
5. HTAs showed these thinking biases most markedly when the scenario was ambiguous.

It appears HTAs think more negatively about potentially provoking events, and that this difference is exaggerated in ambiguous situations. When things are not clear, assume the worst!

But is appraisal necessary?

Some find contemporary theories of anger and other emotions to be excessively cognitive. Is anger necessarily preceded by appraisal and attribution of the person causing offence? Might anger sometimes be an automatic and immediate reaction, with little extended thought occurring between stimulus and response? It is likely that distinctive cognitive appraisals are not *necessary conditions* for the experience of anger, at least in its less intense forms.

Other components of anger are physiological arousal and the aggressive act itself, which may or may not follow anger arousal. 'I felt my blood boiling', in the anger incident recalled above, probably refers to the effects of the autonomic activation (increase in blood pressure, heart rate, respiration, muscle tension etc.) that we know accompanies the angry state. The precise role of physiological changes in the genesis of emotion is still controversial as is the question of whether the pattern of physiological arousal that accompanies anger can be discriminated from that occurring with other strong emotions such as fear or anxiety. In particular individuals the physiological component of anger can be strong and even overwhelming. One of the authors of this book had in therapy a client whose main problem was his inability to control his temper in a range of situations. He reported intense physical symptoms (sweating, muscle tension) for up to two days following an angry upsetting incident. A reaction of this intensity is probably rare, but it does highlight the importance of physiological events.

Most experiences of anger in everyday life are not followed by physical aggression, as we saw in the two incidents described. James Averill found that less than 10 per cent of angry episodes induced physical aggression. What he called 'contrary reactions', activities opposite to the instigation of anger, such as being friendly to the instigator, were twice as frequent as physical aggression. *Anger may produce a range of other reactions* – the previous learning experiences of the individual are clearly important in determining whether frustration and anger are responded to with withdrawal, help-seeking, constructive problem-solving or what has been called 'self-anaesthetization through drugs and alcohol'.

As suggested above, there are likely to be complex and bidirectional relationships between the environmental, cognitive, physiological and behavioural components of anger. Ways of thinking and appraising may induce anger, but equally the emotional state of anger may make it more likely that we will think angry thoughts. Environmental frustration may cause aggression, but behaving aggressively may also expose the person to even more frustration (being disliked by others or even becoming subject to a retaliatory attack from them). Untangling these complex interrelationships will be a major task for psychologists in the future.

CAN WE TREAT ANGER?

It is likely that our future understanding of anger will be increasingly influenced by psychologists working therapeutically with individuals who have problems of anger control. *Anger management has become an important treatment within clinical and forensic psychology*, particularly for individuals whose anger gives rise to violence. The recent film *Anger Management* describes an individual with anger control problems who is referred to an anger management group. To say the least, Jack Nicholson's portrayal of the anger management therapist is unusual. He would certainly fail his psychology examinations, probably on the grounds that his behaviour in therapy actually made the client worse! In reality, however, anger management is one of the more successful forms of cognitive behavioural therapy with good evidence as to its clinical effectiveness. Treatment of this sort has a number of components, including the following:

- Promoting insight into the sequence of external and internal events culminating in anger.
- Changing the client's biased cognitive appraisals of provocations (see above).
- Training the person in relaxation or other calming techniques to offset physiological arousal.
- Use of role plays to develop new responses to provoking situations.
- Problem-solving techniques.

Anger management treatment of this sort is now delivered on a large scale, particularly as part of the rehabilitation of violent offenders, in many developed societies. One of the major challenges for this therapy is the *low level of motivation to engage in treatment* in the first place that characterizes chronically angry individuals, as described by the psychologists Howells and Day. Such people commonly (see above) see others as responsible for their problems and thus do not believe they need to change. A second challenge is the need to deliver anger management therapies as a *preventative measure*. It is likely that large numbers of young people would benefit from the inclusion of techniques to manage anger and other destructive emotions within the educational curriculum. As yet, such preventative work is sadly undeveloped.

Recommended Reading

Berkowitz, L. (1999). Anger. In T. Dalgleish and M. Power (eds.), *Handbook of Cognition and Emotion*. Chichester: Wiley.

BBC (2005). For a brief account of Spielberger's and others' ideas about anger see a web page accessed 1 April 2005: www.bbc.co.uk/health/conditions/mental_health/coping_anger1/shtml.

Power, M. and Dalgleish, T. (1999). *Cognition and Emotion: From order to disorder*. Hove: Psychology Press.

Steele, H. (2002). State of the art: Attachment theory. *Psychologist, 15(10),* 518–522.

Sternberg, R.J. (1998). *Cupid's Arrow: The course of love through time*. New York: Cambridge University Press.

Sternberg, R.J. and Barnes, M.L. (1988). *The Psychology of Love*. New Haven: Yale University Press.

7

Your Brain

- What's in your head?

- How do we know which bits of brain do what?

- Cells in the central nervous system

- Two hemispheres, one brain

- Feeling emotional

- Consciousness

- Repairing damage

WHAT'S IN YOUR HEAD?

Covered by three layers, or *meninges*, which look like a tough plastic sheet, a thin soft sponge and a network of fine blood vessels, your brain is well protected inside your skull. Your brain weighs about 1.3 kilograms, and under the meninges looks a bit like a large greyish-coloured walnut. In fact your brain is one part of your *central nervous system* (the other part is your spinal cord), and it is made up of different subdivisions that have their own roles although they work together. You could see some of these subdivisions if you looked beneath the outer layer. All of the nervous system works by using a combination of electricity and chemistry. More of that later.

It is quite difficult to describe the brain without introducing a lot of new vocabulary – there are no everyday words for most parts of it. We have already met meninges and they're only the surrounding layers. We'll try to keep new words to a minimum, but we hope you'll agree that there would be very little point in skirting round the appropriate terms. The rationale for the names of some parts of the brain comes from the way it develops before birth. The brain grows around the edges of a single fluid-filled tube: this explains how it comes to have spaces in it. These spaces or *ventricles* are filled with *cerebrospinal fluid* (a little of this is removed from around your spinal cord if you have a lumbar puncture), and they serve an important cushioning role for the brain.

Cerebral cortex and what it does

The walnut-like appearance of the brain is because the brain's surface, or *cortex*, is folded in: an arrangement that allows this surface layer to be much larger than it could otherwise be (think how much more fabric you'd need to make a pleated skirt rather than a straight one). The colour is what gives rise to the description *grey matter*: This part of the brain largely comprises nerve cells and compares with other areas (*white matter*) that appear lighter and mainly comprise the long processes which are those parts of the nerve cells that carry signals to and from other nerve cells.

Much of the brain is in two distinct halves, which are joined at strategic points; hence the cerebral cortex covers the two *cerebral hemispheres*. In the cerebral cortex, many of the ridges, or *gyri* (singular *gyrus*), and grooves, *sulci* (singular *sulcus*, or if it's a big one, *fissure*), have names, and the main ones mark the division of the cortex into distinct lobes. These lobes are the *occipital* (at the back), *temporal* (at the side), *parietal* (on top) and *frontal* (at the front) lobes. These can be seen in Figure 7.1.

Part of each lobe is known to receive information from our senses: the primary visual cortex on the inner surfaces at the back of the occipital lobe receives input from our eyes; the primary auditory cortex on the top of each temporal lobe receives input from our ears; the primary somatosensory cortex in the parietal lobe receives information about touch and position from different parts of the body. Just in front of the somatosensory cortex, in the frontal lobe at the other side of the

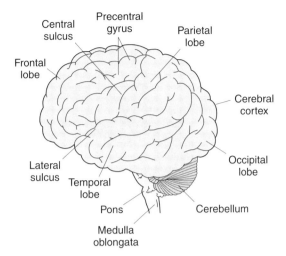

Figure 7.1   The main lobes of the cerebral cortex and other important features of the brain. (From Martini, Frederick H., Timmons, Michael J. and McKinley, Michael P. (2000). *Human Anatomy*, 3rd edn. Copyright © 2000 by Frederick H. Martini and Michael J. Timmons. Reprinted by permission of Pearson Education Inc.)

central sulcus, is the motor cortex which governs movement. The input, though, doesn't go directly from the eyes, ears, hands, legs and so on to the relevant area of the sensory cortex. The nerve signals first pass through relay stations, the most notable of which are in the *thalamus*. The thalamus (actually in two halves), one on each side, but referred to in the singular ('thalam*us*') is deep inside but not actually part of the cerebral hemispheres, and it includes several specialized *nuclei* or clusters of cells that pass on signals to and from different areas of the brain.

So what does the rest of the cortex do, apart from the areas that receive sensory information or that direct movement? Adjacent to the primary sensory areas are areas known as the *association cortex*, which are involved in further processing and integration of incoming information. The distinction between sensation and perception will be outlined in Chapter 11, but it's here in these areas of association cortex that the interpretation of sensory input, which turns a sensation into a perception, occurs. The contribution of these areas to awareness of what we see, hear and so on, and indeed the basis of consciousness in the brain, is amongst the most exciting questions in psychology.

What about the rest of the brain – apart from the cortex?

Areas mentioned in this section are illustrated in Figure 7.2.

We have already met the thalamus, which acts as a relay for incoming information. Immediately below the thalamus is another part that is of great interest to

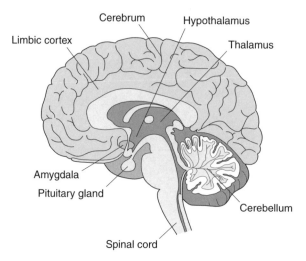

Figure 7.2 A diagram to show some of the structures that can be seen when the brain is sliced down the middle (a 'mid sagittal' view). The thalamus, amygdala, pituitary gland and limbic cortex can be seen here, but not from the outside. (From Wagner, H. and Silber, K. (2004). *Instant Notes in Physiological Psychology*. BIOS Scientific Publishers, Taylor & Francis Group. Figure 7, p. 30.)

psychologists: the *hypothalamus*. The hypothalamus has distinct clusters of cells (*nuclei*) that are involved in regulation of feeding, drinking, temperature control (e.g. sweating), sexual behaviour, control of sleep/wake cycles and aggression. We can think of these as the consequences of forms of motivation.

Just below the hypothalamus is the *pituitary gland*, sometimes referred to as the 'master gland' because of its important role in influencing other glands' hormonal secretions. The hypothalamus stimulates the pituitary gland to secrete its hormones; in fact, it also secretes hormones itself, which are then released from part of the pituitary. The hypothalamus also has connections with another structure whose primary function seems to be in emotion – the *amygdala*.

The amygdala is usually included with other parts of the brain that are distinct in that they are concerned with emotion rather than cognition. These together comprise the *limbic system*. The oldest part of the cerebral cortex (the bit that evolved longest ago and is situated on the inner surfaces down in the deep longitudinal fissure along the middle of the brain) is also part of this system. What actually belongs to the limbic system, though, is unclear, as neuroscientists are discovering more and more about how complicated the brain is and that there are no clear distinctions between areas involved in emotion and in thought.

Before we leave particularly interesting parts of the cerebral hemispheres, we must mention the *hippocampus*, which is below the cortex in the temporal lobe of the cerebrum. This structure (which was once thought to be involved in emotion and used

Figure 7.3 London taxi driver. How much bigger is his hippocampus than most people's? *(Ernst Wrba/Alamy.)*

to be included as part of the limbic system) is now known to be vital for memory to work properly. It was a part of the hippocampus that Eleanor Maguire and her team at University College London showed was enlarged in experienced London taxi drivers.

Prior to this study, we knew that the hippocampus had a role in memory for facts and events: things we can consciously recall and act on or talk about (known as *declarative memory*). We know this from a few cases of people who have unfortunately sustained damage in the hippocampus and who are unable to remember information they are given after the brain damage. In contrast, memories for motor skills, perceptual abilities and simple conditioned responses (of the type we'll look at in Chapter 12) do not seem to be disrupted by damage to the hippocampus.

Apart from the cerebrum, the next most obvious big part of your brain is the *cerebellum* (a confusingly similar name), at the back of the brain. This is important for the organization of movement – a function illustrated by a skill such as riding a bicycle. Deliberate concentration and conscious control of movements are necessary while acquiring the skill, but an accomplished bicycle rider doesn't have to think about how he or she does it – the cerebellum is programmed during the learning phase, to control the necessary muscle activity. In fact, the cerebellum integrates a lot of incoming information, from the senses and from other parts of the brain: it calculates what is needed for rapid and skilled actions and reactions and co-ordinates skilled activities like bicycle-riding.

HOW DO WE KNOW WHICH BITS
OF BRAIN DO WHAT?

The effects of damage and stimulation

Some of the knowledge we have comes from cases of brain damage that have occurred as a result of stroke, head injury, tumours or surgery. When it is known what part of the brain is damaged (sometimes this may be only after the death of the patient), it is fairly safe to infer that that part was involved in a function that has been lost or impaired. This is not the same as saying that, for example, if following brain damage a patient eats excessively, his or her brain area, which controls feeling full (we could call this a *satiety centre*), has been damaged. It could be that the damage has occurred somewhere along a pathway involved in satiety, while the centre, if there is one, remains intact.

A technique that has increased our knowledge about which bits of the brain do what is stimulation of the brain during brain surgery. It is in everyone's interest, for a surgeon who is removing diseased tissue, to know where he or she should stop. If she or he operates on a patient who is awake (this is quite feasible, as the brain itself does not feel pain or even touch), the patient can report experiences during stimulation of the brain with electrical currents, which will indicate the role of the brain area being stimulated. Areas that are not diseased and that are involved in vital functions can then be left alone if at all possible.

Of course, brain surgery and *post-mortem* examination of damaged brains are never carried out on normal healthy brains, so we cannot be sure to what extent we can generalize the findings from this sort of technique to the rest of us. Our knowledge of the brain gained from human patients is extended by research on healthy non-human animals, using these surgical and stimulation techniques and others. However, whatever we feel about the ethics of experimenting on animals, we must in any case always be cautious in extrapolating from one species to another.

Scanning

The traditional methods for studying the brain (exploring the effects of damage, looking at the effects of stimulating electrically and recording electrical activity, which we'll mention later) are all fairly crude and, as we have said, could never (apart from recording with scalp electrodes, discussed later) ethically be carried out on healthy human brain. There is a scanning technique, though, that does not require any injections or potentially damaging rays. This is *magnetic resonance imaging*, which can provide images that reflect activity or malfunction in a person's brain. Probably the most valuable of all the modern scanning techniques for the researcher (a version of this is called *functional magnetic resonance imaging*, fMRI) can give pictures while a patient or research participant is actually carrying out a particular thought process. We need caution in interpreting the pictures, though, because they are not direct measures of changing electrical activity. They reflect

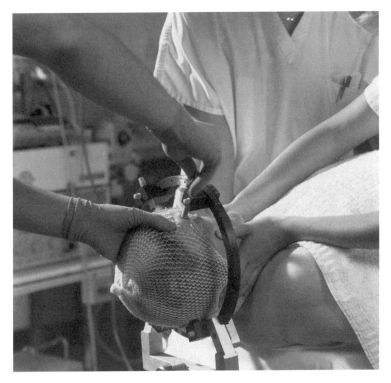

Figure 7.4 Neurosurgeon prepares patient for brain biopsy. Some brain surgery can be carried out without general anaesthetic so that the patient can speak to the surgeon. *(CC Studio/Science Photo Library.)*

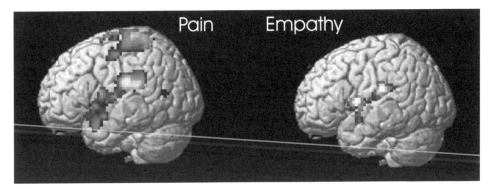

Figure 7.5 Functional magnetic resonance imaging (fMRI) image(s) showing the effects of experiencing (left) and imagining (right) pain. Active brain areas are black, white and grey shaded areas. The scan confirms that similar brain areas are activated in empathy, but that areas producing the actual sensation of pain (at the top of the brain on the left) are not triggered (right). Results from a study by Singer published in *Science* 2004 (Vol. 303). *(Wellcome Department of Imaging Neuroscience/Science Photo Library.)*

changes in oxygen consumption in the brain and we assume that increased oxygen consumption in an area reflects activity in that area.

CELLS IN THE CENTRAL NERVOUS SYSTEM

Neurons and glia

Like all the rest of our bodies, our brains are made of cells. The special cells of the nervous system are called *neurons*, and there are approximately a hundred billion neurons, which essentially all work in the same way, but come in different shapes and sizes according to their positions and precise roles. But neurons are not the only or even the most numerous cells in the brain. About half the volume of the brain is made up of cells that support neurons in different ways. These *glia*, or *glial cells*, provide mechanical support, electrical insulation, nutrition and waste-disposal. Neurons have very specialized, *excitable* membranes that allow them to function by transmitting electrical signals (this is why they need insulation). Each cell has a body (called the *soma*), with its nucleus containing the DNA and general maintenance equipment that cells usually have. It also has an *axon*, which might branch, that carries messages in the form of electrical pulses to other neurons or to muscles, and one or more *dendrites* (branches) that receive information from neighbouring cells and convey it to the soma.

Cells that detect sensations

Sensory receptor cells such as the rods and cones in the retina of the eye, hair cells in the ears or touch-sensitive cells in the skin are specialized neurons that act as transducers, changing the physical energy of light, vibration (sound) and pressure (touch) into a form that the nervous system can transmit. This form is electrical and these cells' special transducer dendrites pass on electrical signals, which are in the form of pulses known as *action potentials*, via the cells' somas to the axons and hence to other cells until the signals reach the relevant primary sensory area of cortex in the brain. Neurons in the sensory cortex pass on signals to association cortex and other brain areas. All neurons use their special electrically excitable membranes, which are able to change their permeability to different electrically charged particles, to transmit signals in the form of electrical pulses. Stronger signals (brighter lights, louder noises etc.) are represented by more pulses.

Messages between cells

When the electrical pulses reach the end of an axon, they cause the release of a minute amount of a chemical that acts as a *neurotransmitter*. This neurotransmitter substance is released into the space between neurons; it diffuses across the space and is taken up by special areas that recognize it on the receiving neuron, where it might trigger more activity in the form of electrical pulses.

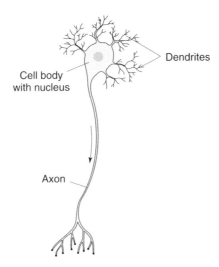

Figure 7.6 A diagram of a typical neuron showing the cell body, axon and dendrites. (From Martini, Frederick H., Timmons, Michael J. and McKinley, Michael P. (2000). *Human Anatomy*, 3rd edn. Copyright © 2000 by Frederick H. Martini and Michael J. Timmons. Reprinted by permission of Pearson Education Inc.)

Neurotransmitters don't always excite the cell that receives them: sometimes they inhibit it, making it less likely to fire off signals. So the means of communication between neurons is generally chemical, in contrast to electrical transmission within neurons. The area where chemical signals pass from one cell to another is called a *synapse*, and the mechanism, involving a neurotransmitter substance, is called *synaptic transmission*.

When communication between cells goes wrong

As you can see, the brain, in fact all the nervous system, depends on some very complicated workings. It is not surprising that things do sometimes go wrong. It seems likely that some mental health problems are linked to the functioning of synapses (the chemical transmission mechanism between neurons). Because this transmission is chemical and we know what at least some of the chemical substances are, we can increase or decrease the activity at synapses by using chemicals (drugs). Some drugs that affect synaptic activity are used by some people for recreational purposes – alcohol, nicotine, cannabis, ecstasy and cocaine are examples. Other drugs are used to treat conditions such as depression. The drugs known as SSRIs (specific serotonin re-uptake inhibitors) for example, enable more of the neurotransmitter serotonin to be available for action at those synapses that make use of it (*serotonergic* synapses). They do this by preventing excess neurotransmitter from being 'mopped up' after its release ('inhibiting' the 're-uptake'). One interpretation of the success of this treatment for many people's depression is that the condition is associated with a reduced working of some of their

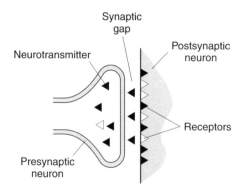

Figure 7.7   A diagram to illustrate how a synapse works. The receptor sites on the post-synaptic cell membrane recognize the neurotransmitter substance so the synapse works like a lock and key. (From Toates, F. (2001). *Biological Psychology: An Integrative Approach*. Reprinted by permission of Pearson Education.)

serotonergic synapses. Amphetamine (speed) and cocaine both act by increasing *dopamine* (another neurotransmitter) activity, although they do it by different mechanisms.

Some effects of larger scale brain damage

On a larger scale, some very interesting things go wrong if whole areas of the brain are not working properly. If a person's primary visual cortex (which receives the input from the eyes) is destroyed by disease or trauma, you would expect that person to be blind wouldn't you? Indeed patients with damage in this area do report that they cannot see. If however you ask such a person to point to something that you 'show' them in their blind area, they are able to do this with remarkable accuracy. This phenomenon was described by Larry Weiskrantz and colleagues at Oxford in 1974 and termed *blindsight*. It seems that people can know where something is even though they are not conscious of the fact that they can see it at all. There is also a complementary condition that occurs when the parietal lobe (where the visual association areas are) on the right-hand side of the brain is damaged. This results in a condition known as *neglect*: patients neglect everything on their left-hand sides, but they can tell you about things on that side if you draw their attention to them (for a review see Leora Cherney, 2002). So blindsight patients know where things are, even though they cannot see them, whereas neglect patients can 'see' them but behave as if they are not there. Thus there are these unusual, intriguing conditions that seem to illustrate a separation of consciousness about objects from some sort of sensation of the objects. See Boxes 7.1 and 7.2 for thought experiments and a case study described by Larry Weiskrantz and colleagues.

BOX 7.1
THOUGHT EXPERIMENTS

Thought experiments have been used for thousands of years, to help students understand difficult concepts, and there are several particularly famous examples from the fields of philosophy and physics. They stimulate us to use our imagination to explore difficult ideas. These experiments usually start with a description of a hypothetical situation, and ask us to question the situation or its consequences. This teaches us something about the assumptions underlying our understanding. We may have to change our concepts as a result of this new way of thinking about things. Some examples of old and new thought experiments can be found at: http://encyclopedia.thefreedictionary.com/thought%20experiment

BOX 7.2
CASE STUDIES

One of the most famous cases in neuropsychology is that of a man known as DB. DB was described by Larry Weiskrantz and colleagues in the 1970s and 1980s. A section of DB's right visual cortex had been surgically removed because it was abnormal. The surgery left DB blind in most of his left visual field. Weiskrantz presented DB with flashes of light, which he said he could not see at all. However when asked to point to were he felt that the flashes had been, DB was able to point with much better than chance accuracy. Later experiments showed that DB could also discriminate between stripes and a plain grey stimulus and between vertical and horizontal stripes.

Several rare and unusual cases of either surgical or accidental brain damage have been famously studied at length to help throw light on the workings of the brain.

Case studies can be particularly helpful when damage in two different areas results in complementary losses of function. For example, if damage to area A results in loss of short-term memory while the long term memory is maintained, whereas damage in area B results in loss of long-term but maintenance of short-term memory; we have evidence of the involvement of different brain areas in the different types of memory. This situation is known as *double dissociation*.

TWO HEMISPHERES, ONE BRAIN

Split-brain cases

Occasionally an operation to cut the main joins (*commissures*) between the two cerebral hemispheres is performed to stop very serious epilepsy. This prevents the uncontrollable epileptic (electrical) discharges spreading from one side of the brain to the other, but it also prevents other signals from crossing over. One result of this is that items can, for example, be presented to one hand or one visual field (not quite the same as one eye, as half the information presented to one eye is passed to each side of the brain – see Chapter 11), and the information will only be processed by one half of the brain. The other visual field, hand and so on does not 'know' what the object was. As the two halves of our brains are not quite the same (language usually only being represented on the left-hand side), interesting phenomena arise whereby 'split-brain' patients are able to say what they have seen, felt and so on only if the image was passed to the left-hand side of the brain. Roger Sperry (1913–1994) whose work with split-brain animals (non-human) informed this surgical treatment in the 1960s, pointed out that the two halves of the brain seem, at least to some extent, to have their own consciousness, and he published several papers on the relationship between the mind and the brain. Sperry shared a Nobel prize in 1981 'for his discoveries concerning the functional specialization of the cerebral hemispheres'.

Hemispheric asymmetry

As we just said, language is usually represented on the left-hand side of the brain only. This is true in most right-handed people, and, as we know from stroke patients and others who have suffered brain damage in these areas, there are two brain areas particularly associated with language. Damage to *Broca's area* in the left frontal lobe results in impairment in speech production; damage to *Wernicke's area* in the left temporal lobe results in speech that may sound normal but is meaningless. Incidentally, children sustaining quite major brain damage often regain function as other brain areas, in the case of language perhaps on the other side, take over. In left-handed people, language is in any case less completely one-sided.

Other functions that are not equally represented in the two hemispheres include the interpretation of some visual stimuli, emotional information and thinking analytically. It is overstating the case to say that the right hemisphere is the artistic, creative, emotional one, while the left is analytic, logical and verbal, as these attributes are complex and interwoven (writing involves verbal skills and creativity; science involves creativity; art requires analytical skills and so on). From brain-damaged patients, though, we have learned that there seems to be a tendency for small detail to be processed in the left hemisphere, while the more general picture is processed in the right.

FEELING EMOTIONAL

Emotions are subjective feelings such as sadness, happiness, anger, fear, so why are we discussing them in a chapter entitled 'Your Brain'? As we saw in Chapter 6, emotions involve bodily changes and also experiences of which we are conscious. It seems likely that both these aspects owe something to activity in the brain. We have already mentioned emotion briefly in the context of the structures in the brain and the side of the brain predominantly involved in processing it.

Questions about what comes first in emotion have a long history in physiological psychology. Do we see something frightening, run away, get all the bodily responses that are linked to the running away (increase in heart rate, mobilizing energy reserves, reducing blood-flow to the periphery and increasing it to the muscles etc.) and then feel scared as a result of the way our bodies have responded? This is the basis of emotional feeling as was proposed by the philosopher William James and the physician Carl Lange in the nineteenth century. However, in an extension to this idea and supported by experimental evidence, Stanley Schachter (1922–1997), working with Jerome Singer, demonstrated that information from the brain about the nature of a situation (bad news, good news, funny sight etc.) determines the *type* of emotion experienced. Even this is an oversimplification, but we do know that emotional feelings result from the integration of our interpretations of situations and our bodily responses. Brain areas involved include areas of the cerebral cortex, the amygdala, the brain stem and the hypothalamus. But how does this integrated brain and body activity give rise to the conscious feeling of being happy, sad, frightened, angry, surprised or disgusted? We'll explore the question of consciousness next.

EXERCISE 7.1
ZOMBIE THOUGHT EXPERIMENT

Suppose that zombies exist, which are exactly the same as human beings in terms of every atom in every molecule of every cell of which they are built. Also suppose that these creatures behave in exactly the same way as humans. There would be no way of distinguishing between these new creatures and normal humans would there?

Are these creatures conscious?

If you feel that the zombies would be conscious, you are effectively saying that consciousness arises 'simply' from the workings of the chemicals that make up our bodies. If, on the other hand, you feel that non-conscious zombies are a possibility, then you are saying that consciousness stems from somewhere other than the physical components of a human's body. Which raises the question again – where is the mind?

CONSCIOUSNESS

What is consciousness? Where is the mind?

We have mentioned consciousness a few times and while questions concerning the relationship between the brain and the mind and the nature of consciousness must be among the most fascinating that psychologists might one day answer, their answers are proving very elusive. Psychology is often referred to as an interdisciplinary or multidisciplinary subject area. This is well illustrated by our attempts to understand consciousness, which include work in practically all areas of psychology as well as collaborations with philosophers, physicians and neuroscientists.

Conscious or unconscious?

Perhaps we could understand what we mean by being conscious, by contrasting it with being unconscious or not conscious? The distinction between conscious and unconscious was fundamental to the psychoanalytic school of psychology founded by Sigmund Freud (1856–1939), but this was not based on any scientific account of what was happening in the brain. We can describe differences in the brain activity of awake (conscious), sleeping (not conscious), anaesthetized (not conscious) or comatose (not conscious) people – are these differences the seat of consciousness? A leading researcher of consciousness in terms of activity in the brain is Antonio Damasio, Professor of Neurology at the University of Iowa. Damasio postulates that neural activity in the brain that is associated with the state of the body interacts with other neural activity associated with perception of things outside the body, giving rise to a further set of neural patterns that represent the core self. By this account, we are not conscious during sleep, anaesthesia or coma, as we do not perceive events outside the body, so this part of the neural circuitry is inactive. The interaction between neural circuits may be what is happening to give rise to consciousness, but Damasio does not explain *how* this neural activity could account for what we *mean* by consciousness, which is surely the more difficult and really interesting question.

A different approach to finding the basis of consciousness in the brain involves studies recording electrical activity before a person makes a voluntary movement. These studies, pioneered by Benjamin Libet, a professor of physiology at the University of California in San Francisco, show that when we make a 'voluntary' action, something happens in the brain even before we know that we're going to move. There is a recordable signal from the brain, showing that the action has been instigated before the decision to move reaches consciousness. It is difficult to understand what this is telling us about the mechanisms of consciousness, but it certainly raises questions about our free will to act. Our plan to act only comes after this *readiness potential* has occurred in the brain.

We will return to consciousness in the context of learning in Chapter 12.

Sleep

Aside from its relevance to the debate on consciousness, we do know a certain amount about the part the brain plays in sleep. The lowest part of the brain, where it joins on to the spinal cord, is known for obvious reasons as the *brainstem*. In this area is a network of cells known as the *ascending reticular activating system* (ARAS), which is important for sleep. The ARAS is triggered by sensory inputs and it in turn sends signals to the thalamus and the cerebral cortex. It seems to operate as a non-specific kind of alerting system – activity here increases alertness and damage here can upset the pattern of sleeping and waking.

You can get an overall impression of brain activity in terms of brain waves by recording minute electrical signals, using electrodes placed on the scalp. Using this technique, which is known as *electroencephalography* (EEG), we can identify different stages of sleep. Each of the five different stages, and waking, has a characteristic EEG pattern. The electrodes are on the scalp, so the cerebral cortex is the closest part of the brain to them and it's assumed that the EEG patterns

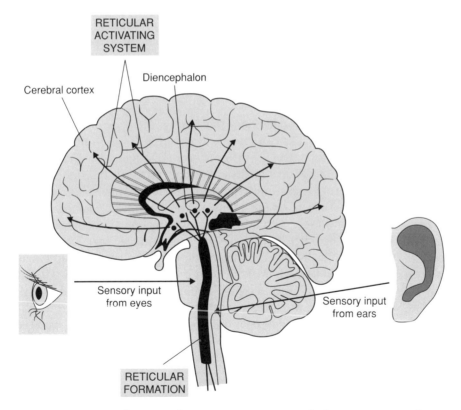

Figure 7.8   The ascending reticular activating system in the brainstem responds to input from the eyes and ears and signals the need for arousal to areas of the brain. (From Minkoff, Eli C. and Baker, Pamela J. (2004). *Biology Today*. Copyright © 2004. Reproduced by permission of Garland Sciences/Taylor & Francis LLC.)

are produced by the overall activity in the cortex. Sometimes when we are asleep, the EEG pattern is similar to when we are awake. This happens during rapid eye movement sleep (*REM sleep*), which is the sleep stage closely associated with dreaming.

The changing patterns of brain waves, sometimes similar to when we are awake but sometimes quite different, provide clear evidence that sleep is not a single condition, nor one of inactivity; in fact, our brains are quite busy when we are asleep.

REPAIRING DAMAGE

Brain plasticity

Until quite recently everyone believed that when the brain or spinal cord is damaged it cannot be repaired. This is not as true as we used to believe, the brain being to some extent *plastic* and able to adjust to change and to damage. In some instances when the brain or part of it stops working properly, there is an associated degeneration of certain areas or types of brain cell. A well-known example is Parkinson's disease, in which sufferers experience a disturbance of movement based on degeneration of some of the neurons that use the chemical dopamine as their neurotransmitter. This occurs in an area of the brain known as the *substantia nigra*.

Stem cells

Parkinson's disease is one of the conditions that doctors are beginning to treat using stem cells. These adaptable cells can grow into any type of cell in the body, so the idea is that stem cells can be injected into the brain of a patient with Parkinson's disease where they will grow into healthy neurons, establish the necessary connections with other brain areas and restore the patient's movement to normal. The main controversy surrounds the supply of the stem cells because, although there are such cells in adults, they are most easily (technically) obtained from a foetus. Foetal cells on the other hand carry the disadvantage of potential rejection because they are genetically different from the patient they are injected into. Probably the ideal would be if some of our own cells could be persuaded to transform into the type of cell we need to repair damage. If the ethical (and technical) difficulties can be overcome, we may see treatment with stem cells become routine for degenerative brain disease and also for traumatic injury to brain and spinal cord.

Recommended Reading

The website www.youramazingbrain.org includes lots of information on the workings of the brain and the body as well as some interactive exercises and games.
Carlson N. (2004). *Physiology of Behaviour, 8th edn.* Boston: Pearson Allyn and Bacon.

8

Your Health

- Psychology, health and illness

- Being healthy

- Preventing illness

- Becoming ill

- Being treated

You might be surprised to find a chapter about health in the middle of a book about psychology! However, some areas of psychology are concerned with the application of psychological theories and methods to the practical aspects of everyday life, and health psychology is one such area. The main areas of *applied psychology* are clinical psychology (discussed in Chapter 10), educational psychology, occupational psychology, forensic psychology, counselling psychology and health psychology. Psychologists working and carrying out research in these fields undergo specialized training, and usually work with individuals or groups in appropriate settings; for example, in schools, the workplace, courtrooms or in hospitals and health centres. Health psychology is a relatively new and exciting area of applied psychology, and represents the interface between psychology and medicine. Broad examples of the concerns of health psychologists include promoting health and preventing illness, seeking healthcare and. In the present chapter, we aim to provide a flavour of some of the ways in which psychological research and theory can help to explain our health-related behaviour.

PSYCHOLOGY, HEALTH AND ILLNESS

Health psychologist Philip Banyard, emphasizes that psychology as a discipline contributes two important strengths to the study of how we behave when we are 'healthy' and how we behave when 'ill'. The first of these relates to the experience of psychologists in studying human behaviour from a variety of theoretical perspectives, many of which are outlined in this book. Health psychology draws upon a number of these perspectives in order to explain our perceptions of health status, and to predict health-related behaviours. For example, the social theories of attitudes and stereotyping described in Chapter 5 can help to explain our way of thinking about people suffering from HIV/AIDS; the study of human development (see Chapter 9) has been highly influential in addressing the needs and shaping the care of children and the elderly in both hospital and primary care settings; finally, the learning theories outlined in Chapter 12 have been applied to a variety of health-related areas, such as eating, smoking and drinking behaviours.

The second strength is the methodology that psychology brings to the study of being healthy and being ill. As described in the various boxes throughout this book, psychology has an enormous amount of expertise and experience in the measurement and recording of what we do, think and feel. Questions such as those introduced in Chapter 1 ('Why did you do it?' 'What were you thinking?' 'How did you feel?') are just as central to our understanding of health-related behaviours as they are to human behaviour in general. However, there is a fourth question that is equally important to health psychologists: 'What would make you change your behaviour?' Why this question is important is discussed in the following section.

BEING HEALTHY

For many of us, being healthy might involve eating fewer fattening foods, reducing stress, taking more exercise, or reducing our use of commonly abused substances; for example, alcohol, tobacco and other 'social' drugs such as caffeine and marijuana. However, engaging in these *preventative health behaviours* can be a different matter. Preventative health behaviours include those mentioned above, which can promote good health, and also actions that can lead to the early detection of disease or disease risk factors. Jane Ogden outlines three forms of prevention: *Primary prevention* refers to attempts to reduce or eliminate risks to health (e.g. smoking cessation, improving poor diet), prior to the development of illness. The recent health promotion campaign concerned with the dangers of smoking, commissioned by the UK Department of Health, is an example of primary prevention. *Secondary prevention* is concerned with interventions designed to detect and treat an illness at an early stage in its development, so that its progress can be stopped or slowed down; *screening* is a form of secondary prevention. *Tertiary prevention* includes the various treatments and actions that can slow down or hold the effects of serious disease or injury, with the aim of rehabilitating the patient.

Being, and staying healthy are also strongly highlighted in the strategy for public health entitled *Saving Lives: Our Healthier Nation* published by the UK Department of Health in 1999. The two key aims of the strategy are to improve health, and to reduce the impact of health on social inequalities such as poverty, employment, housing, education and the environment. The strategy acknowledges that improvements in treatment are important, alongside encouraging health promotion through the development of partnerships between individuals, communities (e.g. Primary Care Trusts, Social Services, Local Authorities) and the Government. A more recent public health document, *Securing Good Health for the Whole Population*, prepared by Derek Wanless, and published in February 2004, goes a step further. This document acknowledges the right of individuals to choose their own lifestyle, but also advocates a shift in focus by the UK National Health Service (NHS) 'from a national sickness service, which treats disease, to a national health service which focuses on preventing it. The key threats to our future health such as smoking, obesity and health inequalities need to be tackled now.'

As we mentioned above, for many people, being healthy involves some kind of lifestyle change. As pointed out by Marion Pitts and Keith Phillips, the challenge for Government and healthcare providers alike is to find ways of motivating people to take on board and carry out these changes. The questions that arise for health psychologists are first, why it is that many of us behave in ways we know are bad for us? And second, why can it be difficult to make changes that might benefit our long-term health, or even survival? Some of the answers to these questions are discussed below in relation to diet, exercise, smoking (primary prevention) and screening (secondary prevention).

PREVENTING ILLNESS

There is a mass of published evidence that links the quantity and quality of Western diets to the development of diseases such as diabetes, heart disease, stroke, orthopaedic problems, and some cancers. Susan Jebb, Chair of the UK Association for the Study of Obesity, recently warned about the seriousness of being overweight, suggesting that by 2010, one-third of Britons could be clinically obese, incurring high costs for both individuals and the NHS.

Related to this, a substantial number of studies have concluded that exercise has an important role to play both in the prevention and treatment of disease. In terms of prevention, people who exercise regularly seem to be less likely to develop and die from heart disease, and also have lower blood pressure than those who do not. In 2003, Min Zhang and colleagues published the startling finding that even simple activities, such as housework and a daily walk, can help to protect women against ovarian cancer. Similarly, with regard to treatment, a number of patient groups (e.g. those suffering from heart disease, diabetes and psychological problems such as depression) were identified in 2001 as being likely to benefit from 'Exercise on Prescription' schemes. Under these schemes, GPs are able to refer their patients for supervised courses at local gyms or leisure centres – either as a preventative measure, or to help recovery.

The news for smokers is similar. Tobacco smoking has been associated with the occurrence of cancers of the lung, larynx (voice box), pharynx (throat), oesophagus, bladder, kidney and pancreas; also, with respiratory diseases that include bronchitis, emphysema and asthma. Moreover, the UK's Scientific Committee on Tobacco and Health has recently reported that not only does smoking affect the health of the smoker, but also that non-smokers are at an increased risk of developing lung cancer from exposure to other people's smoke. However, for the smoker who 'quits', blood pressure and pulse rate return to normal within 20 minutes, and within one year, that person's risk of developing lung cancer falls to approximately half that of a smoker.

We have deliberately written the previous paragraphs in such a way as to provide you with knowledge and information about the severe risks to health of being overweight, not exercising, and smoking. However, and despite the old adage that 'knowledge is power', we will be surprised if you decided to modify or change your current patterns of eating, exercise or smoking behaviour solely on the basis of knowledge about physical risk. Two areas of psychological research are particularly relevant to this conundrum; the first reflects the idea that our beliefs and attitudes, *together with* knowledge, are the most influential predictors of changes in health-related behaviour; the second concerns the way in which health information is communicated.

Beliefs, attitudes and behaviour change

Beliefs, attitudes and knowledge are the key components of what are known as *social cognition* models of health behaviour. Social cognition refers to the ways in which people make sense of situations that occur in a social setting, and the term 'model' is used in psychology to summarize an explanation of a particular behaviour pattern. Therefore, social cognition models attempt to describe the thought processes involved in, and their influence on, health-related behaviour.

One of the most widely quoted and researched of these models is the Health Belief Model (HBM). The HBM was one of the first models that adapted theory from the behavioural sciences to health problems, and it remains one of the most widely recognized theoretical frameworks of health behaviour. It was originally developed by a group of social psychologists (Godfrey Hochbaum, Irwin Rosenstock and Stephen Kegels), working in the US Public Health Service. Their focus was on increasing the use of then-available preventative services, such as chest X-rays for tuberculosis screening and immunizations such as flu vaccines. In its original form, the HBM suggests that it is not just the weighing scales that might motivate individuals to diet, but also the beliefs of those individuals concerning:

- Their susceptibility to illness (e.g. 'Being overweight can cause heart disease.' 'My mother has had two heart attacks, and my father has angina.' 'Heart disease seems to run in my family, so I might be at risk if I don't lose weight').
- The severity of the illness (e.g. 'Heart disease is very serious, perhaps even fatal').
- The costs and benefits involved in carrying out the behaviour (e.g. 'Buying and preparing diet foods can take time and is expensive.' 'On the other hand, I will be able to wear more attractive clothes').
- The cues or signals that prompt individuals to look after their health. These may be internal, such as a symptom of illness (e.g. 'I get out of breath very quickly when climbing stairs'), or external (e.g. 'My doctor has told me that I should lose weight').

The model proposes that these beliefs, alongside demographic variables such as sex, age and socio-economic status, can be used to predict the likelihood that a behaviour will occur. In other words, weight loss and/or exercise behaviours are likely when a person perceives that he or she is highly susceptible to health problems such as heart disease, that heart disease is a severe threat, and when the benefits of weight loss and exercise outweigh the possible costs. Also, when internal or external cues to action such as a symptom of disease, or a comment from a doctor, are present. More recently, and in response to criticisms, further considerations have been added to the model. First, that of 'health motivation', which reflects a person's readiness to act on health issues. Also, 'perceived control' (e.g. 'I am confident that I can lose weight). Including these adjustments, the HBM would also predict dieting behaviour when the individual is confident that weight loss is achievable, and when motivation to do so is high.

A problem with the HBM model is that it reflects the idea of health behaviour as being determined by a variety of individual thought processes (cognitions). However, humans are social beings, and we live within an environment in which our communications with others, and theirs with us, can have a powerful influence on individual cognitions about health.

Communicating health information

Persuasive information about health issues can be communicated in a number of ways, the most fundamental being an exchange of 'medical' opinion between lay-people. Health-related information is also communicated between healthcare providers and patients, as discussed later in this chapter. A third, very powerful source of information about health is the media. Since the 1990s we have seen the development of a number of television and radio campaigns designed to encourage people to stop smoking. The most recent of these has aimed to encourage smokers to quit by depicting the impact that their smoking-related illness or death will have on their family and friends.

The primary principle underlying these campaigns is psychological, and their aim is to raise fear about what may happen as a result of smoking; first, by increasing the extent to which an individual feels at risk, and second, by emphasizing the magnitude of the harm that smoking can cause. Fairly surprisingly, while such campaigns attract interest, they are not always successful in terms of behavioural change. For example, in an early psychological study of the impact of such 'fear appeals', Irving Janis and Seymour Feshbach prepared three 15-minute talks concerned with the dangers of tooth decay and the necessity for good oral hygiene. One talk (minimal fear appeal) described tooth decay, and illustrated its consequences using diagrams and X-rays. The second (moderate fear appeal) presented similar information, but in a slightly more dramatic way, and used 'real' pictures of diseased mouths. A third talk (strong fear appeal) was accompanied by more disturbing illustrations, emphasizing the possible outcomes of gum disease and tooth decay, and highlighting other dangers that can arise from poor oral hygiene, such as cancer. The initial results showed that the strong fear appeal talk was rated more highly in terms of its graphical (although some participants rated the illustrations as too unpleasant) and verbal impact than the remaining two talks. When participants were later interviewed to discover how much they had changed their behaviour to reflect the advice given in the talk they had heard, only 8 per cent of the participants in the strong fear appeal condition had done so. In contrast, 36 per cent of the participants who had heard the minimum fear appeal talk had conformed to its provided advice.

A recent *meta-analysis* conducted by Kim Witte and Mike Allen brought together the findings of more than 100 experiments that tested the effects of fear appeals. In contrast to the findings of the above study, these authors found that strong fear appeals are more persuasive than weak fear appeals, and do produce behavioural changes for the better. However, a problem with such appeals is that they may also lead to high levels of self-protective responses; for example, ignoring the message, or simply deciding that 'it doesn't apply to me'. Psychologists have found that the most effective campaigns appear to be those that not only create a sense of threat, but also produce a sense of *efficacy*; that is, they raise people's beliefs that the proposed behaviour change really will prevent the feared outcome, and that they can actually 'do something' about the threat. The recent antismoking campaign mentioned above undoubtedly attempts to fulfil both of these criteria.

Screening

Screening is another area in which health psychologists have investigated the content of health-related information – in particular, the nature of the messages designed to encourage people to attend screening programmes. Screening is available for a large number of different conditions (e.g. the detection of foetal abnormalities, and screening for heart disease), but the two best-known forms are screening for breast and cervical cancer. Messages about cancer screening can be worded to emphasize gain (so many lives are saved each year by screening), or loss (so many lives are lost because people do not attend for screening). In the case of promoting attendance for breast screening, several studies have indicated that messages highlighting potential loss are more effective than those highlighting possible gain, particularly when combined with a strong fear appeal. Alexander Rothman and his colleagues have developed a framework upon which the effectiveness of each type of message can be assessed. These authors suggest that for screening behaviours (which may detect illness), messages emphasizing loss appear to be most effective; in contrast, messages that emphasize gain are more appropriate for the preventative behaviours (smoking cessation and weight loss) discussed earlier.

This brief exploration of some of the complexities involved in changing our health-related behaviour for the better suggests two related interpretations. The first is that the pathway to change is largely psychological, and depends on our individual beliefs about health, the way these can be influenced by others and the society in which we live. The second is that that ill health can be avoided by individual behaviours and lifestyle choices. Today, health promotion advice is presented as a matter of course within a variety of arenas ranging from supermarkets to hospitals; it is worth noting, however, that its effects are not always positive. In one study, for example, Alison Chapple, Sue Ziebland and Ann McPherson reported that lung cancer patients who had stopped smoking years before felt unjustifiably blamed for their illness. Similarly, Helen Richards and her colleagues have found that some patients in their study blamed themselves for their heart disease, and also believed that health professionals will blame them; for some of these patients, this self-blame and fear-of blame may have contributed to a reluctance to seek professional help.

BECOMING ILL

Self-blame is not the only reason that might contribute to our not seeking medical care. In fact, most of us respond to the 'symptoms' of illness in other ways before doing so. For example, we may ignore the symptoms, we may seek the advice of others (e.g. family, friends) to avoid 'wasting the doctor's time', or we may self-treat – perhaps by using over-the-counter medications or making lifestyle changes. David Locker has described several factors that might trigger a medical consultation, including instances when symptoms last for longer than anticipated, when they worsen, or when there is an expectation that the doctor can do something about them. Other variables are known to influence our decision to consult, including our age and our sex; for example, the elderly and the young consult more frequently than do teenagers and young adults, and it is well documented that women, for a variety of reasons, make much greater use of health service facilities than do men. Therefore, the relationship between the appearance of symptoms and the decision to seek medical advice is not always a simple one.

Seeking medical advice

Psychological studies have addressed both the process of seeking medical advice (e.g. how patients and doctors communicate) and the outcome of the consultation – for example, whether patients adhere to medical advice.

The process through which medical advice is usually sought involves a patient explaining a symptom or symptoms to a doctor, who in turn offers an explanation (diagnosis), and medication and/or advice. However, the parties concerned may have quite different expectations about the consultation, different communication styles and differing opinions about the type and quantity of information that should be communicated; even personal characteristics of the doctor and the patient can affect the communication process.

For example, medicine, like all professions has its own specialist language, and it is quite usual for doctors to use technical language or acronyms, which may be difficult for patients to understand. Sue Langley asked groups of 'professional' (e.g. teachers, solicitors etc.) and 'non-professional' (university students) lay-people for their definitions of some commonly used medical terms, then asked a group of doctors to estimate how many words participants in the other two groups would be able to define. Interestingly, the doctors estimated that 'professionals' would be able to define significantly more words than they actually did! You can test your own knowledge of some of these terms in Exercise 8.1. In contrast, and as Shelley Taylor points out, rather than using medical language, doctors may use overly simplistic terms or even 'baby-talk'. Polly Toynbee, for example, comments that in hospitals, almost everything is 'popped' on or off, and that patients are encouraged to 'pop' everywhere, including to the toilet, and in and out of wheelchairs. Exactly how one 'pops' is never explained!

Furthermore, Kevin Kindelan and his colleague reported that patients and doctors disagree over the relative importance of different types of medical information; patients place the highest value on information about their diagnosis, the cause of their condition and its prognosis, whereas doctors tend to overestimate their patients' desire for information about treatment and drug therapy. Characteristics of the doctor have also been shown to affect their communications with patients, including their physical appearance and sex. In one study for example, Debra Roter and her colleagues reported that consultations with female doctors were viewed more positively by patients than those with male doctors, because they were longer, and contained more positive talk and information exchange.

On the other hand, studies have revealed that patients too can contribute to problems in the communication process. For example, there is evidence that some

EXERCISE 8.1
TEST YOUR KNOWLEDGE OF MEDICAL TERMS

Health psychologists have shown that when doctors employ user-friendly language and clearly presented written information, patients remember more about what they are told about their condition and its treatment. Test your knowledge of medical terms in the exercise below, and then think about the terms your own doctor uses. Do these help or hinder your understanding?

Instructions
All you need to do is to pair the medical terms listed below with their definitions. For example, if you think that Term A, BIOPSY, pairs with Definition 20, Pain in the breast, note down A = 20. Pair all 20 terms with their definitions and then compare your answers with the correct pairs below.

Terms

A. BIOPSY
B. PROGNOSIS
C. MI
D. MENSES
E. DERMATITIS
F. CYSTECTOMY
G. NARCOTIC
H. ENDOSCOPY
I. PRURITUS
J. DYSPEPSIA
K. RHINITIS
L. PSORIASIS
M. EPIDURAL
N. GENERIC DRUG
O. MASTALGIA
P. PANDEMIC
Q. ANTIPYRETIC
R. EPISIOSTOMY
S. CONTRAINDICATION
T. ARRHYTHMIA

Definitions

1. Drug that induces stupor and insensibility, but relieves pain.
2. Abnormal changes in pattern and/or speed from the normal heart rhythm.

3. Itching caused by local irritation of the skin.
4. Drug that reduces fever by reducing body temperature.
5. Drug name that is not protected by trademark.
6. Factor in the patient's condition that makes it unwise to pursue a certain line of treatment.
7. Disordered digestion (indigestion).
8. Chronic skin disease with itchy, red, scaly patches.
9. Local anaesthetic injection into the dura mater on the spinal cord.
10. Surgical removal of the urinary bladder.
11. Incision into the perineum to make delivery easier.
12. A tube with a light at one end and that uses an optical system for transmitting an image to the examiner's eye.
13. Inflammation of the lining of the nose.
14. Assessment of the future outcome of the patient's disease.
15. Myocardial infarction – heart attack.
16. Menstruation.
17. The removal of a small piece of living tissue from an organ or part of the body for microscopic examination.
18. Inflammation of the skin caused by an outside agent.
19. Epidemic so widely spread that vast numbers of people in different countries are affected.
20. Pain in the breast.

Answers

A = 17	B = 14	C = 15	D = 16	E = 18
F = 10	G = 1	H = 12	I = 3	J = 7
K = 13	L = 8	M = 9	N = 5	O = 20
P = 19	Q = 4	R = 11	S = 6	T = 2

(Adapted with permission from Langley, 2000.)

patients have difficulty explaining symptoms that are really bothering them, particularly 'embarrassing' ones, and present them as something of little concern ('Oh, by the way . . . it's probably nothing'). Others regularly fail to ask questions, or voice concerns during medical consultations, and even when information is provided, do not always understand or remember it. In contrast, the wealth of information now available from books and particularly the Internet has transformed sometimes even quite elderly patients from novices to very knowledgeable 'experts.'

As in the case of healthcare providers, individual characteristics of patients themselves can influence the communication process; various authors have alternately described some patients as being difficult, demanding, controlling or manipulative; still others are abusive and even aggressive.

Figure 8.1 From novice to expert: written and particularly electronically available information helps patients to learn more about their condition. *(Photo: Diane Wildbur)*

BEING TREATED

Given the diversity of the factors that might influence effective communication be-tween doctors and patients described above, it is hardly surprising that seeking (and giving) medical advice is sometimes problematic. Nonetheless, having sought and gained such advice, do patients adhere to it? Studies have found that the astonishing answer to this question is 'No, not always', and furthermore that adherence is affected by a number of factors, including the nature of the problem involved, and the type of treatment or advice offered. Robin Di Matteo and Dante DiNicola have estimated that while up to 80 per cent of patients adhere to short-term treatments involving medicine, less than 50 per cent stick to advice about recommendations for lifestyle change. Even more surprising is Jane Ogden's summary of various estimates, which suggests that approximately half of patients, who have *chronic illnesses* such as dia-betes and raised blood pressure, do not fully adhere to their medication schedules.

The reasons why patients do not adhere are complex and probably interwoven. The first and fairly obvious of these is that patients might not like the side effects of their medicines, or may be uncertain about the effectiveness of the treatment offered, or even believe that they have been wrongly diagnosed. Here, patients are making a rational decision not to adhere, and their behaviour is known as *ratio-nal non-adherence*. Rational non-adherence may be further influenced by what the

BOX 8.1
SURVEYS AND FOCUS GROUPS

Surveys can include written questions, interviews or both, and usually provide a numerical, or 'quantitative', summary of people's thoughts, feelings and behaviours with regard to a particular topic. An example of a written survey, and one widely used by general practices in the UK is the General Practice Assessment Questionnaire (GPAQ). Usually around 60 patients per GP are asked their opinions about the services provided by their practice (e.g. waiting times for appointments and aspects of the care provided by staff); the responses are then taken as reflecting those of all of the patients using that practice. Using a group interview or discussion, focus groups also provide a summary of how people think, feel and behave in relation to sometimes sensitive, but always 'focused', topics. The data gathered from focus groups is descriptive rather than numerical, and is usually analysed in terms of the subjects or 'themes' that emerge from the discussion. Focus groups made up from patients of GP practices using the GPAQ mentioned above are sometimes used to add a 'qualitative' contribution to the 'how many?' summary provided by the questionnaire.

Health Belief Model (described earlier in this chapter), refers to as patients' perceptions of their susceptibility to, and the seriousness of, the condition being treated. In other words, the way in which they see their illness will have an effect on whether or not they adhere to treatment for it. Another important factor is the level of social support a person receives from family and friends; Gerry Kent and Mary Dalgleish suggest that when patients are living with their family, adherence to treatment or lifestyle change is double that found for patients living alone. However, according to Philip Ley, adherence or non-adherence to medical advice can be predicted by a mixture of how satisfied patients are with the process of their consultation, and how well they understand and remember the information provided during it. There is considerable research to support this view.

In terms of satisfaction with the consultation process, it has been shown that patients are more likely to adhere to medical advice when their relationship with the doctor is *patient-* rather than *doctor-centred*. In *patient-centred* relationships, doctors aim to seek out and explore the particular concerns of individual patients, and to involve them in treatment decisions. In *doctor-centred* relationships, the doctor simply gathers information and makes treatment decisions without involving the patient. Also, as noted earlier, patients sometimes have difficulty in understanding and remembering what they must do, and this too has been shown to affect rates of adherence. Gerry Kent and Mary Dalgleish provide evidence that patients forget what doctors have told them within a very short period, and other studies have estimated that up to 50 per cent of doctors' advice and other information is forgotten almost immediately after the consultation. Forgetfulness about when or in what quantity to take medication is a particular problem for the elderly, and studies have shown that the rate of forgetting to take medications increases with the number of prescriptions used. How then might adherence be improved?

Improving adherence

At the beginning of the previous section, we suggested that whether or not a patient adheres to medical advice depends on a number of interwoven factors, and clearly these will vary from patient to patient. However, there are a number of strategies that can be effective in improving adherence across a variety of settings. These include providing appropriate support and information, and improving communications between the doctor and the patient.

One of the ways in which adherence can be encouraged is by involving family and friends. As suggested by Philippe Harai and Karen Legge, this could be simply through a friend sitting in on the consultation so that he or she is aware of the treatment programme, or that person taking a more active role such as being involved in the delivery of, or monitoring the patient's use of medication. Alternatively, patient contact or support groups can play a very significant role in providing people with strategies for dealing with both their condition and its treatment. For example, The Expert Patients Programme currently running in many UK Health Trusts is a self-management course for people with long-term conditions (e.g. arthritis, diabetes, asthma) that builds on the psychological principles of *self-efficacy* described above, and aims to give people the self-confidence, skills and knowledge to manage their condition better, and be more in control of their lives.

Based on evidence which suggests that the more information a patient is given, the less he or she remembers, Philip Ley has made several recommendations that might improve communication between doctors and patients. For verbal information, these are principally founded on what psychologists term a *primacy effect*, which is based on the finding that people are prone to remember the information they hear first; also that information be kept specific and simple, should be repeated and that the importance of adherence needs be stressed. Ley and his colleague also reviewed research studies investigating the effects of written information in improving adherence, and found that 97 per cent of the studies reported increased knowledge, 60 per cent reported increased adherence and 57 per cent demonstrated an improved outcome. The above recommendations, with their emphasis on clear, verbal communication by doctors, supported by 'patient-friendly' written information, have been highly influential; first in helping to ensure that patients have access to information that is appropriate not only to their physical, but also psychological, needs; also, in promoting further research into the communication between doctors and patients.

Recommended Reading

Banyard, P. (2002). *Psychology in Practice: Health*. London: Hodder and Stoughton.
Ogden, J. (2004). *Health Psychology: A textbook*. Berkshire: Oxford University Press.

9

Your Development across the Lifespan

- Studying development

- Development in infancy

- 'Theory of mind': perceiving emotions in others

- Language development

- Social cognition in schoolchildren

- Adolescence and adulthood

'Spare the rod and spoil the child.'

'Children should be encouraged to think for themselves and develop independence from their parents.'

'The decline in children's physical fitness stems from far too much time spent on computer games and in front of TV and video.'

'The communications revolution has the capacity to transform the nature of learning and education.'

It goes almost without saying that the future of any society is determined by the way it brings up its young, and so the truth or falsehood of statements like those above are of immense importance. The first two (mutually contradictory) views come from the wealth of 'folk wisdom' that exists about how children should be brought up: the restrictive and permissive views expressed in each of these statements have both come into and gone out of fashion at different times over the last century and longer.

In the new millennium, the rapid growth of digital technology, people's increasing use of the Internet and their effects on many aspects of our lives are only just beginning to be recognized. These changes are beginning to influence the way we conduct business, the nature of our leisure activities, our patterns of working life, the functions of broadcasting and the media, and indeed many aspects of local and national cultural institutions. The third and fourth statements above give just two contrasting views about some ways in which these developments are having an impact upon people's development and learning, showing that these can be negative as well as positive.

The pace of social change is probably as rapid as it ever has been. The traditional nuclear family, with its mother, father and 2.4 children is now the exception rather than the rule, and children are now far more likely to be brought up by caregivers outside the family (e.g. in nurseries or by childminders), or in one-parent families. Working from home and part-time working are now much more commonplace, and this also affects people's patterns of work, leisure and education. Working parents rely on far more nursery provision, childminders and other forms of day care than existed in the past.

These changes are reflected in the *ecological approach* to the study of development, which proposes, in short, that all of these different influences upon the child should be taken into account. Now that mothers are no longer automatically their children's primary daytime caregivers, *ecological* research has begun to look more closely at the influence of fathers, siblings, other relatives, babysitters, childminders and so on.

STUDYING DEVELOPMENT

The field of *developmental psychology* deals with these issues, and has important contributions to make to parenting and educational policymaking. Alongside the ecological approach, we shall highlight two other key features.

The lifespan approach

Quite simply, this proposes that human development should be studied across the full age span, from conception right through to old age and death. This might seem fairly obvious: but until the 1980s or so, developmental psychologists had devoted most of their attention to pre-schoolers and school-aged children. With the exception of some studies of adolescence and old age, relatively little attention was paid to all the other changes that take place in people's lives between the ages of about 18 and 60. This may have been partly because the study of marriage, careers and so on has been in related subject disciplines such as sociology, but lifespan developmental psychology is at last beginning to tell the whole story.

Cognitive and social development

The study of the development of thinking and of social behaviour, again until the last two decades or so, had been separate and distinct. The former includes topics such as language, memory and intelligence, and the latter includes peer relationships, the effects of play, helping others, and moral development, for example. More recently, there has been a growing realization that these two areas cannot be artificially separated from one another, because thinking inevitably takes place in a social and cultural setting.

The concept of *social cognition* is now an important part of many developmental psychologists' thinking, and the *socio-cultural* approach to the study of development and education has become the dominant view. In a nutshell, the basic idea is that children's learning and development can be investigated only within the social and cultural world (they do not occur in a vacuum), and this is summed up by the expression 'situated cognition'. Both of these features will be reflected in this chapter: we shall trace development across the lifespan, as the title suggests, and we shall combine aspects of the cognitive and the social at each stage of development.

DEVELOPMENT IN INFANCY

It used to be thought that newborns came into the world with very few skills other than some basic physical reflexes, and the infant's *learning experiences* were seen as crucial for development. In recent years, psychologists have moved away from this view, and current research is uncovering more and more abilities that seem somehow to be 'built into' babies, or 'pre-wired', at birth. The study of this is now one of the most active areas of developmental psychology.

Perceptual development

One of the first people to try to map out the changes that take place in infancy was the famous Swiss psychologist Jean Piaget (1896–1980). Piaget proposed that, from birth until the age of about 2 years, all children pass through six substages,

128

Figure 9.1   Jean Piaget (1896–1980). *(Piaget Archives.)*

moving from the use of simple physical reflexes through to the beginnings of *symbolism*. In the first three of these substages (up to the age of 8 months or so), 'thought is action'. What babies do to toys and other objects *is* what they think about them: and this idea was captured by the well-known expression 'out of sight is out of mind' – if you can't see your toy any more, then it ceases to exist. Piaget proposed that *object permanence* – the recognition that objects do not cease to exist when they are out of sight – only gradually develops over the fourth, fifth and sixth substages of infancy.

Acquiring object permanence is an extremely significant event, which liberates babies' thinking from the physical world – they can now form *symbols*, or *internal representations*, of objects. As with many parts of Piaget's theory, the idea that 'out of sight is out of mind' has subsequently been challenged by experimental researchers, and further studies have been made of many other aspects of infants' perception and visual preferences. It has been shown that they may have early preferences for particular patterns and shapes; that they clearly prefer to look at faces rather than at jumbled up collections of the same facial features: and that they can recognize depth. This latter feature was demonstrated in a famous study by Eleanor Gibson and Richard Walk in 1960, which used an ingenious device called the 'visual cliff' – this is used to illustrate observational research (see Box 9.1).

129

BOX 9.1
THE VISUAL CLIFF EXPERIMENT

Figure 9.2   Berkeley California baby, ten months old, participating in the 'visual cliff' experiment at the child development research lab at U.C. Berkeley MR. *(TopFoto/The Image Works.)*

This is a famous and often-quoted example of an observational study by Eleanor Gibson and Richard Walk, which used an ingenious piece of equipment to investigate whether or not infants can perceive depth. The photograph shows that the 'cliff' was actually a downwards step of several feet in a chequerboard pattern, over which was placed a glass plate extending horizontally over the 'cliff', and on which it would have been perfectly safe for the babies to crawl. Gibson and Walk argued that if the babies had no depth perception, they would crawl on the glass over the edge of the 'cliff', but that they might hesitate to do so if they could perceive depth.

They tested babies between 6 and 14 months old, and their mothers were standing at the opposite side of the glass plate, encouraging the babies to crawl on it. They found although all of the babies were willing to crawl on the glass on the top of the cliff, very few of them would crawl 'over the cliff'. This is a powerful demonstration of the existence of depth perception in babies over 6 months, because it is based on clear observational data. It could not be used in the same way for younger babies who are unable to crawl, however, and so other methods need to be used to study depth perception in early infancy. Measures of heart rate have frequently been used in more recent studies of infant perception.

Social development

The realization that infants' perceptual development takes place in a *social world* is an increasingly important feature of contemporary research: babies draw on the people around them in constructing meaning from the wealth of sensory input they receive. The most significant early social relationships for most infants are those formed with their parents. Research clearly shows that these relationships are *reciprocal* ones in which the parent responds to the child just as much as vice versa.

In one study by Glyn Collis and Rudolph Schaffer, mother–infant pairs were videotaped while playing together with several toys in a novel situation. Analysis of the tapes showed a typical pattern of *turn-taking* in the timing of the actions of mother and child. For example, a sequence of actions might be started by the child looking at one particular toy. The mother might then look at the same toy and 'elaborate' upon the child's attention towards it by talking, pointing or maybe touching. This response by the mother might in turn stimulate the child to explore the toy further, and so a kind of 'chain' of actions is built up by means of turn-taking. Social development can thus be seen as a whole series of interrelated and increasingly complex 'chains' such as these.

A key feature of each 'chain' is that mother and infant work together, as a team, with their actions very precisely phased in time with one another. This *synchronization* has been demonstrated in vocalizations, as well as in gestures (such as pointing), and in visual gaze. When mothers respond verbally to (non-verbal) babbling noises by their babies, they tend to time their 'conversational' responses just as they would in a normal verbal conversation with an adult. They 'converse' with their infants by creating imaginary replies from the babbling sounds, and these interactions have the important function of laying the foundations of later social interaction.

These imaginary 'conversations' reveal the *intersubjectivity* of early communication – the mothers and babies are interpreting the meaning of these 'behaviour chains', and their interpretations determine the way they interact. Colwyn Trevarthen has suggested a fascinating new explanation; namely, that 'communicative musicality' is what characterizes early interaction and development. He sees the musical features of babies' talk, singing and other rhythmic games with their mothers as being central to many of the expressive actions and emotions that develop between infants and their caretakers.

Trevarthen suggests that music communicates with young babies because it engages with what he calls an 'intrinsic motive pulse' (IMP) that is generated within the brain. This IMP includes a rhythmic time sense that can detect regularities in musical sounds, sensitivity towards the acoustic qualities of the human voice, and the ability to perceive 'narrative' structures in vocal or musical sequences. Trevarthen's basic idea is that the central qualities of early interaction have musical features: and this should be seen alongside a growing body of research which shows that babies seem to be biologically predisposed to recognize musical features in the sounds around them. Sandra Trehub and her colleagues have shown that babies are sensitive to rhythms, to tunes and melodies, to simple musical intervals (e.g. octaves), and even to some aspects of harmony, in ways previously thought impossible.

'THEORY OF MIND': PERCEIVING EMOTIONS IN OTHERS

Another aspect of social understanding is self-awareness – how children perceive themselves in relation to other people, and become aware of others' mental states. The first stage in this is the development of self-recognition. One well-known study by Michael Lewis and Jeanne Brooks-Gunn used the 'mirror test'. In their study, infants in six age groups between 9 and 24 months were placed in front of a mirror, and observed for about 90 seconds. Their noses were then daubed with rouge, and they were then observed again for the same period of time. In the first period, most of the 96 babies in the sample smiled at their reflection in the mirror, and many reached out to touch it, although very few touched their own nose. In the second period, however, whether or not they touched their nose was closely related to age. The younger infants tended not to do so, even though they could see their own red nose, but the majority of the older ones (over 18 months) did. This suggests that the understanding of self, in terms of a reflection in the mirror, develops at about this age (see Chapter 13 for discussion of similar studies in dolphins and primates).

By the age of about 2 years, children have not only developed self-awareness, but are also able to express their own emotional states, and then to recognize and predict beliefs, desires and emotions in other people. Making these predictions has become known as the development of a 'theory of mind', and various suggestions have been made as to how they do it. These include Paul Harris's view that they use an 'as if' or pretence mechanism to imagine themselves in the other person's position, and an alternative view, such as that of Alan Leslie, that the child's developing 'knowledge base' about the world is more important than pretence, or emotional states.

Predicting false beliefs

One way of testing some of these different interpretations has been to use what have become known as 'false belief' tasks. The first of these was devised by Hans Wimmer and Josef Perner, and involved a story about a boy called Maxi who put away some chocolate in a blue cupboard. Maxi went out to play, and while he was playing, the children doing the task saw his mother move the chocolate into a green cupboard. When Maxi came back in, the children were asked, 'Where will Maxi look for the chocolate?'

Wimmer and Perner found that 3-year-olds typically failed on this task, predicting that Maxi would look in the green cupboard even though he didn't know it had been moved – that is, using the actual location of the chocolate rather than an accurate prediction of Maxi's point of view. A higher proportion of 4- and 5-year-olds gave the correct answer, and almost all the 6-year-olds did so. Many other variants of the false belief task have been devised, one of which is outlined in Exercise 9.1: the general conclusion from these is that most children have the ability to form theories of other people's minds by the age of five.

LANGUAGE DEVELOPMENT

The acquisition of language is a remarkable human achievement. Early in their lives, children are able to communicate subtle meanings to each other and to adults, and have internalized some complex grammatical rules. Psychologists have tried to explain the ways in which the speechlike sounds produced in babies' babbling gradually turn into recognizable syllables and words, and how these are put together to form meaningful sentences. Their descriptions and explanations of these developments once again reflect a combination of increasing cognitive maturity, and the influence of the social environment in which the children are growing up.

Children seem to acquire language in a similar series of phases, regardless of the actual language learnt in particular cultures. In the early months, parents are able to identify cries of hunger, anger and pain, and 'oo' sounds are frequently made in pre-verbal 'conversations' with parents. Babies vary the pitch and stress in these vocalizations, and repeat sounds in 'vocal play': this reflects 'communicative musicality', which we mentioned earlier.

By the age of 12 months, the first 'words' start to appear. These are often inventions that refer to whole classes of objects. One of the authors' sons, for example, used the word 'gam' to refer to all the foods that interested him at the time, including porridge, ketchup and other baby foods as well as 'jam'. He also used the word 'jus' to refer to all of his drinks. These 'words' are typically delivered with speech-like intonation and stress.

By the age of 18 months children have typically acquired about 20 words, and this rapidly grows to about 200 by the age of 21 months. Towards the end of the second year babies produce what has been termed 'telegraphic speech', a highly condensed form that contains the first two-word sentences – 'allgone jus'

EXERCISE 9.1
FALSE BELIEFS: THE SALLY-ANNE TASK

Figure 9.3 The Sally-Anne task.

Instructions

Tell the story of Sally and Anne by talking children through the five cartoon pictures shown above. Try this with children aged between 3 and 6 years old. The correct answer is that Sally should look in the basket, since she (unlike the children answering the question) does not know that the marble has been moved. Was there any increase with age in the number of correct answers? (This task is adapted from Frith, 1989) or 'allgone gam' were frequently heard at mealtimes! Sentences then get longer, and three- to four-word sentences, which may appear ungrammatical, but which nevertheless involve the application of grammatical rules (e.g. 'I no want gam'), are produced by 2- to 3-year-olds.

Between 3 and 4 years vocabulary increases to about 1,000 words, and the length and complexity of children's sentences are such that they can easily be understood by adults who have not met them before. By the age of 5, children's speech is very similar to that of adults, and they are able to modify features like the length of sentences and grammatical complexity according to the characteristics of the listener. This developing language system is used within particular social and cultural settings, and for particular purposes. Neil Mercer has coined the term 'interthinking' to explain how language enables joint, co-ordinated intellectual activity to occur between people, and this is a vital means by which children's thinking develops within different contexts and situations.

Conversations at home and at school

The social context of learning changes dramatically for most children when they make the transition from home to school, pre-school playgroup, nursery school or kindergarten. There is usually a substantial increase in the number of children and adults present, and most children form new friends who are unknown to their own parents. Children spend a lot more time away from the home, and are expected to enter into *formal* learning relationships with adults, and sometimes also with other children.

Barbara Tizard and Martin Hughes recorded thirty 4-year-old girls' conversations with their mothers at home and with their nursery teachers at school, and contrasted the language and learning in these two settings. They found that the girls asked significantly more questions at home, and that the adults' answers at home were much more detailed than at school. The girls asked three main types of question; namely, *business questions* (e.g. 'Where are the scissors?'), *curiosity questions* (such as, 'What's that?' 'How do you do that?') and *challenge questions* (e.g. 'Why should I?'). Challenge questions formed only about one-tenth of the children's questions, but seemed to be particularly effective in gaining new information in the mothers' answers.

Formal school or nursery settings, on the other hand, seemed specifically to discourage children from asking challenging questions and from persisting in their questioning. It seems from this research that children's intellectual and language needs are much more likely to be met at home than at school, as there is a great deal more scope for learning by dialogue and interaction. This completely turns on its head the common idea that what teachers do in classrooms is essentially 'educational' and that what goes on in domestic conversation is more humdrum and routine.

Figure 9.4   Varieties of play in children. *(© Nat Bocking/Pixlink.)*

SOCIAL COGNITION IN SCHOOLCHILDREN

Piaget's stage theory

We referred earlier in this chapter to Jean Piaget's famous *stage* theory of child development, which he sets out himself in an introductory book with Barbel Inhelder. The theory has undoubtedly generated more theoretical development, empirical research and educational applications than any other single theory in developmental psychology. Researchers inside as well as outside psychology have questioned its underlying assumptions about the nature of development, the existence of stages, the focus on logical thinking, the methods Piaget used to collect his evidence, and much more besides. Nevertheless, the fact is that the theory is still discussed and assessed, rather than ignored, which perhaps speaks for itself.

We referred earlier to the acquisition of *object permanence*, which was a central feature of the first *sensori-motor* stage (0–2 years). This acquisition is part of the ability to form and use internal symbols or representations, and heralds the move into the second, *pre-operational* stage (2–7 years). The main feature of this is that children are 'egocentric': they can see things only from their own point of view. At around the age of 7, Piaget believed that egocentrism declines, and that children enter the third *concrete operational* stage (7–11 years). This is characterized by the ability to carry out logical, scientific thinking about the effects of variations in the properties of physical ('concrete') objects, such as their volume, mass, density, weight or speed. After the age of 11, children enter the stage of *formal operations*, in which they can perform the same logical operations internally – that is, without the objects being physically present.

Piaget's account of the changes that occur between the second and third of these stages, around the age of 7, stimulated various curriculum schemes for mathematics and science in the first school, and perhaps generated more research than any other aspect of his theory. One main idea in Piaget's account of these changes is that of *conservation*. He proposed that the ability to 'conserve' the properties of objects – to understand that certain features stay the same regardless of changes in other properties – only arrives by the concrete operational stage. In the number conservation task, for example, children are shown one line of six white counters and a second line of six black ones, spaced out at the same distance. When questioned, they typically say that there are the same number in each. When the spacing between the counters is changed in one of the rows, however, pre-operational children may say that there are more in the longer (more spaced out row), and this would display non-conservation.

Making 'human sense'

This aspect of the theory has received a great deal of criticism, and many experiments have been able to show that under certain conditions young children can display conservation abilities at a much earlier age than the theory would predict. One of the most striking of these experiments is based on the idea that the social

Figure 9.5   Co-operative learning. *(Martin Riedl / Science Photo Library.)*

understandings inherent in test settings exert a strong influence upon the judgements that children make. Margaret Donaldson suggested that children try to
make 'human sense' of the test situation rather than simply responding literally
to the questions.

She carried out a pioneering study at Edinburgh University with James
McGarrigle, which found that most of the 4- to 6-year-olds they tested showed
non-conservation on the number test when the spacing out of the counters was
intentionally carried out by the experimenter. When they ingeniously made the transformation appear to be accidental, however, by means of a 'naughty teddy bear'
who 'spoilt the game', the number of children who succeeded on the task more
than doubled.

This demonstrated that pre-operational children can display conservation abilities when the conditions are appropriate, and also illustrates the importance of
the social context of learning. Relationships between peers can be particularly
powerful, and a great deal of peer learning takes place in informal relationships,
such as children's friendships, and also in formal learning relationships, such as
co-operative groups.

Figure 9.6 L. Vygotsky. *(Archives of the History of American Psychology – The University of Akron.)*

Learning together

The Russian developmentalist Lev Vygotsky's theories of development and learning were based on *social co-operation*: on the idea that children draw on the more experienced members of the social groups of which they are part, absorbing cultural expectations, approaches and methods as a natural part of the learning process. Development will take place when a more experienced child, parent or teacher guides the child's participation in particular tasks; and this process of guidance has been described as 'scaffolding'. By recruiting and maintaining the child's attention, setting appropriate task limits, and drawing attention to its critical features, the instructor provides a kind of framework or 'scaffold' that makes it much easier for learning to take place. Instructors are often adults or teachers, but peer learning is equally important.

'Co-operative group work' is widely used in schools, as is 'peer tutoring', in which a more able or experienced child works with a less able or experienced child. Working together in co-operative groups can be done in many different ways, and can have different purposes and outcomes: there is growing evidence that it is effective in promoting cognitive gains, that it can lead to social and emotional developments, and that it can specifically be used to promote team work and co-operative attitudes.

Peer tutoring, particularly when used in the teaching of reading, has been shown to produce improvements in children's attitudes and achievements regardless of gender, race and social class divisions, especially for the children who act as tutors. Keith Topping's review shows that it can be particularly beneficial in multi-ethnic classes, where improvements have been demonstrated in social relationships, liking for others, and in reduced negative stereotyping of other racial groups.

ADOLESCENCE AND ADULTHOOD

The abrupt and profound physical changes that mark the onset of puberty have far-reaching consequences. They affect the whole of psychological development, and one of the most obvious outcomes is the awakening of sexuality itself. Adolescence is a time of major readjustment; the teenager must suddenly come to terms with new-found sexual feelings, and powerful emotional attachments towards others. The whole pattern of social relationships is changed, with parents and family, with peers and with those in the world of school or work such as teachers, supervisors and other authority figures. The adolescent is neither a child nor yet an adult, but is in a confusing, embarrassing and sometimes bewildering period of transition.

Is there an 'identity crisis'?

This idea derives from the theories of the psychoanalyst Eric Erikson, who proposed that there are eight stages in the life cycle, each of which has a particular developmental 'challenge' that must be resolved: the main challenge of adolescence is of wrestling with this 'identity crisis'. The idea is that this creates a great deal of 'storm and stress', and that protest, rebellion and *regression* to earlier forms of behaviour are fairly common and natural reactions.

Sociological theories, on the other hand, emphasize the changes in social roles that teenagers suddenly experience, and there are three main types of these. *Role conflicts* are common: to be a 'son' and a 'boyfriend' at the same time might well lead to problem situations when parents and girlfriend are both present. Role *discontinuities* are experienced, for example, when the 'schoolchild' is suddenly thrust into work experience, and has to relate to adults in a quite different way than hitherto. Role *incongruence* can also occur because the adolescent is torn between two conflicting sets of values: with the conventional social attitudes represented by parents and school, on the one hand, and with those of peer cultures, which quite often oppose authority, on the other. The mass media play a large part in defining peer cultures, which are often linked to current styles in pop music, and which in turn determine fashions in clothes, hairstyles and leisure interests.

Modern-day psychologists draw on both of these types of explanation, and tend to play down the idea of an 'identity crisis' in which the problem issues just described surface together. The basis of John Coleman's 'focal theory', for example, is that different issues 'come into focus' at different parts of adolescence. Anxiety over sexual relationships is a common worry early on, for example. Fears of rejection from, and problems with, different peer groups typically surface somewhat later: and conflict with parents may come to the fore later still. This theory sees the adaptation to adult life as gradually unfolding over time with respect to these different issues of concern, so that the idea of a period of intense 'storm and stress' is not now widely accepted.

The modern world is a rapidly changing place, and today's teenagers are sophisticated and well informed to an unprecedented degree. It is important that they are, since survival depends on avoiding the dangers of crime, drugs and sexual health at earlier ages than ever before. Other social changes such as increasing youth unemployment, different patterns of working and of family structure mean that the world is an increasingly uncertain place. This might explain some feelings of immobilization and depression: but the experiences of different social and cultural groups are so diverse that few contemporary psychologists would want to make generalizations about a teenage 'identity crisis', or about the existence of a 'generation gap'.

Adult careers and life transitions

The course of development in adulthood is probably best explained in terms of the ways, as individuals, in which we fit into patterns of work and career, of parenthood and family life. The career aspirations of today's young people are also rapidly changing: the prospect of a permanent job, or indeed of employment on more than a temporary contract, is much less of a realistic expectation than it was for the previous generations. As the number of graduates rises, the competition for those jobs becomes even more severe.

People's *identities* are influenced by these life transitions: there is a good deal of current psychological interest in how identities develop, and what effect they have on our behaviour across the lifespan. We all have a number of different *self-concepts*: these are the different ways in which we see ourselves in different activities or situations (e.g. how I see myself as a manager, or how I can work under pressure). Our *self-identities* are our overall view of how these all work together: and our *self-esteem* refers to our self-evaluation: how worthy we think and feel we are. Our *self-efficacy*, finally, refers to how effectively we feel we are at working in different activities and situations.

All of these perceptions are constantly changing and continually evolving in our interactions with others in the world around us: and the life change decisions we all make are closely bound up with our developing personal identities. The Teacher Identities in Music Education (TIME) project, led recently by one of the authors, investigated one very important life transition: that from student to employee.

This project was a longitudinal study of the identities of music teaching students, who typically experience a conflict between 'myself as a musician' and 'myself as a teacher'. Some students in music colleges even see going into teaching as a sign that one cannot make it as a musician, and so this is an important issue for them, and a source of internal conflict. We found surprisingly few changes over period in the self-efficacy measures that we asked them to complete, but we did find some quite clear differences between the group of students, and also that their attitude towards what was thought important in teaching changed considerably once they were working in a school. The TIME project is used to illustrate the longitudinal approach in Box 9.2.

BOX 9.2
A LONGITUDINAL STUDY OF IDENTITY
TRANSITIONS

In the Teacher Identities in Music Education (TIME) project, David Hargreaves, Graham Welch, Ross Purves and Nigel Marshall questioned a group of music education students first in their training course, and then after they had been in their first teaching post for a few months, and compared them with an equivalent group of music students who were questioned twice over a similar time period. By following the same two groups over this period of time (i.e. by using a *longitudinal* approach), the project authors were able to get far more direct insight into the transition from student to teacher than would have been possible by simply comparing different groups (age cohorts) of students and teachers at the same point in time. The latter is called the *cross-sectional* approach, and is often used by researchers when it is impractical, too time-consuming or too expensive to carry out longitudinal research.

We hoped to find some clear identity changes over this period, and some differences between the groups, on various measures of self-identity, including 'self-efficacy as a musician' and 'self-efficacy as a teacher'. The rather disappointing result was that neither measure revealed any clear differences in either respect. We did find, however, that the attitudes of the music education students towards the purposes of music education, and towards the skills they thought the job demanded, changed considerably when they became practising teachers, they began to see teaching skills such as communication, and controlling a class, as becoming far more important than musical performance skills.

Early career transitions such as this are experienced by men as well as women: but the general pattern or sequence of transitions across the lifespan seems to be quite different between the sexes. In Western society at least, most men have a clearly defined career pattern, followed by retirement, with parenting largely as a background or support role. The typical female lifespan is much more inconsistent: the relative importance and priority of the roles of worker, caregiver and homemaker vary considerably over adult life.

Traditional gender role behaviour may be at its strongest in the years of active parenting, in the 20s and 30s. In later life, at least in married couples, 'role blurring' occurs, and the interests, attitudes and behaviour of both sexes become less stereotyped. This is likely to be a direct result of retirement for men. They give up their role as active 'breadwinner' and are based at home, and so it seems fairly natural to take on some of the characteristics of the 'homemaker'. In women, the picture is much less clear. One suggestion is that they may suffer from the so-called 'empty nest syndrome' – having devoted time and effort to parenting and home-making over a long period, they suddenly find that their 'birds have flown', which can be another disruptive change in self-identity.

This picture of later adult life is of course based on conventional two-parent married families in Western society, and therefore leaves a great deal unexplained. Today's women are much more likely to have full-time or part-time jobs than in the past, and the possibilities of working from home using computer networking seem to be increasing female employment in particular. We are only just beginning to appreciate the potential of developments such as these. The course of our development over life – patterns of lifestyle, working, careers, leisure, family relationships, and much more besides – is changing more rapidly than ever before.

Recommended Reading

Berryman, J., Smythe, P.K., Taylor, A., Lamont, A.M and Joiner, R. (2002). *Developmental Psychology and You, 2nd edn.* Oxford: BPS Blackwell. [A 'companion volume' to this book, specializing in developmental psychology and using the same approach and style.]

Bremner, G. (1993). *Infancy, 2nd edn.* Oxford: Blackwell. [A comprehensive guide.]

Donaldson, M. (1978). *Children's Minds.* London: Fontana.

Durkin, K. (1995). *Developmental Social Psychology.* Oxford: Blackwell.

Smith, P.K., Cowie, H. and Blades, M. (2003). *Understanding Children's Development, 4th edn.* Oxford: Blackwell.

Wood, D. (1998). *How Children Think and Learn, 2nd edn.* Oxford: Blackwell.

10

Psychological Problems

- Anxiety and related problems

- The complex nature of fear and anxiety

- Sources of phobias and anxiety

- The treatment of fear and anxiety

- Social anxiety

- Schizophrenia

- Personality disorders

- Keeping critical about methods of classification: some limitations of diagnostic systems for personality disorder

Throughout this book we have been trying to show ways in which psychologists have attempted to understand and explain particular aspects of human experience and behaviour. Some areas of psychology are explicitly concerned with applying psychological theories to the problems and distress that arise in everyday life. Clinical psychology, for example, is about the application of psychological theories and methods in psychiatric, medical and related settings. The range of clinical psychology is now great, encompassing the fields of behaviour problems in childhood, the difficulties of the elderly, the effects of brain damage, delinquency and anti-social behaviour, as well as mental disorders such as depression and schizophrenia. In recent years, other branches of professional psychology have developed and advanced very rapidly. Health psychologists focus on the interface between medical illness/health and psychological processes. Counselling psychologists use psychological principles to help individuals cope with the wide range of problems that occur in everyday life. Forensic psychologists, on the other hand, work with the social problem of crime and its management by the justice system.

While there are many types of applied psychologists, in general these various professionals have much in common. They share basic training in *psychology as an applied science* and endeavour to increase human well-being and reduce distress through the application of psychological theory and research. Clearly psychologists are not the only professional group applying their theories and skills to the alleviation of human problems. Psychiatrists, social workers and others engage in comparable activities. What distinguishes psychologists is the attempt to apply psychological theories and findings and also their reliance on particular methods for gathering information about the problem at hand.

It is not possible in a short chapter to give an overview of this work. What we shall try to do is to give a flavour of the psychological approach by picking out three areas. It is worth stressing that it would be possible to pick out 20 or more fields of disorder in which psychologists have made a contribution. The problem areas we have chosen are those of fear and anxiety, schizophrenia and personality disorders. Applied psychologists were not the first to tackle these problems, but they have brought new perspectives to bear on them. Psychology's contribution has often been to *test and evaluate the theories* that have been put forward to explain particular difficulties and also to evaluate the effectiveness of interventions or treatment systematically.

ANXIETY AND RELATED PROBLEMS

Let us start by considering in detail one particular case (personal details have been changed for confidentiality).

Ms J. is a 23-year-old nurse. She was referred for help with a problem that had developed over the preceding year. She had always viewed herself as the 'nervous' and 'emotional' member of the family but never considered herself as having any major problems. A year prior to her referral she had been working a series of night shifts at a general hospital. When alone on the ward during the night a patient to whom she was very attached died. She was upset at the time but not unduly so. Two weeks later, while working on the ward at night, she was telephoned from home and told that her grandmother was seriously ill. She died a few days later. Over the ensuing weeks bouts of anxiety would arise if she was working alone on a night shift. She would feel dizzy, her legs would shake and she had a feeling of desperately wanting to leave the ward. On occasions she actually left the ward at night when these 'panics' came on. She eventually gave up night shifts, but her fear generalized to some degree to working during the day. She was then unable to go to work. Even the thought of work upset her. She was concerned to re-establish her normal work pattern as she was planning to marry and needed the income.

Phobias

Problems of fear and anxiety, of the kind just described, formed the bread-and-butter work of many clinical psychologists in the 1960s and early 1970s, particularly for psychologists of the behavioural school, who saw problems as learned according to the conditioning principles discussed in Chapter 12.

Today, even though the range of problems tackled is much wider, fear and anxiety are still a common reason for consulting a clinical psychologist. The problem just described is an example of a phobic disorder: the degree of fear experienced is out of all proportion to the objective threat the feared situation poses and is of such an intensity as to restrict and impair the individual's daily life. Phobias are fairly common. One American survey found that more than 7 per cent of the population reported a mildly disabling phobia, but that severe, crippling phobias were found in only two persons in every thousand. A range of phobias can be found in the community, including fears of illness, injury, storms, animals (rats, mice, spiders, cats, dogs etc.), heights and crowds. The most commonly treated one is agoraphobia.

Agoraphobia

Agoraphobia begins most commonly between the ages of 18 and 35 and is found predominantly in women. Fear-arousing situations include being away from home, being in crowds, being confined, travelling on trains or buses, and even going shopping. As with other phobias, the feared situation is often avoided and the person's life becomes very restricted as a result. Agoraphobics often experience a state best described as 'panic' in the feared situation. Their heart may thump; they may feel dizzy, sweat or experience a range of other unpleasant sensations. Panic symptoms like these can seem like a real physical disorder such as heart disease, and sufferers may even believe they will pass out or die.

Panic disorders of this sort are usually distinguished from generalized anxiety disorders in terms of the duration of the anxiety experience. For panic disorder the anxiety is sudden and limited in duration. For generalized anxiety disorder the feeling of apprehension is present over a long period of time and is unrelated to the perception of any specific danger.

THE COMPLEX NATURE OF FEAR AND ANXIETY

Psychologists and doctors have made a number of contributions to our understanding of conditions of this sort. An important beginning has been to reveal the *complexity of fear and anxiety*. Anxiety seems to involve four systems that interrelate in a complex and, as yet, poorly understood way: a cognitive/verbal system, a physiological system, a subjective/emotional system, and a behavioural system. In some instances of anxiety, all four systems are activated. The person perceives and expects danger (cognitive), he or she sweats, trembles and feels dizzy (physiological), feels anxious and frightened (subjective), and avoids the threatening situation (behavioural). But it is possible that these systems can become desynchronized. The person may show all features, except the cognitive perception of a particular threat (as in generalized anxiety, where the person does not perceive any particular danger). It is also possible to be fearful without marked physical changes, and vice versa. Equally the person may experience the cognitive, physiological and subjective aspects of anxiety in a particular situation and yet not avoid it. The clear implication of all this is that treatments may need to tackle these many different aspects of the problem if they are to be effective.

SOURCES OF PHOBIAS AND ANXIETY

One of the authors of this book has a daughter who, for some time as a baby, became upset and cried if the word 'hot' was said in the course of conversation. This puzzled many visitors to the house, though it had a simple conditioning explanation – in the preceding months she was at the stage where she spent much time exploring the house and its corners. She would often be spotted about to put a hand on something that might burn, such as a radiator; she would be warned, 'Don't touch that: it's hot,' typically just at the moment when she did in fact touch it. 'Hot', then, became a conditioned stimulus signalling pain.

Some clinical cases of phobia can be shown to be based on *conditioning experiences* of this sort. The case of Ms J. seems to be explainable in this way. Her avoidance of the feared situation (the ward at night) prevents her 'unlearning' her fear reaction. She gives herself no opportunity to learn that she can be on the ward at night without anything tragic happening. In many, perhaps most, clinical cases, however, conditioning experience of this sort cannot be found in the person's history. What the other routes to a phobia might be, are not yet clear.

Passing on fear

Social modelling may be an important factor. It can be demonstrated in laboratory studies that young monkeys with no experience of snakes can develop a strong fear by observing their parents react with fear to a snake. It is not difficult to see how agoraphobic reactions, phobic fear of illness, or a range of other fears could be acquired by humans in this way. Parents may teach fears by direct modelling and such learning may be accentuated by the parents' and child's capacity to encode such experiences in a verbal way. A fear of mice or spiders can run in the family.

Phobias can make good sense

Recently, it has been argued that the assertion that phobias can be acquired by conditioning needs considerable qualification. The conditioning of phobias is highly selective. Only some objects and situations are easily linked with fear, while others are not. Martin Seligman and others have pointed out that the objects or situations most feared by phobic people are the ones that *were* dangerous in the early stages of human history. The argument goes that evolution will have selected for those individuals who would readily associate particular dangerous situations with fear. People and other animals who quickly learned to be afraid of heights, or strangers or separation would have reproductive advantages over those without this capacity. Learning of this sort is referred to as *biologically prepared*. People do not readily acquire phobic reactions to electrical plugs or guns, because such objects have appeared too recently in human culture for them to have featured in natural selection. Clearly, we are primed to develop only particular kinds of fears or phobias. What other factors, apart from biological preparedness, promote the acquisition of particular fears, is, as yet, largely unknown.

Who is vulnerable?

Conditioning theories have been relatively unsuccessful in accounting for more complex phobias such as agoraphobia or for generalized, non-specific, anxiety states. For agoraphobia, there is rarely an obvious traumatic conditioning event that can be pointed to. A theory of the origin of agoraphobia, therefore, will need to look at a broader range of influences. For example, British researchers have suggested the following factors may predispose the person to develop agoraphobic symptoms:

- The early family environment. Families in which there is instability, over-protectiveness or lack of parental care may increase the tendency to be dependent on others and to avoid difficult situations.
- A general 'anxious' temperament (possibly influenced by genetics).
- Exposure to general stress in the environment.

The likely sequence for the development of the disorder is as follows. The anxiety-prone person with a 'bad' family background is exposed to stress (conflicts, domestic crises etc.), which induces a high level of anxiety and physical arousal. When the person then finds himself or herself in an overstimulating environment (for instance, a crowded shopping centre or shop in the case of agoraphobia), the physical arousal is increased and, eventually, the person experiences a full-blown panic in that situation. An additional factor then determines whether the person becomes agoraphobic or develops a generalized anxiety state. The person will become agoraphobic if he or she attributes the panic experienced to the external situation (the crowded place) rather then internally. The person now sees the panic as caused by the setting and learns to avoid it in future. Once the agoraphobic habit has been produced it will be maintained and confirmed if staying at home is rewarded by family and friends and if the person now avoids going out from fear of having another panic attack. It may be that the panic attack itself is now feared as much as the crowded street or shop.

Looking for danger

This account, of course, does not fully explain why some people are anxiety prone in the first place, nor why only some individuals are made anxious by life stresses. One promising line of recent research suggests that *anxious people 'selectively process' information relating to personal danger*. It is as if the anxious person is attuned to threats in the environment in a way that the non-anxious person is not. The 'dangers' in this case may be social (e.g. rejection) as well as physical (e.g. illness). Andrew Mathews has suggested that the anxious person may be locked in a 'cognitive-anxiety loop'. Cognitions or thoughts about danger cause a state of anxiety. The state of anxiety, in turn, activates 'danger schemata'. In everyday terms, perceived danger produces anxiety, which makes the person even more aware of thoughts and memories relating to danger. Such a loop produces an escalation of distress until a state of panic is reached.

THE TREATMENT OF FEAR AND ANXIETY

The treatment of phobias has been one of the success stories of modern clinical psychology. A very large number of studies have been conducted since the 1970s, evaluating the effectiveness of various therapeutic approaches. With considerable consistency the research points to the *effectiveness of exposure* to the feared situation in reducing phobic reactions. There have been several variants of exposure treatment that have been popular for a time, and one example is given below.

Systematic desensitization

In the 1950s, Joseph Wolpe developed systematic desensitization as a treatment for phobias. The technique has three components. First, the client is trained in deep muscle relaxation, to produce a physical state that is incompatible with the experience of anxiety. Second, the client is helped to devise a hierarchy of fear-inducing situations. At the top of the hierarchy are situations of maximum fear; at the bottom, situations of low fear. Finally, the client is asked to imagine each scene, starting at the bottom of the hierarchy, while deeply relaxed. When the fear diminishes the client moves up the hierarchy until the most frightening scene can be imagined without fear. This simple method proved to be effective with a number of simple phobias. Subsequent experiments showed that the relaxation was not essential for this method to be effective.

Treating panic

One of the most rapidly developing areas in the last few decades has been the psychological treatment of one type of anxiety – *panic disorder*. Panic refers to recurrent attacks of intense fear and anxiety. During an attack the sufferer may experience a range of disturbing symptoms, including a racing heart, sweating, shaking, nausea, numbness and choking. Sometimes panics of this sort are associated with agoraphobia (see above). It is the intensity of the physical symptoms, and their short duration, that distinguish panic disorders from generalized anxiety disorder. While pharmacological interventions play a part in the contemporary treatment of panic, psychological intervention is essential. Generally speaking, effective treatment programs for panic include a broad range of procedures and methods. These include training the person to modify his or her overbreathing (a likely contributor to feeling panicky) and teaching the person to produce the physical symptoms of panic consciously. There is also an important emphasis on helping the person to identify automatic catastrophic thoughts ('I'm going to die') that accompany physical sensations of panic and to substitute more realistic thoughts ('My heart is racing because I have been overbreathing'). Using such methods, many clients are able to control and reduce the terrors of a panic attack.

SOCIAL ANXIETY

Many mainstream clinical psychologists use *cognitive behavioural therapy (CBT)* to treat a wide range of clinical problems. We have already alluded to cognitive and behavioural methods in our previous discussion of fear and anxiety. CBT practitioners typically explain the presenting disorder in terms of underlying beliefs and assumptions (*schema*) that the person has and on patterns of behaviour that follow from these beliefs and assumptions (see also Chapter 14, Box 14.1, Case 2). Typically, treatment involves trying to change the problematic beliefs and assumptions and also modifying the coping behaviours the individual has acquired. To illustrate the approach in more detail we shall describe the application of CBT to a problem that is common in the community – social anxiety (sometimes called social phobia).

In various surveys, between 20 per cent and 50 per cent of college students report problems of anxiety and shyness in social situations, though only a small proportion of these have a problem that is so severe that it would lead to a formal diagnosis. Social anxiety is characterized by marked and persistent fear of social or performance situations (examples: eating in a restaurant or giving a talk at a seminar at college). The sufferer typically experiences feelings of panic in these situations, avoids them and fears that she or he will act in ways in these situations that will be humiliating or embarrassing.

Most people experience these feelings occasionally. What is different about the socially anxious person is the intensity and enduring nature of these feelings – they often form part of the personality rather than being a response to particular situations (see the discussion of *personality disorders* and of *avoidant personality disorder* below).

150

Contemporary theories (e.g. that put forward by the British psychologist Adrian Wells) propose that socially anxious people engage in three types of problem behaviours when they are exposed to the feared situation, for example when asked to do a speech in front of others in the classroom. These problem behaviours are as follows:

- Negative automatic thoughts ('I don't know what to say'; 'People will think I am stupid').
- Excessive focus on the self (self-consciousness, seeing an image of self from the viewpoint of others).
- Safety behaviours (attempts to control or avoid the situation, which often makes matters worse. 'I will avoid making eye contact. I will let my partner do the talking').

In addition to these problems, the socially anxious person is prone to unhelpful anticipatory thinking before entering feared situations ('I will look an idiot and have to rush out of the room) and to destructive 'post-mortem' thinking ('I have blown it now!').

SCHIZOPHRENIA

Schizophrenia is a severe psychiatric disorder affecting approximately 1 per cent of the population. Its presentation varies in different individuals, but among the most common symptoms are *delusions, hallucinations* and *thought disorder*. Delusions are false and abnormal beliefs (e.g. that the Government has implanted a radio transmitter in your brain to control your actions). Hallucinations are sensory experiences in the absence of an external stimulus. The most common form of hallucination is 'hearing a voice' that often gives instructions, or comments in a negative way on the person's behaviour. Hallucinations commonly cause much distress to the person, though not necessarily so. Thought disorder refers to a disorganization of speech, sometimes in the form of a loosening of associations, so that speech becomes confusing and disjointed for the listener.

The psychological perspective

Psychologists are increasingly making a contribution to the understanding and treatment of schizophrenia, often in innovative ways. The general view of psychologists tends to be that the likelihood of a schizophrenic episode occurring depends on people's vulnerability (which has a likely biological/genetic basis) in combination with the level of stress they experience. It is generally believed that the psychosocial stressors may be more relevant to the maintenance of schizophrenia (why it continues or recurs) than to its initial onset.

In addition to the psychosocial contribution to the maintenance of schizophrenia, it is also clear that *schizophrenia causes major impairments* for the affected

151

individual. Apart from the symptoms of the condition itself (delusions, hallucinations, thought disorder), the person suffers subsequent disabilities (poor social and community survival skills, poor self-image) and social problems (unemployment, family discord, diminished social networks).

How to intervene?

Psychologists such as Max Birchwood and Nicholas Tarrier in the United Kingdom have described and evaluated a range of interventions for schizophrenia. These are normally complementary to medical interventions rather than alternatives to them. One approach has been to tackle directly the symptom itself and to assist the person to cope more effectively with it. For hallucinations, for example, the first step would be to conduct an analysis of the factors controlling and influencing the hallucinatory experience, of the emotional consequences, of how the person copes and of how she or he might cope more effectively. Treatment would involve *devising and enhancing coping techniques* through practice and rehearsal. Max Birchwood and Paul Chadwick have shown that the person's appraisals and interpretations of the hallucinatory agent (the voice) are important determinants of adverse emotional and behavioural reactions to the hallucinations. If follows that in therapy we may need to help individuals change their interpretations and beliefs concerning the voice. Cognitive therapy for schizophrenia is a new but rapidly developing area of psychological practice.

Change through the family

There is evidence that family stresses contribute to the likelihood of a person with schizophrenia relapsing after discharge from hospital. For this reason, interventions need to focus on the family as well as on the individual sufferer. Nicholas Tarrier suggests that family interventions need to include educating the family about schizophrenia, stress management, goal setting for the patient and improving communication. It appears that a consensus is emerging that the problem of schizophrenia requires a multidisciplinary response in which the biological, psychological and social aspects are all addressed in an integrated and co-ordinated way.

PERSONALITY DISORDERS

In the early years of the twenty-first century there has been considerable interest in applying psychological ideas to a type of psychological/psychiatric disorder called *personality disorder (PD)*. This particular disorder is very relevant to the readers of this book in that it illustrates how psychiatric diagnostic systems work, the major problems that exist in classificatory systems and it alerts us to the fact that ways of thinking about problems and disorders are not set in stone but can and should change over time. In addition, consideration of this particular type of disorder requires us to think about *what is normal and what is abnormal* in

EXERCISE 10.1
IS THIS 'AGGRESSIVE PERSONALITY DISORDER'?

Chris is aged 27. For the past two years he has been drinking heavily. During this time he has become very aggressive, both verbally and physically, to his wife and young child. He has never been aggressive outside his home and gets on well with others at work and at his sports club. He also has periods when his home life is happy and free of incidents. Could Chris be described as having an 'aggressive personality disorder'?

The answer is no. Although he undoubtedly behaves in an aggressive way, aggressiveness is not a pervasive (he is not aggressive at work), inflexible (he is often non-aggressive at home) or stable (he showed no aggressiveness until he was 25) trait in his case.

personality. You should read the following section in conjunction with Chapter 3 on normal personality.

First, though, we need to define what 'personality disorder' means. In the past, there have been many different, and often inconsistent definitions of personality disorder. In recent years a consensus has begun to emerge. The most authoritative description of personality and other psychiatric disorders is provided by a well-known manual, which is used by psychologists and psychiatrists in many countries – *The Diagnostic and Statistical Manual of the American Psychiatric Association* – often referred to as the *DSM*. The DSM Manual (currently in a fourth revised version) sits on the desk of thousands of mental health professionals across the world. According to the DSM, a personality disorder is

> an enduring pattern of inner experience and behavior that deviates markedly from the expectations of the individual's culture, is pervasive and inflexible, has an onset in adolescence or early adulthood, is stable over time, and leads to distress or impairment.

We can see from this definition that it has been strongly influenced by trait theory (already discussed in Chapter 3). The critical words in the DSM definition are 'pervasive', 'inflexible' and 'stable'. For a personality trait to become a disorder it would need to be shown across many areas of the person's life (pervasive); the person would almost always act in the same way (inflexible) and the trait would need to be an enduring and ongoing feature of the person's behaviour over time (stable).

How many personality disorders are there? Just about any personality trait, if taken to an extreme, could, in theory, become a personality disorder, provided it met the general criteria suggested in the DSM definition above. This would apply even to traits, which at first glance, appear to be positive. Although there are, in principle, thousands of different potential personality disorders, in practice a small number of disorders have been described as common among those seeking help from psychologists and psychiatrists. The personality disorders described in the DSM are shown in Table 10.1, along with some of the characteristic features.

Personality disorders have a relatively high *prevalence* in the general community. Scientific surveys suggest that between 5 per cent and 13 per cent of individuals may suffer from a personality disorder, depending on the assessment measures used in the study and the particular population looked at. Antisocial personality disorder is very common indeed in offenders, particularly those in prison.

Table 10.1   DSM personality disorders

Paranoid personality disorder	Pervasive distrust and suspiciousness of others and their motives; since early adulthood; in a variety of contexts; beliefs about being deceived; sees hidden meanings; grudges; sexual fidelity suspicions.
Schizoid personality disorder	Detachment from relationships; restricted emotional expression; low engagement in sexual and social relationships.
Schizotypal personality disorder	Social and interpersonal deficits; eccentricities; odd beliefs and thinking; unusual perceptual experiences.
Antisocial personality disorder	Fails to conform with social norms; deceitfulness; impulsivity; irritability and aggressiveness; irresponsibility etc.
Borderline personality disorder	Instability of relationships, self-image and affect; marked impulsivity; identity disturbance; suicidal and self-mutilating behaviour; affective instability; intense anger; transient paranoid ideation or dissociative phenomena.
Histrionic personality disorder	Excessive emotionality and attention seeking; inappropriate sexually seductive or provocative behaviour; shallow range of emotions; theatricality and self-dramatization.
Narcissistic personality disorder	Grandiosity of fantasy or behaviour; need for admiration; lack of empathy; sense of self-importance; interpersonally exploitative.
Avoidant personality disorder	Social inhibition; feelings of inadequacy; hypersensitivity to negative evaluation; avoidance of social situations.
Dependent personality disorder	Excessive need to be taken care of; submissive/clinging; fears of separation; needs others to take responsibility.
Obsessive-compulsive personality disorder	Preoccupation with orderliness; perfectionism; need for control; low flexibility.

It will occur to many readers that *many forms of psychological problems and distress are not personality disorders* in the sense of being a trait that is pervasive and stable over time. Some disorders (e.g. mood disorders such as depression or anxiety, as described above) are usually time limited rather than enduring personality problems. Thus depression is not a personality disorder. The inclusion of personality disorders within the DSM reflects an important fact: that many of the severe problems of social adjustment encountered in clinical practice are not simply the product of a current neurotic or psychotic condition but reflect long-term personal attributes of the individual.

Having said that, it also needs to be pointed out that a high proportion of individuals with current, time-limited disorders *also* have accompanying personality disorders. It is common, for example, for a psychiatric patient to be diagnosed as having a current mental disorder such as a mood or anxiety disorder but also as having long-term problems of personality – thus multiple diagnoses are not unusual. What the link is between long-term personality problems and current states such as anxiety, depression or schizophrenia is uncertain, but this is an area likely to receive research attention in the future. It is known that diagnosed personality disorder is often associated with problems in social relationships, with abuse of alcohol and other substances and with self-harm.

KEEPING CRITICAL ABOUT METHODS OF CLASSIFICATION: SOME LIMITATIONS OF DIAGNOSTIC SYSTEMS FOR PERSONALITY DISORDER

It may be apparent to the reader by this point that a *psychological approach to human problems differs from a psychiatric one.* Diagnostic systems such as the DSM are mainly the product of a psychiatric/medical taxonomic approach. Psychologists have often been suspicious of diagnostic systems of this sort and have been quick to point out some of their inadequacies. One unresolved problem, for example, is how we define abnormality. Judging someone as abnormal or disordered involves broader criteria than straightforward biological abnormality – issues of statistical abnormality, the breaking of social norms and negative moral evaluation are also involved. We do not wish to take sides in this debate but, as an illustration of the critical psychological perspective, we would like to point out some criticisms that can be made of a psychiatric classification such as personality disorder.

Description, not explanation?

The concept of traits has been severely criticized by some psychologists (see Chapter 3 on Personality). A trait is a convenient descriptive summary. A trait is not an *explanation.* When we have observed a person acting as if she or he is suspicious of others and saying that she or he feels others are out to get her or him, we may label her or him as 'paranoid'. This term, however, merely restates

BOX 10.1
A CLINICAL INTERVENTION OUTCOME STUDY

As indicated in this chapter, cognitive behavioural therapy (CBT) is the treatment of choice for social phobia. In this study, a randomized control trial was used to compare individual CBT with group CBT and with waiting-list controls (the latter participants received no treatment). Seventy-one patients meeting DSM IV criteria for social phobia participated and were reassessed post-treatment and at 6 months follow up.

On measures of social phobia there was a significant pre-treatment to post-treatment improvement in both individual and group treatment. Individual CBT was superior to group CBT on several measures at post-treatment and at follow-up. The study confirms the effectiveness of CBT for social phobia. Why individual treatment should be better than group treatment is unclear. For further details see:

Stangier, U., Heidenreich, T., Lauterbach, W. and Clark, D.M. (2003). Cognitive therapy for social phobia: Individual versus group treatment. *Behaviour Research and Therapy*, 41, 991–1007.

our observations in a brief and cogent form. To explain her or his behaviour as caused by paranoia would be circular. Similarly, to describe a person as suffering from 'anti-social personality disorder' tells us, usefully, that she or he has the long list of characteristics listed in DSM IV, but it does not, as yet, tell us why she or he has those characteristics. The presence of descriptions of personality disorders in a big and authoritative tome such as DSM IV should not tempt us to think that somehow the person's problems are explained away.

Categories or dimensions?

The DSM IV system is categorical rather than dimensional. Many psychological researchers have questioned the usefulness of the categorical approach, which requires an either/or dichotomy. Either you have a personality disorder or you do not. Psychologists have pointed out that a dimensional approach is probably more valid and useful in describing traits. The appropriate question is not so much whether or not an individual has a particular personality disorder, but where on the continuum they can be placed. Thus, it is argued, it would be more useful to say he or she is at the seventy-fifth percentile on say, Dependency, than to say they have or do not have a 'dependent personality disorder'. One of the positive effects of adopting a dimensional approach is that it democratizes problems. We all share problem traits to some extent, rather than viewing the world as clearly divided into pathological and non-pathological.

Absolute or relative?

The listing of categories of personality disorder may be mistakenly taken as an indication that such disorders have some objective special status when compared to aspects of personality that do not feature in the DSM IV. It has been estimated that many thousands of trait descriptions exist in English (see Chapter 3 on Personality). The question may be asked: Why isolate these particular personality disorders? Could any trait, when taken to an extreme, become dysfunctional for the person? The selection of personality disorders for psychiatric classification systems may reflect (a) clinical realities within a particular society. Individuals with these particular traits come the way of psychiatric services. (b) Historical factors within psychiatry that lead to a focus on these particular extreme personality types. (c) Cultural values defining which kinds of behaviour are highly desirable and which are problematic. Does the existence of dependent and histrionic personality disorders, for example, say something about cultural values in the West, emphasizing the importance of autonomy and self-restraint? In brief, it may be that *we need to think about personalty disorders relativistically*. In a different society, with a different history and values, with different theoretical influences, the list of disorders may look rather different?

Stigma?

Although there is relatively little research investigating how people with particular diagnostic labels are perceived by others, it is plausible to suggest that personality disorder is one of the least attractive psychiatric labels, both to those who have the disorder, the general public and even health professionals themselves. The term suggests (consistently with the actual diagnostic criteria – see above) an entrenched, unchangeable, even lifelong, deficiency. This can be compared with disorders such as anxiety or mood disorders, which are less pejorative as labels and are probably viewed as temporary states amenable to therapeutic change. Many mental health professionals have felt they have little to offer those with personality disorders and have been reluctant to take them on for therapy. At the time of writing this book, however, we are witnessing increased optimism about therapeutic work with this group of people. Whether the stigma attached to the label of personality disorder diminishes as a result remains to be seen.

A positive approach to human problems

As you have read the chapters of this book, it may have occurred to you that psychology seems excessively concerned with what is bad or problematic in human experience and behaviour. There are many reasons why this should be so. One factor is undoubtedly the strong association (both in reality and in people's perceptions) between psychology and psychiatry, the latter discipline being concerned with the study and treatment of mental disorders. Applied psychologists are often employed in settings (psychiatric hospitals and clinics, prisons) associated with distress and with problems in living. Some have even suggested that the excessive concern of psychologists with negative traits and experiences is traceable to long-standing views in Western culture that people are 'rotten to the core' (original sin) and that happiness and goodness are illusions. The famous American psychologist Martin Seligman has pointed out that we have relegated the study of what makes life worth living to the back seat.

In very recent years this has started to change. Martin Seligman has promoted what has become known as 'positive psychology'. Positive psychology is concerned with understanding and developing happiness, well-being, optimism, enjoyment of activities (the good life), strengths and virtues and 'the meaningful life' (people's use of their strengths in the service of something much larger than they are individually). It is likely that this change of perspective will influence what applied psychologists study and also the interventions they deliver. Positive states and traits may not be simple opposites of negative states and traits. The psychological experiences producing happiness, for example, may not be simple mirror images of those that produce unhappiness and depression. *Dealing effectively with human problems may require a focus on developing a good life.*

Recommended Reading

Bennett, P. (2003). *Abnormal and Clinical Psychology: An introductory textbook.* Milton Keynes: Open University Press.

Cheshire, K. and Pilgrim, D. (2004). *A Short Introduction to Clinical Psychology.* London: Sage.

11

Your View of the World: Perception and Thinking

- Perception is more than sensation

- Attention affects perception

- Memory mechanisms

- Thinking and the nature of thoughts

- Differences in thinking and creativity

How does a blind person whose sight is restored make sense of what he or she is seeing? Or how does a profoundly deaf person, given a cochlear implant, know what he or she is hearing? Does the meaning of every pattern of light or sound have to be learned and remembered? Does the significance of sensations have to be learned so that the important sights and sounds can be attended to? How do thinking and memory work? Do we think in words? If so, how do babies think and how does the deaf person, who uses sign language and hence has a visual and not acoustic representation of words, think in terms of signs or the written word?

In this chapter, we shall look at the processes involved in perceiving things, paying attention, thinking and remembering. These aspects of human functioning are all linked, as without memory, how would we think? How would we recognize things around us? How would we know what to attend to and what to ignore? We shall look at each aspect of behaviour in turn, although we shall see some overlap in the explanations of the processes involved.

PERCEPTION IS MORE THAN SENSATION

Making sense of the world

How do you know that the thing you are looking at is a book? This knowledge needs more than the visual image you are receiving from your eyes and the feel of the book from your hands; it depends also on your existing knowledge of what a book is.

The sensory receptors in your eyes, ears, nose, tongue, skin and joints receive information from your environment and transform this into electrical impulses, which are transmitted to your brain. This is the subject of sensory physiology. As psychologists we need to have some knowledge of these processes. Perception, though, involves more than just taking in information from your senses. Perception is concerned with your interpretation of the sensory information you receive. You perceive something only when you become aware of it, and this occurs in the 'higher centres' of the brain where the sensory information is not just received but is processed.

Perception involving the sense of vision is the area that has been most studied, as for the majority of us this is the modality (the type of information) on which we are most dependent, although other species rely on scent, hearing, touch or even perception of electrical impulses to a greater extent than sight. We shall be using vision to illustrate perceptual processes.

The eyes and vision

The retina at the back of the eye contains two types of cell that are sensitive to light energy. These rod and cone cells (so called because of their shape) form one of five layers of cells in the retina and can be thought of rather like the film in a camera. There are approximately 100,000,000 rods in the retina of each eye, which are highly sensitive to light but give us no information about colour. This is why in dim light in the evenings you may be able to see, but everything looks grey. When it's brighter, we use our cones (approximately 3,000,000 per eye) and so can see in

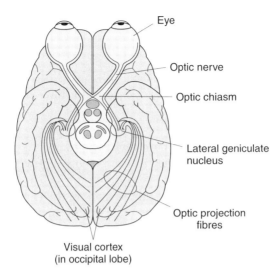

Figure 11.1   Light enters the eye and is transformed by the retina into electrical signals which are transmitted to the brain. As these signals pass through the optic chiasm, some of them change sides before being passed on for further processing in the lateral geniculate nuclei and then the visual cortex. (From Martini, Frederick H., Timmons, Michael J. and McKinley, Michael P. (2000). *Human Anatomy*, 3rd edn. Copyright © 2000 by Frederick H. Martini and Michael J. Timmons. Reprinted by permission of Pearson Education Inc.)

colour. After passing through the retina, where light energy is converted into electrical impulses that can travel along nerves, signals proceed along the optic nerves to the optic chiasm. Here, some of the signals from the right eye cross over to be transmitted to the left side of the brain and vice versa, as shown in Figure 11.1.

When the signals reach the primary visual cortex at the back of the brain, recordings from single nerve cells have shown that they are received by cells sensitive only to specific shapes, directions of movement, sizes and so on. This major discovery was made by David Hubel and Torsten Weisel in 1959. But finding these *feature detection cells* still leaves us a long way from understanding how we interpret the light patterns falling on our eyes as corresponding to particular objects in the environment.

What you get is not necessarily what you see

When we look at an object, it is situated on a background. Indeed, it has to be sufficiently distinct from the background in order for us to be able to see it (this is also true of hearing sounds, touching, smelling and tasting). Moreover a group of German psychologists pointed out that the distinction between figure and background cannot be considered simply in terms of physical boundaries. The demonstrations by these *Gestalt* psychologists of what they called 'laws of perceptual organization' show that in perception, the whole is greater than the sum of its parts. For example, the three isolated dots shown in Figure 11.2a are perceived by most people to be

Figure 11.2 Patterns of dots that illustrate the principle of good form, or *prägnanz*, which Gestalt psychologists described. Many people see the three dots in '(a)' as a triangle and the three in '(b)' as an arrow.

the corners of a triangle, but tip them on their side, as in 11.2b, and they become an arrowhead. In neither case are they just three dots. This illustrates the Gestalt principle of 'good form'.

More examples of Gestalt principles can be seen on the webpage to be found at http://www.sapdesignguild.org/resources/optical_illusions/gestalt_laws.html.

If you look at this book while you're holding it close to you, the light reflected from it stimulates large areas of your retinae. If you put the book on the table at the far end of the room, it stimulates a much smaller area of retina. So does the book look smaller the further away it is? A silly question perhaps, but why? Almost certainly the book looks to be about 20 centimetres by 15 centimetres by 2 centimetres however near or far away it is. This is because of a phenomenon known as *size constancy*. One way in which we can explain size constancy is to assume that the brain is receiving information not only about the size of the retinal image but also about the distance between object and viewer.

Visual illusions can fool the brain by giving it conflicting clues. One clue as to the distance away an object is, is perspective. Parallel lines such as railway lines or the edges of a straight road, appear to converge in the distance. Figure 11.3 shows a variation on the famous Ponzo illusion, which uses this perspective phenomenon to demonstrate size constancy.

Most of us perceive the two ladders as being of different lengths, when in fact they are the same (measure them if you're not convinced). The explanation of this is that the converging lines are interpreted as parallel lines receding into the distance. To some extent then, your view is based on your experience and expectations. For more visual illusions see http://www.michaelbach.de/ot/. There has recently been a proliferation of road signs in Britain exhorting road users to 'Think bike'. These signs are designed to raise your expectation that you will see a cyclist. Research in psychology shows that this should actually increase your chances of seeing any cyclists. There is a category of accidents known as 'looked but failed to see' (LBFS) accidents, first labelled in 1975 by Barbara Sabey and a colleague, which occur when we collide with things we are not expecting to see and we don't see!

Theories of perception

This sort of evidence, that we seem to make assumptions about objects in our environment, led Richard Gregory in 1966 to propose the theory of perceptual hypotheses. The idea is that we use what we already know in order to make the best guess we can about the sometimes sketchy and ambiguous material that our

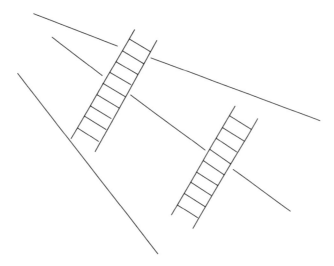

Figure 11.3   A version of the famous Ponzo illusion. Are the two ladders the same length?

senses present to us. One difficulty with this is that it cannot explain how we come to learn what things are in the first place. Gregory's theory can be classed as a *top down* theory, as it is based on the idea of information, stored in the brain, being used to interpret incoming information from the senses.

A completely different approach to perception was hinted at earlier when we mentioned feature detection cells. This is the idea that information is processed from the 'bottom', where it enters at the sensory receptors, 'up' as it progresses through the various levels of analysis in the central nervous system. One problem here is that there would have to be a huge number of feature detectors in order to discriminate not only between all the variations in shape, directions of movement, colours and so on, but also between the same information in different contexts. A fluent reader of the English language interprets the ambiguous shape in Figure 11.4, as an H in the first word but as an A in the second, although they are identical.

This is difficult to explain by a purely *bottom up* or *data driven* theory of perception. Perhaps a theory incorporating top down and bottom up approaches may come nearer to explaining how perception operates. Whichever way it works, there are going to be problems for the person with restored sight or hearing mentioned in the introduction to this chapter.

Figure 11.4   Is it an 'H' or is it an 'A'? The shape is exactly the same but we 'see' different letters, making an explanation of perception in terms of feature detection seem inadequate.

ATTENTION AFFECTS PERCEPTION

Your view depends on what you attend to

When in a crowded room at a party for example or in a club, you may be concentrating on a conversation you are having with a friend and be quite unaware of what other people around you are saying. However, even under those conditions, your attention will be caught if someone mentions your name or says 'help' or 'fire'. This shows that the unattended conversations are not completely blocked. They can catch your attention if their content is potentially relevant to you. Anne Treisman suggested that unattended information is attenuated, but not lost and that our attention has different thresholds depending on the interest we have in the information. Some earlier experiments had suggested a *single channel theory* whereby only one channel could pass information to the brain at one time.

While reading this book you cannot also read the newspaper or watch the television. When listening to music you may focus on the brass section of the orchestra and be unaware of the violins. These examples suggest that you have some control over what reaches your awareness. But this is only partly true: becoming aware of someone mentioning your name in the crowded room example at the beginning of this section is not a matter of choice.

Dual tasking

Anyone who has tried to listen to a small child while helping an older one with homework, planning what to cook for dinner, sorting the laundry and wondering what the puppy is up to in the next room, will be all too well aware that there is a limit to the capacity we have to process information. Perhaps, though, you can knit and watch television or read a book? Sing a melody while strumming the accompaniment on the guitar? Or perhaps you can drive a car and hold a conversation? If you are an accomplished keyboard operator, perhaps you can copy-type one passage at the same time as repeating another passage being spoken to you over headphones.

Under certain circumstances we can pay attention to or do more than one thing at a time. We can usually do this only if the two tasks require the use of different input and different output modalities (channels). Another important point is that with practice we become able to carry out some tasks without having to pay attention to what we're doing. That is to say, some processes are carried out automatically. If one task is being done automatically, for example driving a car, another act such as holding a conversation can easily be performed. However if, as the driver of the car, you should suddenly find yourself having to carry out evasive action because the lorry in front has jack-knifed, the chances are that your conversation will come to an abrupt end. Your driving skills have become attentional processes again and you are no longer able to attend to your conversation.

Generally speaking, then, two tasks can be performed at the same time if they use different modalities or if one of them is so highly practised as to have become automatic. As the person, familiar to many of us, at the beginning of this paragraph is experiencing, there is a limit to our capacity to divide our attention. Automatic processes take up very little of this capacity, which is why they can usually be performed at the same time as other tasks. Indeed, problems can arise when automatically completed tasks conflict with something you are trying to attend to. In general though, our resources seem to be allocated by a central processor and may be spread over several tasks that require little mental capacity, or they may be concentrated on one more demanding task.

See Box 11.1 for experiments using a split-span or dichotic listening procedure.

BOX 11.1
EXPERIMENTS ON ATTENTION, USING REPEATED MEASURES

In 1954, Donald Broadbent published the first of a series of experiments using his *split-span* procedure to explore the common experience of being able to attend to only one stimulus at a time. In his 1954 paper, he describes *within participants* or *repeated measures* experiments. This is an experimental design where each participant is presented with every condition or 'level' of the *independent variable* under investigation. Each participant's recorded response on one level can then be compared with his or her response on the other level(s) (the responses are the *dependent variable*). In other words, each participant acts as his or her own *experimental control*.

We shall describe a much more recent study using the split-span procedure (sometimes called 'dichotic listening') and a modern twist involving fMRI (see Chapter 7).

Lutz Jancke from Zurich and colleagues played simple tones through headphones and asked participants to direct attention either to both ears, or the left or right only. Their hypothesis was that the auditory cortex (an area of the brain specifically involved in processing sound) on the opposite side to the attended ear (opposite because the left side of the brain processes information from the right ear and vice versa) would show signs of greater activity than that on the same side as the attended ear. Because the same participants were included in all conditions, Jancke was able to compare the MRI pictures (dependent variable) on different conditions for each participant. There is a statistical procedure called a *repeated measures ANOVA* (repeated measures because all the measures are taken on each individual participant and ANOVA stands for analysis of variance) for analysing the results in order to show whether or not differences between measures made under the different conditions are statistically significant and unlikely to have occurred by chance. Jancke found significant differences between some areas under different conditions of paying attention.

Criticisms of experimental research in cognitive psychology

One problem with carrying out experiments on topics such as attention is that they inevitably involve creating on artificially simple situation, because the real question is often too complicated to experiment on. It is said that they lack *ecological validity*. What we really want to know is how these processes work in real-life situations. The best way to find this might be to use a combination of research methods. This was what Martin Langham and his colleagues at Sussex did in their analysis of looked-but-failed-to-see (LBFS) accidents. They first explored police records of accidents where drivers had collided with stationary police cars they claimed they had not seen. It turned out that most of these accidents involved experienced drivers on familiar roads close to home, where the police cars were parked in line with the traffic. After collecting this survey data, Langham carried out experiments using driving simulators, to work out which factors could be involved in these kinds of accidents.

MEMORY MECHANISMS

Much of what has been said so far in this chapter has depended on the existence of memory. Indeed, without memory of how written language works, we would have been unable to write any of it and you would have been unable to read it. So how does memory work?

Stages and codes in memory

One way to look at memory is to consider it in three stages. The first, *encoding*, involves transformation of input from our senses to a code suitable for the memory to store; the second is *retention* or holding the information in a store or stores, and the third, *retrieval*, the processes involved in getting information out of the store(s). At any one of these stages something may go wrong and we shall have forgotten the information we hoped to remember. The types of errors we commonly make show us quite a lot about the codes used and the organization of information in our memories. We can use this knowledge to help improve our memories.

In short-term memory, material is often stored using an *acoustic* code; that is, according to the way it sounds. We know this because we often 'recall' wrong but similar-sounding words to those we were actually trying to remember. This happens even when material is presented visually: most of us, shown a list of letters and asked to recall them, would be more likely to substitute F for M (which begins with the same sound) than for E (which is physically more similar). A visual code is sometimes used in short-term memory, though, for information such as the positions of shapes in a grid, which cannot easily be 'read' in an acoustic form. These general findings may not apply to people with specific reading difficulties.

Linking items and categorizing seem to be key to the way we remember things in the long term. Long-term memory has been classified into *episodic* memory for personal experiences and particular events in our lives, and *semantic* memory for general knowledge and meanings of things. Following brain disease or injury, there is sometimes a problem with memory for specific categories of item and this has led neuroscientists to use brain scans (positron emission tomography, PET, and functional magnetic resonance imaging, fMRI) to look for particular brain areas that may be involved in memory for certain categories of information. This is a fascinating idea, which is still under development.

One theory for the way in which material is organized for long-term storage is known as the *spreading activation model*. This assumes links, which may be more or less long and strong between words. 'Car', 'truck' and 'bus' for example are connected by strong short links to 'vehicle'. This means that thinking of one concept, for example 'vehicle', would make it easy to recall 'car', 'bus' or 'truck'. 'Wheels', 'carburettors' and 'exhaust pipes' would also be more accessible if you were thinking about vehicles than they would if you were remembering along different lines, for example houses. Drop-down menus in Microsoft Windows computer operating systems use this type of hierarchical structure to organize information and make its access intuitive. Try to recall the names of teachers you had at your first school. The chances are that you will recall the names of other teachers you have known (category: teachers) or of other people you knew when you were at that school (category: people I knew when I was aged 4–11), perhaps before you are able to come up with the appropriate names.

Improving memory

Strategies for improving memory make use of this linking. One method involves mentally allocating items from a to-be-remembered list to different places. A mental walk through the places in order will then allow you to recall the list of items. This is known as the *method of loci*. An example for remembering a shopping list of bread, lemons, cheese, nuts and eggs would be to picture your local playground with bread on the slide, lemons rolling around the soft-play area, cheese on a swing and nuts and eggs on either end of the see-saw. This may sound silly but it works surprisingly well – try it and see. Another method, *story linkage*, involves building up a story around the items to be remembered. A variation on this involves making up a story using the initial letters of the words to be remembered. In order to remember the recent presidents of the United States for example, with their election dates, a story might be something like this: '4 times I went out with Brian. He was my *1st* boyfriend and he was a bit of a 'lad'. He boasted that he had been out with *93* classy girls, once drunk *89* bacardi breezers in a weekend and wooed me with *81* roses. They were nicer than the *77* carnations my new man gave me but he's been *faithful* for *74* days now.' (Bush, '04; Bush, '01; Clinton, '93; Bush, '89; Reagan, '81; Carter, '77; Ford, '74.) Most of us will never be able to remember lists of over 50 items as exceptional mnemonists can do, but we might improve our memories a bit if we employ one of these strategies.

Short- and long-term memory

The memory storage system is often thought of as being divided into short- and long-term memory stores. According to this way of looking at things, anything that passes the encoding process is passed on to the short-term memory. This is as far as something like a telephone number that we look up, use immediately and then forget, ever gets. This type of memory has a capacity of about seven items (when telephone numbers are longer than this, we have to group the digits together in order to remember them) and lasts for a few minutes at the most. Material to be stored for longer must be held in another store. The traditional view is that it is passed from the short-term to a long-term memory store. This store is thought to have almost unlimited capacity and storage duration.

The simple explanation of memory in terms of encoding, retention and retrieval assumes that information transfer occurs in one direction only. However, telephone numbers appear in telephone directories in the form of black squiggles on a pale background. You could not encode a telephone number in the form of the sounds the digits would make if you said them (acoustic code), unless you had already learnt how to interpret the squiggles. This means that there must be information flowing from the long-term to the short-term memory as well as the other way round.

More ways to improve your memory: context

Successful memory can depend on contextual cues. Have you ever gone upstairs to get something only to forget what it was by the time you got there? Chances are that you went back downstairs and promptly remembered what it was. You are likely to remember more in an exam if you sit the exam in the same surroundings as you learnt the material.

More ways to improve your memory: state

A person's own internal state at the time of encoding can be important for later retrieval. The phenomenon whereby you may be told something when under the influence of alcohol or other drugs, be unable to recall it later when sober, but be able to do so when again similarly intoxicated, is known as *state dependent learning*. Emotional state and attitude also affect memory. Many of us watch soap operas on our televisions. Imagine a storyline in your favourite soap that parallels an upsetting episode in your life. When discussing the previous evening's episode at work the following day, would you and your colleague 'remember' the same details? Probably not. Our attitudes to things we see, read and so on affect the way we interpret and remember them. This has major implications for witnesses to crimes, as their memories will certainly be influenced by the, probably fearful, state they were in at the time the crime was perpetrated.

EXERCISE 11.1
THOUGHT AND LANGUAGE

What you need to do:
The words below are common in the English language. Look through them and mark them according to whether you think they are linked to universal categories or whether they have meanings specific to the culture of a particular English-speaking society.

fortnight	pants	blow
feminine	adult	teenager
student	weekend	morning
afternoon	teatime	mother
housewife	chair	magazine
book	treat	reward

This exercise makes us consider the relationship between language and thought. Just to look at one example: 'teatime' has a clear meaning for most British families. To many people in North America though, there is no such thing as teatime. Do Americans have difficulty with the concept of teatime because they have no word for it, or do they have no word for it because it is a concept they do not have? There are also words listed that have different meanings for different groups, or different meanings according to the context.

Why not try out this task on a few other people? Try to include some who are from cultures other than your own. You could also change the words, adding some of your own choosing.

THINKING AND THE NATURE OF THOUGHTS

If memories are coded in terms of their acoustic features or their meanings, does this mean we remember and think mainly in words? What do we mean by 'thinking'? We use this word in a variety of ways. For example, we might say, 'Try to *think* where you put it,' using the word as a synonym for 'remember'. Or 'What do you *think* about the present government?', meaning what is your opinion? Or 'What do you *think* about God?', meaning what do you believe? '*Think* what you're doing' means 'concentrate'. So is each one of these asking people to do very different things? What is thought and what processes are involved in thinking?

Psychologists who adopt different theoretical standpoints have explained thought in different ways, and we shall look at some of these.

Where and what are thoughts?

Sigmund Freud, whose theory of psychodynamics put great emphasis on levels of consciousness, distinguished between rational conscious thought of which we are aware, and less logical, emotionally based, repressed thoughts and fantasies stored at an unconscious level. The latter are only retrievable, he believed, under the special conditions of psychoanalysis. Other people have been more concerned with what form thought takes, rather than 'where' it takes place. Most importantly, the relationship between language and thought has been the topic of several signific-ant theories. Do we need language in order to think? Or perhaps we need thought in order to be able to use language? Perhaps language is irrelevant and thought can occur in the form of visual or other sensory images?

In the 1920s and 1930s, two men working independently came up with the idea that the way each of us thinks depends on how we express concepts in our par-ticular language. The theory, named after the two linguists Edward Sapir and Benjamin Lee Whorf (Whorf was an amateur linguist), is known as the Sapir-Whorf hypothesis or the *linguistic relativity hypothesis*. The main idea, that language affects the way we think about things, can be supported by examples from the world's different cultures. For example, in European languages we have different tenses to indicate the passage of time (past, present and future) and we tend to regard time as an object rather like a tape, which we can mark off in spaces or cut up. The Hopi Indians of North America, on the other hand, have no time referents in their language and apparently (maybe consequently?) have no use for the idea of the passage of time.

Another often-quoted example is of the Inuit people who may have many words for snow in their language (although studies have not always found this). The suggestion based on the Sapir-Whorf hypothesis is that this actually enables these people to perceive many more different kinds of snow than people living in other parts of the world.

Some experimental evidence also seems to support a relationship this way round between language and thought. If you show line drawings to people and then later ask them to reproduce the drawings, the outcome depends on the label given with the original drawing (see Figure 11.5). This experiment was first published as long ago as 1932. Participants were given either one of two different sets of labels with line drawings, or no labels at all. When asked to reproduce the line drawings from memory, what people actually drew was clearly influenced by the label they had read: the original ambiguous drawing was modified to resemble the descrip-tion given. The language (label), in other words, had influenced what the person thought she or he had seen.

But does it follow from examples such as these that the whole nature of thought is based on language? Could it be the other way round?

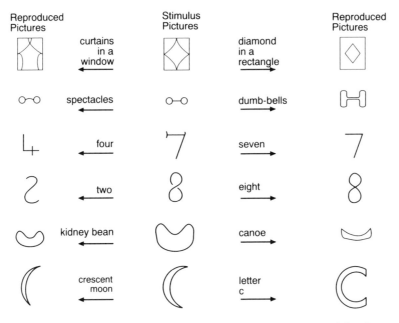

Figure 11.5 The label associated with a figure affects your memory of the shape you have seen. This experiment was originally carried out by Carmichael, Hogan and Walter in 1932.

The great developmental psychologist Jean Piaget (discussed in Chapter 9) based his theory on universal stages in thought processes through which all children pass as they mature, regardless of the language they are learning to speak or the culture in which they live. For Piaget, then, language was secondary to thought, depending on maturation of thought processes and reflecting the complexity of thought of which the person was capable, according to her/his developmental stage. This idea is more or less the opposite to the linguistic relativity hypothesis, which considers thought to depend on grasp of language. It is supported by an increasing body of evidence that non-human animals (so far as we know without language, see also the discussion in Chapter 3) may be capable of thinking through the consequences of their and others' actions.

Perhaps the true answer to 'Which comes first, language or thought?' is that neither does. The Russian psychologist Lev Vygotsky (see Chapter 9) was among the first (in the 1930s) to suggest that at least from the age of two, language, thought and social development are all inextricably linked. No one factor can be singled out as coming first and enabling the others.

An example of the consequences of problems arising somewhere in this three-way package is autism. The child with autism typically has problems with language and other aspects of communication, with relationships and interactions with others and with flexibility of thought, especially understanding another person's point of

BOX 11.2
DISCOURSE ANALYSIS: A QUALITATIVE RESEARCH CHALLENGE TO TRADITIONAL METHODS IN COGNITIVE PSYCHOLOGY

Cognitive psychology has traditionally been dominated by the experimental tradition. Language has been regarded only as a means for communicating information about cognitions, and cognitions are seen as definite representations of objects we can perceive, information we have committed to memory and so on.

However, an alternative viewpoint is that we interpret the world around us in different ways and that we actually construct the things we perceive and remember through our use of language. Thus we can use a version of qualitative methodology known as 'discourse analysis' to study cognition. This is a 'hermeneutic' approach; that is, it involves interpretation of meanings and is completely different from the scientific approach that involves measurement or counting (in this context) items recalled.

Discourse analysts argue that putting thoughts into words actually changes the thoughts, giving them meanings, rather that simply reflecting them. Use of this method to study memory, then, emphasizes the importance of looking not for accuracy of recall, but at how the language used in recalling an incident suits the requirements of the individual recounting the incident. The words she or he uses construct her/his position with respect to the incident and in the context of the audience to which it is related. Psychological processes (in this case memory) can be revealed by analysis of the social context and the language used, rather than language merely being a tool to access the memories stored inside our heads. We 'remember' differently according to our audience or how long ago the incident occurred and so on, and the meaning is constructed jointly by speaker and listener. Discourse analysts break down or 'deconstruct' the language used into its meaning as shared by the speaker, listener(s) and the analyst.

view. It is not clear where the initial difficulties lie, but the spread of difficulties indicates that the three areas of language, thought and social interaction are tied up.

DIFFERENCES IN THINKING AND CREATIVITY

Do we all think in the same way? Do you think in colour? In pictures? In emotional feelings? In words? In musical sounds? If words are important for thought, how do babies think? What do they think about? Presumably a person profoundly deaf from birth might think in a form of language, but his/her memories will not be represented as the sounds of words. Someone blind from birth will not think in visual terms. People with a relatively common and sometimes mild disorder of language, dyslexia, with its characteristic difficulties with reading and writing, are reported to use visual imagery in their thinking (some have superior spatial skills) more than most of us. In his book on the development of thought in childhood, Peter Hobson concludes that self-awareness is key to the ability to think. This allows for differences between people in the form of thoughts, and indeed Hobson describes how experience has an important influence in determining not just what we think but how we think.

Creativity

We are all capable of creative thinking in that we put together thoughts in unique and original ways. Some people though, seem to be more creative than others: thinking up ideas that are markedly different from anything already around. Graham Wallas suggested in 1926 that creative thinking occurs in four stages: preparation, incubation, illumination and verification. The idea of incubation in this context brings us back to the whereabouts of thought processes, as the idea describes our experience of the creative process taking place outside conscious awareness. The evidence for this is the way that original ideas sometimes appear to pop up in our minds (the illumination stage) when we are carrying out some completely unrelated task (but incubating). Creativity is notoriously difficult to assess and much of what is written about creativity is concerned with commerce (see for example the review by Jaafar El-Murad and Douglas West).

Recommended Reading

http://www.sapdesignguild.org/resources/optical_illusions/gestalt_laws.html [Designers make use of gestalt laws.]

http://www.michaelbach.de/ot/ [Excellent and amusing site of visual illusions with explanations.]

http://www.opprints.co.uk/gallery.php [Another site with good illustrations of optical illusions.]

Posner, M.I. (2004). Neural systems and individual differences. *Teachers College Record, 106,* 24–30.

12

Learning about Your World

- Learning by linking

- Learning by consequences

- Learning what to expect

- Learning from others

- Consciousness, intelligence and learning

Learning involves change in an individual, the acquisition at least temporarily of some form of information. But how do you learn? Almost every day you meet new people, learn their names and learn to recognize their faces and voices, you learn items of news from the media or from other people. You may also have learned your times-tables by rote as a child; you learn all sorts of things as you move about in your daily life. But how do you do this? Do you learn by forming associations between pairs of things, building on these and accumulating a big bank of linked items of information? If so, how come you can't 'teach an old dog new tricks'? Or can you? *Behaviourism*, an influential 'school' of psychology, was built on the premise that learning could all be explained by the forming of associations.

LEARNING BY LINKING

Classical conditioning

Ivan Pavlov (1849–1936) was a Russian physiologist investigating the digestive system of dogs. He became famous in psychology for describing a form of learning-by-association, which became known as classical conditioning. Pavlov was studying dogs' reflex salivation in response to food, and was surprised to observe that the dogs salivated on some occasions when they had no food. He went on to investigate these 'psychic secretions' as he called them and found that they were responses to cues that the dogs had come to associate with food. Food (which always induced salivation) was now called an 'unconditional stimulus' (UCS) and the response of salivation was called the 'unconditional response' (UCR). In his experiments, Pavlov sounded a bell every time the dogs were fed, immediately before they were given their food. When this had been repeated a number of times, he sounded the bell without giving any food and still the dogs salivated. The bell had now changed from being a 'neutral stimulus' and had become a 'conditional stimulus' (CS), and the response to the bell (salivation, which would not naturally follow hearing a bell) had become a 'conditional response' (CR) (see Figure 12.1).

Behaviourists explained this in terms of the dogs having linked the two stimuli: food and bell. They responded to the bell as if it were food. Further experiments showed that the classically conditioned response may be *generalized* to stimuli similar to the original CS, although following repeated exposure to one specific CS, animals may also show *discrimination* between other possible CSs. This discrimination in classical conditioning is shown by the pet cat which responds excitedly (CR) when its owner goes into the kitchen at feeding time (CS) to get its food (UCS), but not when someone else goes into the kitchen (neutral stimulus). Following classical conditioning and whether generalization or discrimination occurs, the CR will be *extinguished*, and stop occurring, when the CS is presented a number of times without the UCS.

From the early work it was thought that the time gap between the CS and the UCS during the conditioning period was very critical. A principle of *temporal contiguity* was suggested, or a need for the two stimuli to be very close together in time, which we shall see later, does not quite fit all the evidence.

Figure 12.1　Pavlov explained his dogs' salivation at the sound of a bell as being a result of their linking of the two stimuli: bell and food. *(From www.CartoonStock.com)*

Watson's Behaviourism

Psychology in the late 1800s and early 1900s had depended on people's introspections concerning their feelings and sensations, in order to gain understanding of consciousness. The new Behaviourism was something of a reaction to this, and now only behaviour that could be observed and recorded objectively was considered acceptable data for study in psychology. This new type of psychology was founded by an American called John B. Watson (1876–1958). Watson extended Pavlov's work and showed that classical conditioning worked in humans, by inducing, in a child named Albert, a conditioned fear of furry white animals.

Poor little Albert, who initially had no fear of a pet rat (a neutral stimulus), was subjected to a loud bang (Watson banging a piece of metal just behind his head) whenever the rat came near him. This bang (a UCS) frightened Albert who started and began to cry (UCR). After several pairings of the bang with the rat, the rat was presented alone and Albert's response was now to start (a CR). He had been conditioned. Over the course of a few months, Albert's conditional fear response was shown to have generalized to a rabbit, a dog, a fur coat and a Santa Claus mask. It was probably as well that the process of extinction was never studied: one thing

EXERCISE 12.1
CLASSICAL CONDITIONING

What you will need
You will need a lemon, a bell or buzzer (a kitchen timer with seconds would do fine) and a willing friend.

What you need to do

- Position yourself so that you can put a drop of lemon juice on your friend's tongue.
- Sound the buzzer and get your friend to confirm that it doesn't make him or her salivate. Also try putting a drop of lemon juice on your friend's tongue – your friend should salivate.
- Now try sounding the buzzer and immediately afterwards giving the drop of lemon juice.
- Repeat this pairing of buzzer and lemon juice several times.
- Sound the buzzer alone.

Did salivation occur in this last stage?

   If your friend salivated in the last stage, you have turned an initially neutral stimulus (buzzer) into a conditional stimulus for the salivation response. This response is now a conditional response, having been originally an unconditional response to the unconditional stimulus (drop of lemon juice). In terms of expectancy, your friend has learned to expect that E1 (the buzzer) will be followed by E2 (the juice). Note that the behavioural response conditioned here is a reflex behaviour – one over which we do not usually have any voluntary control. These are the responses usually susceptible to classical conditioning.

Watson considered trying was 'reconditioning' Albert, to remove his fear, by showing him the fear-producing objects while simultaneously stimulating his erogenous zones; first lips, nipples, then sex organs. We should stress that this was not done and would certainly not be considered ethical today!

   Although we know now that the mechanistic kind of theory proposed by Watson is too simplistic and that we cannot explain all learning by stimulus–response associations, we do know that associations aid recall in our everyday lives as well as in experiments. For example, if you revisit your old school or another place you have not been to for a long time, come across an odour you last smelled in your childhood, play a piece of music you last heard years ago or look at an old group photograph; memories of people, place names, conversations, incidents may all come flooding back with associated emotions. The conditional stimuli (photograph, music etc.) are associated with actual events in your past (unconditional stimuli) and you respond with embarrassment, pleasure, anxiety and so on (conditional responses) as you did on previous occasions when the UCSs were present.

LEARNING BY CONSEQUENCES

A puzzle for cats

Other pioneers of the new American psychology based on learning were Edward Thorndike (1874–1949) and the more famous Burrhus F. Skinner (1904–1990). Thorndike developed a puzzle box from which a cat had to escape by pulling a string or pressing a catch in order to get to food. Cats would take less and less time to escape over a series of trials in the box, which Thorndike explained as the gradual formation of an association between the stimulus situation of the box and the response that was instrumental in securing the cat's escape. This type of learning was known as *instrumental conditioning* and the explanation was, as with classical conditioning, in terms of stimulus–response associations. However, in this case the animals' own actions are instrumental in their gaining the rewards, whereas in classical conditioning, two stimuli become linked so that either elicits the same reflex, involuntary response. The emphasis has therefore shifted towards the consequences of action. Thorndike's major contribution was his *Law of Effect*, which holds that those behaviours that produce desirable outcomes will be those that are repeated and vice versa. This was an important advance, although we would now interpret Thorndike's experimental findings rather differently.

The Skinner box

Burrhus F. Skinner, whose name is associated with the famous box, investigated instrumental learning in greater detail. (See William O'Donohue and Kyle Ferguson's review of Skinner's life and work.) The Skinner box is a piece of apparatus containing a lever that can be pressed or a button that can be pecked and a tray for the automatic delivery of a reward (usually food). The lever-presses or button-pecks are recorded automatically over time. When an animal (e.g. a pigeon) is first placed in the box, it may have a food reward for moving around investigating. After this, it may be rewarded only if it approaches the button; later it will have to touch the button in order to receive a reward; next it will be rewarded only when it pecks the button. Versions of this process of *shaping* of the desired behaviour can be seen in everyday life when we use money to increase the productivity of workers or praise or stickers to increase desirable/good behaviour in children. Once the pigeon has learned to peck the button in order to gain food, or the child to sit quietly in order to get stickers, their discriminatory abilities can be investigated as they can be rewarded, for example, for responding only when a red light shines or only when a triangle is illuminated, or, in the case of the child, when the story has finished.

178

The Skinner box method is generally known as *operant conditioning*, as the animal in the box performs some operation on the environment in order to bring about change. The changes that animals will work for are, as we know from Thorndike's work, changes in the animal's desired direction and are known as *reinforcement*. Operant conditioning has been particularly useful in the study of the effectiveness of different forms and different schedules of reinforcement.

Reinforcement and punishment

Positive or negative reinforcement can be effective in teaching a desired behaviour. The food rewards and stickers we have been describing constitute positive reinforcement, whereas if by responding appropriately, a rat is able to *avoid* receiving an electric shock. We call this shock a negative reinforcer. The Skinner box may also be used to demonstrate the effects of punishment. If pressing a bar results in a rat *receiving* a mild electric shock, the rat will soon stop pressing the bar. However, following a punishment routine such as this, the rat may show signs of stress and stop performing

"That large, rolled-up newspaper is a reminder -- mess up in this office, and you'll pay the price."

Figure 12.2   Skinner explored reinforcement in his box, which automatically records an animal's actions and delivers rewards. He concluded that punishment was not a good aid to learning. The cartoon illustrates the effect of a more useful aid to learning: negative reinforcement. If the worker doesn't 'mess-up', he will avoid ill effects. *(From www.CartoonStock.com)*

all the behaviour it was doing at the time or may start to perform unpredictable behaviour. These findings led Skinner to recommend reinforcement rather than punishment for shaping behaviour in humans (as well as rats) (Figure 12.2).

Working with the Skinner box, it was difficult to use associations between stimuli and responses to explain what was going on. As the experimental animal in the box was free to press the lever at any time, what stimulated it to respond in this way? Learning would have to be explained in a different way if a stimulus could not be identified. Because of this, Skinner dropped the idea of a stimulus eliciting a response, from his explanation of conditioning, and instead divided responses into *elicited* responses like the salivation in Pavlov's classical conditioning experiment and *emitted* responses such as touching a lever in a Skinner box. The latter was a freely performed response, which an animal may perform at any time. This dissent from hard-nosed Behaviourism was also cropping up in other guises elsewhere, as we shall now see.

LEARNING WHAT TO EXPECT

Predicting behaviour

So far, we have given little thought to the processes involved between stimulus and response, or between response and reinforcement. There was no place for cognitions, or facts animals may learn and use when faced with new situations, in the early Behaviourists' explanations of learning. Work being carried out while stimulus–response psychology was still in its heyday, by Edward Tolman (1886–1959), pointed to the conclusion that the behaviour of rats running mazes was purposive and flexible, not mechanistic as suggested by the mainstream researchers. One experiment that led Tolman to this conclusion was performed by his student, Donald Macfarlane, in 1930.

Macfarlane's experiment involved training rats (which are good swimmers) to find their way through a maze flooded with water. When the rats had completed this task, the maze was drained and the rats were once again placed at the start. Using a completely different set of responses (running instead of swimming), the rats were able to complete the maze without error. According to Tolman, the animals had learnt, not a series of responses to be performed, but information about the experimental situation, such as 'at the T-junction turn towards the window, go right by the window then right again on to the path that brings you to the food'. In other words, the rat forms a *cognitive map* or internal representation of its environment, which it stores in its brain. It is then able to use this information with the aim of reaching its goal (Figure 12.3).

Many ingenious experiments have followed Tolman's early work and have allowed a new interpretation of classical and operant conditioning to be made. Without going into too much detail, the new interpretation states that the occurrence of event E1 can lead an animal to expect event E2. It is an animal's ability to form this E1 → E2 expectancy that gives it an advantage as it goes about its daily life, as this is the ability that allows it to form possibly life-preserving predictions

Figure 12.3 Edward Tolman suggested that animals form 'cognitive maps' of their environments, rather than learning to produce a fixed set of responses to a given stimulus situation. *(From www.CartoonStock.com)*

about what is going to happen. Without the ability to predict events, the animal may not act in the most appropriate way to maximize its chances of survival.

Can any event become a predictor for any other event?

The expectation that a stimulus might, for example, be harmful, need not be based on experience of its immediate noxious effects as would be predicted by the rule of temporal contiguity to which Pavlov, Watson and others subscribed.

A famous experiment by John Garcia and Robert Koelling in 1966 showed that if rats were ill *several hours* after consuming water flavoured with saccharine, they refused saccharine-flavoured water subsequently, apparently having learned to associate the taste of saccharine with their illness and to expect a nasty outcome to result from consuming something with this taste again (i.e. E1, drink flavoured water → E2, feel ill). This expectancy can be formed despite a gap of several hours between the first and second event. Another remarkable thing about this experiment was that the learning occurred after only *one experience* with the taste. It is rats' capacity for this type of learning that makes them such good survivors and so difficult for us to poison.

It is quite common for a very similar type of learning experience to occur in us. Perhaps you were ill years ago after eating a particular food or drinking too much, and have been unable to face the same food or drink again? Even though you may know that the foodstuff was not the cause of your illness or that the drink in moderation is very unlikely to produce adverse consequences now, you are still unable to bring yourself to try it.

Another very interesting finding that emerges from this work and that also goes against the earlier understanding of classical conditioning is that rats will not learn an aversion to plain water. Our understanding of this is that it would not be biologically possible for rats to have evolved the capacity to associate water with illness and to avoid it, as there is no other adequate source of fluid for them: avoiding harmless water would inevitably lead to death, whereas drinking water that just might be poisonous will usually have no repercussions. As an omnivore, though, the ability to reject a foodstuff that has once made you ill has obvious advantages. This shows that not everything can be taught to any animal (and that includes us).

Examples of this constraint on learning come from attempts to use operant conditioning to teach tricks to animals for show business or advertising purposes. Keller and Margaret Breland were completely unable to persuade pigs to carry coins consistently to a piggy bank and drop them into it, even though this would appear to be a simple task for these highly intelligent animals. The pigs repeatedly dropped the coins and rooted them along the ground. The point here is that an animal working for reinforcement with food will tend to gravitate towards its natural food-getting behaviour and will not learn to carry out a different behaviour in order to get food.

LEARNING FROM OTHERS

So far, the learning we have considered has involved one animal or person learning from experience, a likely outcome of an action or event. We know though that a lot of learning takes place in a social context. A particular concern in many Western societies is the effect that television and computer games might be having on anti-social behaviour in children and young people. The American psychologist Albert Bandura argued that if we pay attention to the actions of others, we remember what they do and can reproduce their behaviour ourselves at a later date. This learning appears to occur without direct links to benefits (reinforcement).

Bandura's 'Bobo' doll

An experiment Albert Bandura (1925–) published in 1961, which is still quoted by those concerned about the effects of violence in the media, involved groups of nursery school children. One group watched an adult playing with a set of small toys but ignoring a large inflated 'Bobo' doll that was in the room. Another group watched an adult shouting at and hitting the doll. When the children were later allowed to play with the doll, those who had seen the adult being violent towards it, acted in a similar way, whereas those in the first group played pleasantly. How much light this experiment throws on the effects of media violence is still controversial and not the subject of this chapter (see Chapter 5). The point is that the children had learnt through observation and imitated their adult model's behaviour. Young chimpanzees have been filmed watching their mothers fishing for termites and subsequently trying the behaviour themselves, something they do not necessarily do without the adult model. But this learning by observation is not confined to highly intelligent primates. Hens (not generally thought of as being particularly clever) have been shown to peck more at red than blue food containers after seeing a video in which food was presented in red containers (or vice versa).

Learning, then, is influenced by your social or cultural experiences. Learning is intimately tied up with the use of culturally shared tools, and perhaps our most important tool is language. Through talking things over with others, explaining and discussing, you gain understanding and actually jointly create meanings. By reading this book, you are not simply learning interesting facts about psychology, but by immersing yourself in the language of the book and understanding its content, you are actually learning to become a student of psychology. Before you read anything on the subject, you will have had ideas about behaviour and what makes people 'tick', but perhaps you lacked the tools to carry your thinking forward and to talk or write about the subject matter of psychology. In a similar way, a child starting school has to learn the ways in which this new society operates, before he or she is able to make progress with the timetabled lessons.

CONSCIOUSNESS, INTELLIGENCE AND LEARNING

Does all learning involve the same principles and mechanisms? The rather different explanations of learning we have introduced are not mutually exclusive. From the simple experiments described at the beginning of the chapter, we can extract two general principles: some things are easier to learn than others and what we learn today builds on what we learnt yesterday. One feature of the learning we have described is that it occurs for the most part without deliberate, conscious effort. Clearly, though, some of our learning (e.g. when we learn times-tables or course material for an exam) does need conscious effort. We shall now look briefly at the role of consciousness and of intelligence in learning.

Consciousness and learning

Most people find that when learning for an exam, or even when trying to commit a shopping list or 'to-do' list to memory, they can remember more if they actively engage with the material, rather than simply reading it. The act of writing a shopping list enables this author to remember more of what is needed from the supermarket, even if the list is subsequently left behind on the kitchen table! Indeed, people who need to remember long lists of information consciously employ various mnemonic devices that involve actively and deliberately manipulating the

EXERCISE 12.2
MEMORY, MEANING AND RHYME

What you need to do

Look down the list of words below. If a word has 'M' beside it, think of a different word related by meaning to the word given. The meaning need not be the same: 'fork' would do for 'spoon', for example. If the word has 'R' beside it, think of a word that rhymes with the word given. For example, 'moon' for 'spoon'.

rat (M)	bike (R)
book (R)	fence (M)
bag (M)	stool (M)
rock (R)	mug (R)
tree (R)	hair (M)
rain (R)	cloth (M)
desk (M)	rug (M)
lake (R)	bread (R)

Now put the list out of sight and write down as many of the original words as you can recall.

Check how many of your answers were M words and how many were R words.

Prediction: you have remembered more M words than R words.

The levels of processing theory predicts that you will remember more M than R words in this task, because semantic processing (involving meaning) occurs at a deeper level than acoustic processing (using the sound the words make). This usually works, although there is an alternative to the explanation that it is the depth of processing which the two tasks require that leads to this effect. It usually takes us longer and we find it more difficult to think up synonyms than rhymes, so is it perhaps the time it takes or the effort involved that determines how well things are remembered, rather than the way in which they are processed?

material to be remembered. The success of these strategies is explained by the *levels of processing* theory of memory. Fergus Craik and Robert Lockhart proposed this theory in 1972, and it is based around the observation that we remember more material if we process it 'deeply' than 'shallowly' or superficially – this is what the mnemonic devices, some of which were outlined in Chapter 11, involve. The *Memory, Meaning and Rhyme* exercise is a good demonstration that a deeper level of processing results in better retention.

Information you have learned, whether or not the learning involved conscious effort, requires you to be conscious of it in order to be able to use it later or to relate it to another person. To be conscious, or aware of something and to be able to express this in language is one way of thinking about consciousness. But is consciousness really more than this? Is it more than the sum of the things we are aware of at any one time? Probably we would all agree that it is: that there is a fundamental aspect of consciousness, which you experience, but which is very difficult to define. This is an area philosophers have grappled with for centuries, but has now had a revival in psychology, with a multidisciplinary effort involving philosophers, neuroscientists and psychologists all trying to understand the nature of consciousness. Some progress is being made in the light of various phenomena such as blindsight and visual neglect, which we looked at in Chapter 7. However, the fundamental aspect of consciousness, referred to above, or the 'feel' of being conscious, sometimes termed *phenomenological consciousness*, is proving very difficult to understand in scientific terms because of its qualitative and subjective nature. Indeed, some claim it does not exist – we just think it does because of the way we conceive of consciousness.

The relationship between intelligence and learning

To return to learning, as we saw above, not all animals can learn everything. It is also true that people are different in the things they find it easy to learn. To some extent this is attributable to differences in intelligence. Intelligence, though, is notoriously difficult to define, let alone measure, in a meaningful way. In 1996, a task force, established by the American Psychological Association (APA), published its report about the nature of intelligence. While not giving one definition of intelligence, the report considers the substantial, though not consistent, differences in individuals' 'ability to understand complex ideas, to adapt effectively to the environment, to learn from experience, to engage in various forms of reasoning, and to overcome obstacles by taking thought'.

Most agree that there is a relationship between intelligence and ability to learn. The role of learning in intelligence, though, and particularly the contribution of learning to intelligence continue to cause controversy. Some of the interesting questions revolve around the relative contributions of environmental and hereditary (genetic) factors to intelligence: an aspect of the so-called 'nature/nurture debate'. Estimates of the extent to which intelligence is inherited necessarily relate to heritability within populations, although they are often misunderstood as being indicative of the inherited component within individuals. There is evidence that experience of an enriched environment can lead to higher scores on intelligence tests; that is, learning does contribute to intelligence as we measure it.

So learning and experience influence intelligence, but the definition above refers to a link the other way round: intelligence influencing learning ('to adapt effectively to the environment, to learn from experience'). We are, then, looking at a complicated two-way relationship between learning and intelligence.

185

BOX 12.1
CORRELATION USED TO ASSESS DEGREE OF CONCORDANCE

In order to assess the contribution of genetics to a particular trait, behaviour geneticists use the degree of concordance (or agreement) on a given measure in differently related family members. The principle is that a trait which is under genetic control is more likely to be shared by more closely related than less closely related people, even though they are exposed to different environments. On the other hand, if a trait is greatly affected by environmental factors, people occupying similar environmental niches are likely to be similar with respect to that trait. There are some striking anecdotal reports of similarity between identical twins who find each other in adulthood after having been adopted by different families in childhood. But systematic studies using this method have provided estimates that genetics accounts for about 50 per cent of individual variation in IQ.

What you do is simply get measures on a trait (e.g. IQ) from, say, identical and non-identical twins and carry out a statistical test of correlation (association) between each twin pair. The closer the correlation is to the known genetic relationship (i.e. the greater the concordance), the greater the evidence for the trait being governed by genetics. This approach is confounded by the fact that the effects of greater or lesser similarities in people's environments cannot be ignored.

Nevertheless, if it turned out that the concordance on a particular trait for identical twins (who have identical genetic material) was 100 per cent (a correlation coefficient of 1), and that for non-identical twins (who on average have 50 per cent of their genetic material in common as do other sibling pairs) was 50 per cent, this would be strong evidence for a 100 per cent contribution of genetics. This does not happen where measures like IQ or personality, which involve complicated behaviour, are concerned, but the method has proved useful for giving an indication of the strength of the genetic contribution to a trait or a clinical condition.

Fluid and crystallized intelligence

In an effort to clarify what we mean by intelligence, it has been divided up and looked at in different ways. The division into *fluid* and *crystallized* intelligence helps explain the two-way relationship between intelligence and learning. Fluid intelligence depends on the speed at which your brain can process information. This will affect what you can learn and how fast you can learn it. Crystallized intelligence, on the other hand, reflects experience and general knowledge, so is affected by what you have learned. We all have varying degrees of each type of intelligence. Incidentally, although some measures of fluid intelligence suggest that it decreases with advancing age, crystallized intelligence definitely does not show a decline. Although you may become less quick at learning new things and solving new problems, the accumulated learning of the years compensates for this. Intelligence is different in the elderly, not inferior overall.

Brain scanning techniques are being used to explore brain activity during intellectual tasks, and evidence is accumulating for the involvement of different brain structures and differences between individuals in this. See the review of this work by Richard Haier and colleagues.

Intelligence, IQ and learning

One way of assessing the effect of learning on intelligence is to estimate the hereditary contribution. This is done by comparing the associations between measured intelligence (IQ test scores) of more and less closely related family members. If, for example, identical twins (who have identical genes), had identical IQ scores, you might conclude that IQ was governed entirely by genes. In fact, we know from many of these *behavioural genetic* studies, which have looked at twins as well as other family relationships and cases of adoption of non-blood-relatives, that while there is a genetic component of intelligence, it can be affected by the environment in which a child is raised. In particular, a stimulating environment, which provides plenty of opportunity for learning, raises a child's IQ score. See Box 12.1 on 'Concordance studies'.

The inverse relationship, the effect of intelligence on learning, probably accounts for some of the difference between people's school performance. The APA task force reported more learning in school among those with higher intelligence test scores. Other factors such as interest and encouragement from home will obviously affect school learning as well and particular styles of teaching might enhance any effects of intelligence.

Recommended Reading

Sternberg, R.J., Lautrey, J. and Lubart, T.I. (eds.) (2003). *Models of Intelligence: International perspectives.* Washington D.C.: American Psychological Association.

Stimulus Response Video (1995). Association for the Study of Animal Behaviour, 82A High Street, Sawston, Cambridge CB2 4HJ, UK.

BOX 12.2
HUMAN GENOME PROJECT/GENOMICS
AND PROTEOMICS

This project has led to the publication of the biochemical make-up of DNA in the human genome. Deoxyribonucleic acid (DNA) is a very big chemical molecule, which is made up of many copies of only four different amino acids, arranged in a 'double helix' shape. Not all the DNA belongs to genes, which make an identifiable contribution to the way we function by coding for the proteins that make up our bodies. The human genome project has allowed identification and description (in biochemical terms) of genes. Surprisingly, we have only about 30,000 genes.

Increasingly, knowledge is being gained about what genes do what, but we are a long way from labelling genes as 'the gene for intelligence', 'extraversion', 'good memory' and so on. These complicated psychological functions are almost certainly affected by numerous genes, which are acting, we must never forget, in association with environmental influences. We should think only of genes giving us predispositions to certain traits; they do not provide blueprints for behaviour. There is no imminent danger of designer babies being created by the insertion of the gene for, say, a sympathetic personality, a beautiful face, a potential Picasso or a 'party animal'.

13

You and Other Animals

- Can other animals think?

- Intelligence, tool-use and culture

- Is language unique to humans?

- Sensory sensitivity in other animals

- Awareness and consciousness

- Human uses of other animals

- People with other animals

Should a book essentially about people include a section on our links with other animals? There are several different rationales that can be used in answering this question. First, we are animals. Thus by studying ourselves in relation to other animals, we may gain insights into our place in the scheme of things within the animal kingdom. *Comparative psychology* is a branch of psychology in which animal species are investigated with the emphasis on finding similarities between them. In this, humans are seen as just one important species among many. But, due in part to the very strong reaction against research on animals that burgeoned in the 1970s and 1980s, there has been a reduction in animal behaviour research, which has had an impact on how we see the place of non-human animals in psychology.

A wholly different way of looking at this issue is to recognize that other animals play a significant part in the lives of many people. We work with them, live with them and play with them; animals are farmed for food and a range of other products such as wool and silk. They play a vital role in research (e.g. medical and pharmacological), and we use them for pleasure as pets and in recreation in a multitude of different ways (in horse racing, jumping and hunting, greyhound racing, bull fighting, and circuses, to name just a handful of ways). Viewed in this way, our relationships with animals, how we interact with them, and why, can be seen as just another part of our psychology.

A third view is to see psychology as more than just a 'human science', but as a subject essentially about behaviour, emotion and cognition and which includes *all* species that display these characteristics.

Whatever perspective you take, there seems to us to be a good argument for considering other animals in an introductory text. And so, before reading further, you might like to pause and think about your responses to the statements in Exercise 13.1 which deal with some of the issues often discussed concerning the way humans may differ from other animals.

This chapter explores some of the issues raised in Exercise 13.1. We shall look at the research evidence on areas of difference between humans and other animals, and the unique and special characteristics other animals have, which we lack, will also be highlighted. The ethical issues involved in using other animals will be discussed, and, finally, we shall look at our relationships with other animals.

CAN OTHER ANIMALS THINK?

In his book *The Question of Animal Awareness*, Donald Griffin suggests that mental experiences are 'the objects and events that are remote in space and time' that we think about, or have in mind. A mental image of a future event in which the 'intender pictures himself as a participant' is what he means by intention, and this is another quality that has often been said to be uniquely human. Human thought and language are often considered to be so closely linked that some would argue that one cannot exist without the other; however, studies in other animals make this assumption questionable.

EXERCISE 13.1
HOW UNIQUE ARE HUMANS?

Read the following statements. Which of these statements applies only to humans and not to other animals? Circle TRUE or FALSE

Humans are

• the peak of evolution	True	False
• the only intelligent species	True	False
• the only species that can think	True	False
• the only species that can use language	True	False
• the only species that can lie	True	False
• the only species that can show intention in behaviour	True	False
• the only species that can show cultural transmission of behaviour	True	False
• the only species that can show self-awareness	True	False
• more sensitive than other animals	True	False
• the only species that can feel pain	True	False
• the only species that can show empathy	True	False

You will find out our current state of knowledge on the truth of each of these statements in this chapter.

Non-human animals can solve a variety of abstract problems. Fredrick Rohles and James Devine demonstrated that chimpanzees can learn the concept of 'middleness': they can learn to select the middle one from various numbers of objects arranged in different ways. Four to 6-year-old children can also solve this type of problem. A number of researchers report evidence of counting in non-human animals – examples come from a range of bird and mammal species, including parrots, ravens, magpies, pigeons, monkeys, chimpanzees and gorillas. Hank Davis and John Memmott, in a critical evaluation of this research, believe that counting 'can and does occur in infrahuman animals'. In a study by Sarah Boysen and colleagues, a chimpanzee trained in counting arrays of 0–7 items and also to comprehend number symbols was able to show behaviour 'comparable to similar behaviours observed in children in the early stages of learning to count'.

The use of mental images by other animals is hard to demonstrate, and a study of pigeons raises more questions than it answers. Pigeons were taught to discriminate between geometric shapes, and their mirror images were presented in various orientations. They were then required to indicate which of two symbols a sample symbol most resembled. Humans given this task were found to have a similar accuracy rate to pigeons, but the pigeons were *quicker* at selecting the correct response than were humans. The humans' reaction times increased with the angular disparity between the sample and comparisons, but this was not the case with the pigeons. Humans appear to require some form of mental representation in order to do this task, but it is not clear if this is so in pigeons. If not, in what way can this ability in pigeons be explained? At present the best way for us to explain this ability in other animals is to consider it in terms of thinking, but thinking that may not include mental images and language.

If intention requires imagery, as Donald Griffin believes, then if it can be shown to occur in other animals, this too would indicate 'thinking' in these creatures. A number of birds will feign injury. The broken wing display of the sandpiper is one such example, and it is shown by incubating birds as they move away from the nest when a predator threatens. This behaviour has been accounted for in terms of a ritualized display characteristic of a species, but it is possible that intentionality may play a part. Donald Griffin points out that primates and members of the dog family can show intention, because they can learn to 'mislead' in a situation where there is competition for food. If so, then the goal of the behaviour is not what it outwardly appears to be, and evidence for thinking in Griffin's terms will have been found to occur in other animals.

INTELLIGENCE, TOOL-USE AND CULTURE

Reasoning power is often said to be central to the concept of intelligence. Although psychologists argue over the definition of intelligence, problem-solving ability is frequently included in any assessment of an individual's intelligence. Experiments comparing problem-solving abilities in humans and other animals have been devised. See Box 13.1.

On the face of it, this kind of comparison shown in Box 13.1 may seem perfectly sensible as a way of studying intelligence in different species, but in reality it is fraught with problems. Every species is uniquely adapted to a particular environment and way of life. A deep-sea fish, for example, is likely to rely much less on eyesight than do birds, and it has probably never encountered a vertical face, such as the wall of a fish tank, in its natural setting, whereas a rat is used to walls and confined spaces. In the past, maze learning tests were frequently used when comparing learning abilities in different species, but such a test is quite inappropriate for many species. Once we find problems appropriate for each species, it then becomes hard to equate the degree of difficulty of each problem in any comparison.

There is another approach to this question. William Riddell discusses an index of brain development as a way of assessing the intelligence of animals (this is an estimate of the number of nerve cells in the brain that are over and above those needed for the control of bodily functions). When animals are given a series of

BOX 13.1
AN EXPERIMENT IN COMPARATIVE PSYCHOLOGY

Morton Bitterman sought to compare five different species on a habit reversal task. In this task the animal is rewarded for choosing alternative A rather than B; when a preference for A is established, then B rather than A is rewarded (habit reversal). This procedure is repeated several times. Bitterman used spatial and visual problems. In the spatial problem, two altern-atives look the same, but the reward is correlated with the position. In the visual problem two alternatives look visually different, for example a blue and green disc, and the reward is correlated with one of these colours. Bitterman compared five species: monkeys, rats, pigeons, turtles and fish. He found that fish were the least successful, and the two mammals showed the best performance. Does this tell us that fish are the least intelligent? See the text for further discussion of this question.

problems and ranked in terms of their rate of improvement, their rank can be predicted on the basis of this index.

However, the notion that humans are at the top of an evolutionary scale is highly misleading. Evolution is not a simple progression: mammals and birds, for instance, evolved at the same time from different groups of reptiles. Birds did not evolve before mammals, as is often thought. Because each species is uniquely adapted, it is not possible to arrange them in a linear hierarchy from least to most intelligent.

In our own terms, we are undoubtedly the most intelligent animal, but we should not ignore or disregard qualities in other animals simply because we do not share them.

Tool-use and culture

Extending the body with a tool, in order to attain a goal, has often been viewed as intelligent behaviour. Human culture has been built on this ability, and yet it is not uniquely human. Other primates have been observed using tools. Chimpanzees use twigs to gouge insects from cracks and crevices, and leaves as 'sponges' to soak up drinking water from inaccessible sources. Elephants may use a stick to scratch their backs. Sea otters use two stones to crack open shellfish – one stone is used as the anvil and the other as the hammer. Crows sometimes use a stick such as a matchstick to aid grooming, and the woodpecker finch uses sticks to find its insect prey.

Some forms of tool-use in non-human animals seem to be passed on by genetic means – the woodpecker finch may be an example of an innate predisposition to tool-use (although not all authorities accept this). However, other forms of tool-use do *not* appear to be 'built-in' adaptations, but are spontaneous solutions to problems confronting particular individuals, which are then passed on to others by observation and imitation. This seems closer to our idea of intelligence or reasoning behaviour.

Some delightful examples of cultural traditions have been recorded in Japanese macaques. In a macaque colony, whose diet was supplemented with sweet potatoes by scientists, one female was observed to wash the sand from her potatoes in a stream. Soon other macaques imitated her and over some years this new practice was established virtually throughout the population of the area. Another example concerns snowball-making, also in macaques. Again, one monkey started this practice and it rapidly spread throughout the population and became a characteristic of their winter behaviour.

Although these examples of tool-use and culture are quite limited in type and range, it is clear that other animals, and in particular other primates, share the ability to solve problems that we believe characterize intelligent behaviour. While the reasoning abilities of humans may go far beyond what is demonstrable in other animals, it is clear that the basis of this behaviour *is* found in these creatures. Probably the major difference between us and other primates is that while tool-use is essential for our survival, it has only a minor place in the life of other primates.

IS LANGUAGE UNIQUE TO HUMANS?

Language has been said to be unique to humans. But what do we mean by the term 'language'? It is not easy to define because it has many characteristics. *The Shorter Oxford Dictionary* mentions 'speech' and 'words and methods of combining them in the expression of thought' in its definition. Charles Snowden discusses the design features of language put forward by Charles Hockett; 18 features are described, such as: language is *symbolic* and the symbols are *arbitrary*. It enables us to *communicate about things remote in time and space*. Language is *learned* and is *passed on by tradition*. Language enables us to express our thoughts honestly or to *prevaricate*. These are just a few of the 18 features. Are these found in communication in other species?

Take communication in honeybees. Bees, on returning to the hive, can convey information about the distance and location of a food source, by performing a 'waggle dance'. The dance seems to be *symbolic*, although some suggest that since the rate of waggling is related to the distance of the food source, the relationship is not truly symbolic. In fact, different bees have different dialects. For a given distance, a German bee waggles more slowly than an Egyptian one.

The ability to communicate about something *remote in space* is found in other animals. A dog's marking behaviour enables it to convey information when it is no longer present. This *displacement*, as it is called, is also found in the alarm calls of some species, which can indicate whether a predator is in the air or on the ground.

The fact that language is *learned* and *passed on by tradition* is not exclusive to human language either. Chaffinches, for example, learn their local dialect song from other chaffinches in a particular critical period during development. Thus the song is passed from one generation to the next. Fostered birds reared by chaffinches from another locality learn the song of their foster parents: they do not sing like their biological parents.

So we see that some of the qualities of human language are found in the communication systems of other species. However, there are other qualities over which there is still much debate, and these are highlighted next.

Language in non-human animals?

Numerous attempts have been made to teach other animals to speak our language or some analogue of language. Animals such as chimpanzees, bonobos, orang-utans, dolphins and parrots have all achieved some level of success. Sounds, symbols presented on a keyboard, signs from ASL (American Sign Language) and spoken language have all been used in these attempts. With the exception of parrots, vocal signals have not been too successful, as in chimpanzees; for example, the larynx is not designed for language as it is in humans. Apes have achieved large vocabularies of signs or arbitrary lexigrams to represent words (sometimes in the range of 150–200 elements) and have combined them according to simple syntax. *Duality of patterning* has been shown too. For example, dolphins and apes can respond appropriately to reverse order messages such as 'Take the ball to the chair' and 'Take the chair to the ball.' Showing here that word order is crucial for meaning, and these animals can recognize this.

Openness or the ability to coin new phrases has been reported occasionally in chimpanzees, such as 'water bird' and 'candy drink', but only a few examples of this kind have been recorded.

There is no doubt that dolphins and apes, in particular, have shown abilities not previously suspected (in terms of displaying many of the qualities of language), but as yet we do not have all these features together in a non-human species. Thus language does appear to be unique to humans, but as David McFarland points out, 'Language should not be defined as a uniquely human activity because there are many features of animal communication that are language like.' He goes on to say that 'Apes cannot learn to speak, but they can learn to communicate with humans using symbols to represent words.'

SENSORY SENSITIVITY IN OTHER ANIMALS

We are very aware of the sights, sounds and smells around us, so it is perhaps surprising to learn that our sensory sensitivity is not exceptional in the animal kingdom. Many animals are more aware than we are in one or other sensory modality, and some creatures have senses about which we know nothing.

Seeing other colours

Honeybees see a world in colours that we cannot see. For example, they can see ultraviolet, a colour invisible to us, but they are less sensitive to the red end of the spectrum. Honeybees can orient themselves using the polarization patterns of the blue sky, an ability totally lacking in humans.

Long-distance smelling

Although we might expect to be able to see another person at a distance of perhaps half a mile, the idea that we could smell them at such a distance seems laughable, and yet such an ability would be nothing to the male silk moth. It can detect the presence of the female moth, by odour alone, at a distance of several miles. Similar feats of sensitivity exist in the salmon too.

Hearing other sounds

Many animals have the ability to hear sounds well outside our audible range – they may also communicate using ultrasonic cries. Rodents, for instance, make ultrasonic cries audible to cats. Bats, whales, dolphins and porpoises all have hearing outside our audible range, and they can produce signals that enable them to echolocate objects or prey. A dolphin can detect even a small object beneath the seabed by this means.

Sensing electricity

Sensitivity to electric fields is another sense beyond our imagining. Electric fish can produce an electric current from special organs, and are so sensitive to electric fields that they can locate the objects around them in dark and muddy waters. They can also identify other electric fish species and their own mates by this means.

Telepathy

The ability in humans to know what someone else is thinking is an area of parapsychology that has been researched. Evidence indicates that experiments can demonstrate an above chance likelihood that some people have this ability. Can the same be said of non-human animals?

Rupert Sheldrake investigated what appears to be a particular form of telepathy between dogs and their owners – an ability of dogs to know when their owners are coming home. He collected 580 reports of this type of behaviour where dogs waited at the door or gate just prior to their owner's time of arrival. One particularly clear example of this comes from a dog called Jaytee, which was carefully investigated by Sheldrake. The dog seemed to change its behaviour at whatever time the owner set out for home – whether this was 4 or 40 kilometres away.

AWARENESS AND CONSCIOUSNESS

David McFarland believes that awareness is a form of perception, while consciousness involves a special kind of self-awareness. It involves 'a propositional awareness that it is I who am feeling or thinking, I am the animal aware of the circumstances'.

Of course, sensitivity to the environment tells us nothing about how *self-aware* other animals are, but there are experiments which show that animals can be made aware of what they are doing. A rat can be trained to press one of four levers depending on which of four activities it is engaged in when a buzzer is sounded. Thus if the buzzer sounds when it is grooming, it can press the 'grooming' lever to receive a food reward.

Self-awareness and mirrors

A dog will bark at itself in a mirror, treating its reflection as another dog, but chimpanzees and orang-utans can look in a mirror and recognize themselves if they have a little time to become used to mirrors. Gordon Gallup painted small red patches on lightly anaesthetized chimpanzees in places that could not be seen unaided. These animals looked long and hard at the patches when later they were given mirrors. Chimpanzees will also use mirrors to groom parts of their bodies they cannot otherwise see. Diana Reiss and Lori Marino studied self-recognition in bottlenose dolphins and found evidence that they too are able to recognize themselves.

Consciousness and self-awareness are not thought to be identical. Donald Griffin suggests that consciousness involves the presence of mental images to regulate behaviour. Evidence of intentional behaviour would therefore in his view be a sign of consciousness. The issue of how other animals feel about themselves is a very difficult field of study. One person cannot really know whether another person's experience is the same as their own. We have evidence, however, that some non-human primates can recognize themselves and this is perhaps very close to, if not the same as, our own consciousness. Indeed Gallup goes so far as to suggest that if a chimpanzee can contemplate itself, and hence perhaps its own existence, this is not far from the contemplation of its non-existence or mortality.

Consciousness, suffering and empathy

We have no idea of what the conscious experience of other animals might be, and we must avoid being anthropomorphic about how they feel. We cannot assume 'they' feel as we do when they appear to show facial expressions or postures we associate with particular feelings in ourselves.

Nevertheless, we do tend to assume that, if other people react or behave as we do when we experience a particular emotion, then their experiences are like ours. We give people the benefit of the doubt. When it comes to suffering in other animals, while we may still wish to avoid being anthropomorphic, should we not also, as McFarland suggests, give them the benefit of the doubt? Should we not strive to help other animals in distress, or to prevent their distress?

If non-human animals have some self-awareness, then it is argued that they may also show some empathy (an awareness that others have feelings similar to their

Figure 13.1   Does this animal have self-awareness? *(Shaun Cunningham/Alamy.)*

own), because in children mirror recognition and the beginnings of empathy occur at the same time (16–24 months).

There are a number of interesting anecdotal cases of non-human animals helping distressed humans, such as dolphins saving a person from drowning, or a gorilla gently picking up a boy who fell many metres into the enclosure. It is hard to know how we can explain these examples, but an explanation involving empathy may perhaps be one possibility. Alternatively, such responses may be seen as merely being elicited by cries or distress, or bodily postures indicating injury, and the species showing the 'helping' responds to these just as a robin will attack a bunch of red feathers placed in its territory.

HUMAN USES OF OTHER ANIMALS

Ethical issues involved in using other animals for food and in research cover many areas, two of which we shall briefly consider. The first issue concerns whether there is any moral justification for placing ourselves before all other animals, and the second issue revolves around the problem of how such animals should be used, if they are used, to ensure they do not suffer.

198

The Bible tells Christians that 'man' has 'dominion' over all animals – this view has been used by some Christians to justify using animals in any way they choose. It is probably fair to say that Jewish people and Muslims also subscribe to this view. 'Speciesism' is a term coined by Richard Ryder to describe the view that humans are uniquely important in the scheme of things, and discrimination against other species is possible simply because they are other species. Ryder suggests that speciesism, like racism or sexism, has no moral justification.

Another less extreme form of speciesism is 'speciesism with a reason'. Here discrimination is practised because other animals are held either to lack, or to possess to a lesser extent, attributes we have. An example might be that other animals lack consciousness, or feel no pain. The problem here is to justify the reason, for, as we have seen, it is hard to differentiate between other animals and humans on clear-cut grounds.

If we accept the use of animals, for instance, for food or research, then how can we ensure minimal suffering or distress? Knowing when an animal suffers is not always easy. It is often said of domesticated animals that if they breed, then their living conditions must be adequate for their needs. Similarly, that given a choice between its usual living conditions, for example, a battery cage, or a free-range environment in the case of domestic fowl, then if the animal prefers what it has, this is a sign that it cannot be suffering. Marion Dawkins has investigated habitat preferences in domestic fowl and her work is described in her book *Animal Suffering*.

Marion Dawkins studied hens' preferences for a battery house environment versus an outdoor run in a garden. Hens in the study lived in one or the other of these environments. Dawkins found that given a choice, each group chose the familiar environment. Battery hens chose batteries; those who had lived outside chose outside runs. But after repeated choice tests, battery hens started choosing the outside runs, whereas the hens that already lived in such runs continued with their initial choice.

Thus brief experience of outside runs was sufficient to alter the battery hens' choices, but experience of batteries did not alter the choices of hens from outside runs. This study highlights the importance of careful research to establish appropriate rearing conditions for animals which humans use – whether as pets, as farm animals or in research. Only by research of this type can we establish ways of using them humanely.

PEOPLE WITH OTHER ANIMALS

Humans can form close associations with other animals as companions or pets. All human societies have tamed and domesticated animals, and humans and other animals living together often exchange food for protection, or milk, or wool, and such an association need not harm the latter. It is likely that there has been no time in our evolution when humans have not enjoyed other animals as pets, and other animals have also provided valuable services for humans.

199

Service animals and therapeutic effects of other animals

Many people share their lives with animals because these animals assist them in some way. We are all familiar with guide dogs for the blind, but hearing dogs for the deaf and assistance animals such as monkeys helping people with various disabilities are less widely known. These animals can vastly improve the quality of life of their owners: they can enhance their independence and increase their chances of employment.

Animals can also have a therapeutic value, as has been recognized for centuries. The first known use was recorded in the ninth century in Belgium, where caring for animals was thought to re-establish the harmony of soul and body for handicapped people. Today animals are widely used with psychiatric patients, children, and the elderly and dying. Pet visitors, for example 'PAT dogs' in hospitals and hospices, are now a common occurrence and are said to reduce patient stress and improve their quality of life. Although there is a dearth of well-designed research exploring the effects of pets on people, partly because there are clear ethical problems in introducing animals into healthcare settings, there are some studies showing beneficial effects, such as beneficial physiological changes. Nevertheless, it is unlikely that pet therapy can ever be recommended for all.

Figure 13.2 Humans can form close associations with other animals as companions or pets. *(Photo: Julia C. Berryman.)*

Relationships with pets

People's feelings for their pets can be very strong indeed. Research by two of us (Julia Berryman and Kevin Howells) on the relationships people have with their pets produced some intriguing findings. We assessed people's relationships with those who were important to them, including their pets, using a modified version of the repertory grid technique (described in Chapter 3). All the people we tested were able to make comparisons between relationships with humans and relationships with other animals. We found that for about one-third of our 30 participants, the pet(s) were rated as *more important* on a range of *personal constructs* (discussed in Chapter 3) when compared with other significant human relationships. A dog might be more loved, easier to talk to, or missed more, than a spouse, for example. Of course, not all our participants described themselves as pet lovers, and for these the pets were not rated so highly.

If our study reflects a general tendency, it seems that the potential of pets to satisfy many of our needs can be just as great as that of friends, parents or partners. Obviously more research is needed, but our research suggests that the important things for humans in their relationships with other humans are not necessarily unique to us as humans, but are very much the qualities that relationships with other animals can provide – if we choose to have a pet. This is not of course the same as saying that people *should* have pets, or that pets are 'people substitutes', but for many people other animals form a very important part of their lives.

Recommended Reading

Dawkins, M.S. (1980). *Animal Suffering: The science of animal welfare.* London: Chapman and Hall.

Griffin, D.R. (1981). *A Question of Animal Awareness: Evolutionary continuity of mental experience.* Los Altos: Kaufmann.

Manning, A. and Stamp Dawkins, M. (1998). *An Introduction to Animal Behaviour.* Cambridge: Cambridge University Press.

McFarland, D. (1999). *Animal Behaviour: Ethology and evolution.* London: Pitman.

Serpell, J. (1986). *In the Company of Animals.* London: Pitman.

14

What Psychologists Can Do – for You?

- Becoming a psychologist

- Teachers and researchers

- Clinical and counselling psychologists

- Health psychologists

- Educational psychologists

- Forensic psychologists

- Occupational psychologists

- Sport and exercise psychologists

- Psychologists in other areas

Even if you have never met a psychologist it is likely you have picked up some ideas about what they are like from the media. Most of us are aware there are psychologists behind the very popular *Big Brother* TV programme, where Peter Collett and Geoff Beattie are seen commenting on the behaviour of the contestants almost as if the latter were creatures in a natural history programme. Psychologists are also portrayed in TV programmes like *Cracker*, while *The Real Cracker* shows professional forensic psychologists Julian Boon and Richard Badcock working with the police to uncover psychological clues in complex criminal cases. Relationship experts such as the psychologist Tracey Cox, for example, are seen on such TV programmes as *Would Like To Meet*, helping individuals to improve their social skills to increase their chances of finding a partner. Paranormal and other unexplained events are discussed in the media by psychologists such as Chris French, who considers the plausibility of claims of such phenomena. These are just a few examples of the way, at an everyday level, you may have come across psychologists if you have not encountered them in their professional capacity.

Psychologists are now to be found in many areas of life (education, health and the law, to name just a few), and psychology has become an extremely popular subject of study at degree level, due in part no doubt to the recent burgeoning of psychological themes in the media. What kinds of opportunities are there for the would-be psychologist and in what situations might you encounter a psychologist or seek her or his help? This chapter briefly surveys some of the ways in which psychologists work and how they may have an impact on all our lives.

BECOMING A PSYCHOLOGIST

The emphasis in this book has been on describing the findings of psychologists who have carried out research in each of the areas covered by a chapter. Our understanding of people has been greatly enhanced by psychological research, but not all psychologists do research, as we shall see.

In Britain, becoming a psychologist is achieved by taking a qualification in psychology that is recognized by the British Psychological Society (BPS) as being equivalent to the BPS Qualifying Examination, or by being a graduate who has passed the BPS Qualifying Examination. Once a person has achieved either of these routes to accreditation they can become a Graduate Member of the BPS. However, in order to become eligible for Registration as a Chartered Psychologist, further BPS-accredited postgraduate training in an area of applied psychology must be undertaken. The BPS is the professional body of psychologists in Britain and as such sets standards for the profession. The following sections show a variety of areas in which psychologists may specialize.

TEACHERS AND RESEARCHERS

In the first half of the twentieth century, most psychologists worked either as researchers or teachers of their subject. Today, psychologists can be found in a wide range of settings, but the majority of graduates will not go on to take up either of these areas. However, for those who do pursue a research and teaching career (in universities, for example, lecturers will generally do both), they will usually work within specific areas of psychology, each with its own particular methods of study. Physiological psychologists study the brain, nervous system, and other bodily processes to discover how each influences the others. The study of brain-damaged patients mentioned earlier is carried out by them. Experimental psychology and comparative psychology are both fields in which experimental methods are applied to assist in understanding the behaviour of humans and other animals. Traditionally, experimental psychology is often used to explain how people respond to external stimuli (as in visual perception), but the use of experimental methods is not confined to this area, as the numerous examples throughout this book show.

Human development is the province of developmental psychologists who are concerned with explaining development throughout life. This topic may seem to embrace every aspect of human psychology, but in fact, personality, cognition and social psychology are generally considered to be separate, though interrelated, specialities. Influences in human development shape our personalities, but the latter field has become so specialized, and is often concerned with devising methods of personality assessment so that the field is generally considered to be a separate one of individual differences. Cognitive psychologists study how the mind processes the information received – for example, processes involved in memory or problem-solving. The influence of others on the individual is the concern of social psychologists and, as we saw, a person's behaviour can be greatly challenged by the social context within which it occurs.

Today psychologists are found in many applied fields outside academic research and teaching; for instance, there are educational psychologists, prison psychologists, occupational psychologists and those working in the areas of sport and exercise. We shall now consider some of these other areas.

CLINICAL AND COUNSELLING PSYCHOLOGISTS

Clinical psychologists

Clinical psychologists are occupied with people of all ages who have psychological problems. Their concern ranges from the treatment of relatively minor stresses to major forms of disorder, such as schizophrenia (see Chapter 10 for further details). Their aims are to diagnose the nature of the illness and to effect its treatment. Clinical psychologists may work within universities in teaching and research or outside in the National Health Service or private healthcare. Under certain circumstances, they may also work within Young Offenders institutions or in Penal Reform or Special Care units.

If you sought help from a clinical psychologist the most common route is by referral through your GP, but some self-referrals are also accepted. The range of work the clinical psychologist encounters is extremely broad. In addition to the problems already noted, others may include adjustment to physical illness, addictive behaviours, neurological disorders and problems of childhood. Problems with personal and family relationships, including sexual problems, may also form part of their work. Box 14.1 illustrates two cases of the clinical psychologist helping clients with sexual problems.

BOX 14.1
CASE STUDIES OF SEXUAL PROBLEMS ENCOUNTERED BY A CLINICAL PSYCHOLOGIST

Below are two cases that are part of the caseload of a clinical psychologist; the psychologist's name is not given and the patients' names have been changed to maintain full confidentiality.

Case 1

Hannah was a 24-year-old woman who was referred to a clinical psychologist because she had become extremely distressed by symptoms of abdominal pain, a feeling of constant pressure in her bladder and a sexual problem. Her first serious relationship had just ended because she was unable to have sexual intercourse. Whenever this was attempted she found it extremely painful and very little penetration was possible, because of a reflex spasm in her vaginal muscle.

She had undergone many tests and investigations, which were all negative. Despite this, Hannah was convinced she had something seriously wrong with her.

She was tearful and negative about herself and the future. She was very worried that she would never be able to have a normal relationship with a man and never have children.

Hannah was initially very resistant to the idea that her symptoms had a psychological basis. A diary of her mood and symptoms, however, revealed a clear relationship between the occurrence and severity of her symptoms and her mood. She was taught various psychological strategies to help reduce her anxiety and distress and break the pain–tension–pain cycle. Her vaginismus was successfully treated with a programme of education and systematic desensitization.

Case 2

John is a 32-year-old single man who was diagnosed with HIV, three months ago. He was referred to a clinical psychologist because he was feeling angry, anxious and depressed. He was tearful as he described the shock and devastation he felt when he was given his diagnosis. He felt he had nothing to look forward to and that no one would want a relationship with him. He was also experiencing panic attacks, tiredness and insomnia. He had been active on the gay scene since the age of 16. He had had many casual partners and one long-term relationship, which ended four years ago.

He was brutally raped three years ago and believes he contracted HIV from this man. John wanted help accepting his HIV diagnosis and dealing with the trauma of the rape and a difficult and unhappy childhood.

John's negative beliefs about himself and the future will be explored and challenged with cognitive therapy. He will be taught stress management techniques including relaxation and assertiveness training.

Clinical psychologists also work closely with other professionals such as nurses, doctors and social workers, and with counselling and forensic psychologists.

After completing a degree, those aspiring to be a clinical psychologist must have work experience as an assistant psychologist, plus a three-year accredited training course to qualify. Clinical psychology is a highly competitive field and gradu-ates need a very good degree to gain entry on to a recognized course.

Counselling psychologists

In addition to the work of clinical psychologists described above, some psychologists work with individuals in counselling psychology. Such psychologists work with individuals as well as with couples, families and groups. Their aim is to help people improve their sense of well-being and cope better with the difficulties of everyday life. To become a counselling psychologist, completion of a degree in psychology and postgraduate training is required, such as a doctorate in counselling, or the BPS's Diploma in Psychology. Both routes also require three years' full-time independent study/practice.

HEALTH PSYCHOLOGISTS

Health psychology is another growing area of psychology that seeks to promote changes in people's attitudes and thinking about health. They may work in a number of settings such as hospitals, health authorities and academic departments. Health psychologists are concerned with the promotion and maintenance of health, the prevention and treatment of illness and the improvement of the healthcare system (see Chapter 8).

To become a health psychologist it is necessary to take an accredited postgraduate course after graduating in psychology, such as an MSc and Part II of a qualification in health psychology.

EDUCATIONAL PSYCHOLOGISTS

Educational psychologists specialize in helping children both in the classroom and in the home, and are concerned with children's learning and development. Currently, they are qualified in both psychology and education (having trained and worked as teachers) but training in England, Wales and Northern Ireland is about to change and is likely to become a three-year postgraduate course that will include an educational component. One of their most important functions is the assessment and diagnosis of children who are not doing well at school and where there is concern about a possible problem. For example, a child who has difficulties in reading, but otherwise seems able and bright, might be diagnosed as having dyslexia. The educational psychologist will be the person assessing the child, and once he or she has diagnosed the problem, she or he may also be involved in the

Figure 14.1 Psychologists at work. Dyslexia testing, Egham Dyslexia Institute. *(Annabella Bluesky/Science Photo Library.)*

treatment. Educational psychologists can work directly with the child (ages range from birth to 19 years), involving some form of assessment perhaps through observation, interview or testing. Or they may work indirectly with other professionals such as speech therapists, social workers and medical consultants. Generally, educational psychologists are employed by local education authorities. See Box 14.2 for a day in the life of an educational psychologist.

You might have encountered such a person at school helping you or other children with some learning problem, or your children might be assessed in this way should the need arise.

BOX 14.2
A DAY IN THE LIFE OF AN EDUCATIONAL PSYCHOLOGIST

This is a diary of a typical day in the life of an educational psychologist working for a large Local Education Authority. Our educational psychologist writes:

'This year, our work is organized around three themes – reducing bullying, improving emotional health and behaviour and increasing the inclusion of vulnerable children into school and everyday life. All the work I do comes under one or more of these themes. Most educational psychologists nowadays work with the adults who care for or educate children rather than directly with the children themselves. Using a consultative approach, my aim is to influence and empower people to use untapped resources to manage more successfully the complexities and challenges of their professional and personal lives.

'This morning I will be visiting a large secondary school where I will be working with a group of teenage boys who need help to manage their anger more effectively. We use role-play and video to rehearse different ways of responding to possible scenarios in their lives, so that the boys can discover which approach is most successful for them. The group is run with two teachers from the school, and gradually I will pass over responsibility for the work to those school staff. I act as a link between the Service and a group of about 18 primary and secondary schools. I also have a specialism that involves me working for part of the week with pre-school children and their families. The work involves identifying children who might have difficulty once they reach school age, and intervening as early as possible to improve their social, communication, play and early learning skills, and to think about the arrangements that will need to be in place to make their school life as successful as possible. This afternoon I am visiting a child and her mother at home to introduce the idea that the youngster might need a place at a special nursery school to help her make best progress. Later this afternoon I will be offering training to a group of school staff with the aim of helping them improve the communication skills of the pupils they teach.

'This is an immensely satisfying job, and it really does feel that I am making a difference to improve people's lives.'

FORENSIC PSYCHOLOGISTS

In the prison setting, or other penal institutions, the forensic psychologist's role is concerned with assessment and diagnosis. Prison inmates, like the rest of the population, may suffer from a range of psychological disorders, and their particular circumstances are likely to add to the stresses they experience. Being isolated from family and friends, feeling guilt and the stresses associated with being incarcerated with people one would not necessarily choose to be with, are just some of the problems that prison itself causes. The forensic psychologist's role is to identify such problems and to help to treat them. They will also work closely with prison staff and medical practitioners. More recently forensic psychologists have become widely known for their work in crime analysis and criminal profiling. They may give expert evidence in court, or assist the police by identifying kinds of individuals likely to have performed crimes of particular types. Box 14.3 illustrates how psychological profiling of offenders is carried out.

After completing a psychology degree, typical training involves either an MSc in Forensic Psychology plus elements of the BPS's Diploma in Forensic Psychology.

BOX 14.3
PSYCHOLOGICAL PROFILING OF OFFENDERS: A CLINICAL APPROACH

When criminal profiling is required in an investigation the normal procedure is for a referral to be made, by a Senior Investigating Officer (SIO) at the National Crime and Operations Faculty, located in Hampshire, to a recognized profiler with expertise in the relevant crime domain. Once the profiler and the SIO have made contact, they discuss their requirements and mutual perspectives for the particular investigation.

Three principal areas of enquiry are generally required for the SIO: (1) gaining an understanding of why an offender has behaved in what often appear as bizarre ways; (2) asking whether such an understanding has any implications for honing down the search net parameters (lives near/far from crime scene, known to victim or a stranger, previous offence history, likely aspects of offender lifestyle etc.); and (3) whether and when the offender is likely to offend again. For the profiler operating from a clinical perspective (there are other approaches, including the statistical, geographical and 'investigative') this necessitates a request for access to *all* available detail relating to the case. This information often comprises a full set of crime scene photographs/videos, as much victimology information as can be garnered, a crime scene visit for very intensive inspection and access to the relevant witness statements.

The need for meticulous examination of this information *in minute detail* cannot be exaggerated. This is because the successful use of the clinical approach requires the most precise identification of the cognitive and affective dynamics contained within the offender's commission of the crime. In principle, there is no reason why two apparently near identical offences that differ in say just one or two respects could not emerge as being radically different in terms of their interpretation from a psychological perspective. In turn, this can have correspondingly radical differences in terms of the nature of the offences, the offenders and the advice offered to the SIO. The most precise possible analysis of the modus operandi can reveal critical things about the offender, such as the possible presence of sadistic tendencies, obsessional behaviour, fantasy enactment and psychopathy.

Accordingly, the collation of the report for the SIO is an intensely detailed, careful and considered process. This involves highlighting the salient case details from the potentially infinite array of information – prioritizing them from the perspective of the mindset of the offender and then moving on to consider the implications for offender characteristics, risk assessment and previous offence history. At all times the clinical psychological profiler must be able to explain the rationale underpinning her/his conclusions. Indeed, one of the most valuable phases of her/his involvement is the discussion with the SIO and the investigating team. At no time must the profiling tail wag the investigating dog. Instead, one of the chief values of profiling is that it comes from a perspective that is different (not necessarily superior to) from that of the experienced detective. In many instances the provision of a different, psychological perspective has been found to result in investigators seeing the offence and the offender from a new viewpoint – one that can result in different suspects being considered and new leads being prioritized for enquiry.

OCCUPATIONAL PSYCHOLOGISTS

Occupational psychologists, or industrial psychologists, work in a wide variety of areas. They may work as independent consultants, who are called in by organizations from time to time, or they may be based in-house and be involved with almost any aspect of the concerns of employed staff. They could be employed as personnel psychologists primarily concerned with selection of staff and staff training, or they may be involved with problems in the workplace concerned with staff motivation or job satisfaction and ways of improving both. Some occupational psychologists work in the area of ergonomics, 'fitting jobs for people'. One aspect of their work might be to ensure that workstations are designed to maximize employee comfort and well-being as well as to maximize performance in the job. They will also be interested in reducing boredom and fatigue in employees. Occupational psychologists may often work at an organizational level rather than just at the level of individual employees. Here they are concerned with how the organization itself works, how it is managed, and the structures within the organization (such as boards or committees) that are part of the administration.

Becoming an occupational psychologist involves taking an accredited MSc course in occupational psychology, following a first degree in psychology, plus two years of supervised work experience.

SPORT AND EXERCISE PSYCHOLOGISTS

Sport psychologists help sport participants and athletes prepare for competition and to cope with the demands of training and competing. They may work with individuals or teams, amateurs or professionals. Their work may involve advising team coaches on how to promote cohesiveness and counselling referees to help them deal with the stress of their work. Sport psychologists may have a permanent post with a professional team or act on a consultancy basis in a variety of settings. Box 14.4 illustrates a case encountered by a sport psychologist.

The role of the exercise psychologist is slightly different from the sport psychologist and is chiefly concerned with motivating people in general, rather than sportsmen and women in particular, to increase their participation in sport. Most practising exercise psychologists combine consultancy with teaching and research.

To join this profession you will need a degree in psychology plus an approved higher degree in Psychology or Sport and Exercise Psychology, and a period of supervised experience. Since 2004, when the Division of Sport and Exercise Psychology was formed in the BPS, individuals can now qualify as a Chartered Sport and Exercise Psychologist, but as this Division is very new, formal training for psychologists in this area has not yet been defined.

BOX 14.4
SPORT PSYCHOLOGY: A CASE STUDY

The parents of Richard, a 14-year-old tennis player, approached a sport psychologist to ask for help in developing their son's psychological approach to competition. Information on Richard's psychological approach to competition was collected from interviews, questionnaires and from observing him compete. It was decided that the intervention should focus specifically on helping Richard serve more consistently and enhance his confidence and ability to cope with pressure.

To help improve Richard's service consistency a pre-service routine was developed that incorporated imagery. Prior to serving, Richard would take a deep breath, bounce the ball a set number of times, 'see' in his mind where he wanted the ball to land and 'feel' himself execute the correct movement pattern.

Richard identified a number of sources of pressure that occurred during a tennis match. Examples included serving to win a set or being a number of games down. Richard was taught a number of skills that would help him cope with pressure, including positive self-talk and a physical relaxation technique he could use if he felt physically tense. Richard practised applying these techniques in a series of scenarios during practice; for example, he would begin a set already a number of games down.

In addition to using positive self-talk and imagery (running success over in his mind) to maintain his confidence levels, Richard also identified the behaviours of confident tennis players (e.g. appropriate body language, maintaining effort even when losing) and made a conscious attempt to engage in those behaviours when on court.

Richard's performance levels improved and he climbed up the rankings. Following the intervention, he reported higher levels of confidence and lower levels of anxiety when competing.

PSYCHOLOGISTS IN OTHER AREAS

We have briefly considered a number of areas in which psychologists may specialize, but many graduates of psychology use their knowledge in a variety of other types of employment such as personnel, advertising and marketing. Because psychology is about people, and most businesses, especially the larger organizations, are concerned with managing people – human resources – it is likely that there will be psychologists around who will assist in this area. Similarly, because a knowledge of psychology enables us to understand more about people's needs, wishes and aspirations it is likely that psychologists can assist in promoting products.

Most large companies will call on experts to help them sell their products, and psychologists are likely to be brought in to research and advise on the best selling tactics. Selling a product is not the only way a psychologist may be used in advertising. Selling an idea or an image may be very much part of this too. Psychologists often play a part in influencing our choices – as you walk round a supermarket to a background of music – a psychologist has probably influenced the type of music played, because research has shown how this may influence our likelihood of purchasing a particular product.

It is not possible to cover all the areas in which psychologists may work but this chapter has explored a variety of occupations in which psychologists may be found, or be encountered by you, the reader. For those who are interested in finding out more, the Recommended Reading section directs you to appropriate material.

Recommended Reading

British Psychological Society (2004). *Careers in Psychology*. Leicester: British Psychological Society.

British Psychological Society (2005). *Careers in Psychology*. Retrieved 23 February 2005 from http://www.bps.org.uk/careers/careers_home.cfm.

Colman, A.M. (1999). *What Is Psychology?* London: Routledge.

Glossary

Ability tests: tests designed to measure people's maximum performance, independent of their learning.

Acoustic: concerning sound and hearing.

Action potential: pulsed electrical signals which are the means by which activity is transmitted within neurons.

Adrenal gland: a hormone-producing, or endocrine gland situated over the kidneys.

Adrenaline: hormone secreted by the adrenal gland and active in emotional excitement.

Adult Attachment Interview: an interview designed to explore adults' thoughts and feelings about relationships. Attachment patterns can then be classified into one of four categories.

Age norms: the average scores obtained on psychological tests by people at given age levels.

Aggregation: a summing together of different instances of behaviour.

Agoraphobia: one of the more common forms of irrational fear or phobia in clinical groups. Strong fear and panic may occur in a range of situations such as crowds, public places, travelling on trains or buses.

Amygdala: a small part of the brain which, as part of the limbic system, is important in emotion.

Androgens: a collective term for the hormones produced chiefly by the testes, the chief one of which is testosterone. Responsible for the maintenance and development of many male sexual characteristics.

Androgyny: the combination of masculine and feminine characteristics within an individual male or female.

Applied psychology: areas of psychology in which psychological theories and methods are applied to the practical aspects of everyday life (e.g. health, education, work).

Ascending reticular activating system: a diffuse structure in the brainstem which influences level of arousal.

Association cortex: parts of the cerebral cortex that process information after it has been received from the senses.

Attachment behaviour: behaviour that promotes proximity and physical contact with the object of the attachment.

Attachment tests: tests designed to measure people's progress, or learning, on a given course of instruction.

Attribution: the perception of the cause of an event.

Authoritarian personality: a constellation of personality characteristics that characterize people with prejudiced attitudes centring on respect for authority.

Autism: a form of disordered behaviour that arises in early childhood and is characterized by communication difficulties.

Autonomic nervous system (ANS): a system of nerve cells and nerve fibres that control the functions of smooth muscles and glands.

Axon: an elongated process which is the part of a neuron which carries a signal away from the soma towards another cell.

Behaviour modification: therapeutic techniques, often involving the use of rewards and punishments, based on operant conditioning.

Behavioural genetic studies: studies exploring the similarities and differences in behavioural attributes in related individuals, in order to estimate the contribution of inheritance.

Behaviourism: a dominant school of psychology, for much of the twentieth century, which limited data to behaviour that could be observed.

Blindsight: a rare consequence of damage to the visual cortex, where sufferers are able to locate objects even though they report that they cannot see them.

Bottom up: processing of information from simple input of signals to more complex 'higher' levels.

Brainstem: the part of the brain that joins on to the spinal cord.

Broca's area: brain area concerned with speech production first described by Paul Broca in the nineteenth century.

Catharsis: the purging or release of an emotion through direct or indirect expression.

Causality: this refers to the person's perception of what the cause of an event was; that is, 'Why did this occur?'

Central nervous system: the brain and spinal cord.

Cerebellum: the second largest and most obvious structure seen when looking at a brain, the cerebellum plays an important role in coordinating actions.

Cerebral cortex: that part of the brain responsible for many 'higher' human mental activities.

Cerebral hemispheres: the largest and uppermost part of the brain (the cerebrum) is divided into two sides or hemispheres.

Cerebrospinal fluid: the fluid that surrounds the brain and spinal cord and fills the ventricles.

Chromosome: microscopic body found in a cell nucleus containing genes, the individual's hereditary material.

Chronic illness: any condition that involves some disability, brought about by pathological change, and that is usually not curable.

Classical conditioning: the learning of a response through association with a previously neutral stimulus, studied by Pavlov.

Cognition: a person's thoughts, knowledge and ideas about him/herself and the environment.

Cognitive behavioural therapy: a psychological treatment approach based on changing the client's dysfunctional beliefs and behaviours.

Cognitive dissonance theory: one of the best-known cognitive consistency theories that was proposed by Leon Festinger, and that explains how people resolve inconsistencies in their knowledge, beliefs and behaviour.

Cognitive map: a plan of the environment that is carried in the brain.

Cognitive processes: refers to mental activities involving evaluation and appraisal. It can sometimes be used as equivalent to thought.

Commissures: structures that join the two sides of the brain.

Cones: receptive cells in the retina responsive to coloured light.

Consciousness: a state in which an individual is aware of, or is 'inside', what is happening. Often used synonymously with 'awareness', but generally thought to be rather more than this.

Conservation: a cognitive advance that Piaget proposed as a central feature of concrete operational thinking acquired at around the age of seven.

Constructive alternativism: the theory that the world may be construed in very different ways, without any one view being 'correct' in an absolute sense.

Control group: a group in an experiment that is not given the treatment whose effect is being studied (see *Experimental group*).

Convergent thinking: the ability to focus on the correct solution to a problem.

Correlational study: a study that is designed to find out the degree of correspondence between two sets of measures.

Cortex: the outer layer. In the context of the brain, used to refer to the outer layer of the cerebellum or, more frequently, the cerebral hemispheres.

Cross-sectional approach: investigation of development that compares groups of people with different levels of age or experience at the same point in time.

Crystallized intelligence: aspects of intelligence that depend on knowledge.

Declarative memory: memory for facts and events.

Delusions: false beliefs, often associated with severe mental disorders such as schizophrenia.

Dendrites: branching nerve cell processes that receive signals from other cells.

Dependent variable: the behaviour or response measured in a psychological experiment that is believed to be changed by the independent variable.

Desensitization: a therapeutic technique to reduce phobic anxiety, through gradual exposure.

Diffusion of responsibility: the tendency for people in a group not to take action, typically in an emergency situation, because the presence of others makes them feel less able or less competent to act and diffuses their feeling of responsibility to act.

Discrimination: making a distinction between stimuli and responding differently.

Divergent thinking: the ability to generate different ideas from a given proposition, or problem.

Dopamine: one of many neurotransmitter substances.

Double dissociation: the situation where one set of circumstances leads to one outcome but not a second, a second set of circumstances leads to the second outcome but not the first. For example damage to brain area A1 leads to loss of function F1 but leaves function F2 intact. Damage to A2 impairs F2 but leaves F1 intact.

DSM: the Diagnostic and Statistical Manual of the American Psychiatric Association. The most widely used diagnostic system.

Echolocation: an animal echolocates an object by emitting high frequency sounds that can be heard and timed by that animal as they are reflected off solid objects in the vicinity. Used by bats for flight in darkness and the location of food.

Ecological approach: a research strategy in developmental psychology that takes account of all the interacting social and environmental influences upon humans.

Ecological validity: the relevance that an experimental or other research procedure has to real life.

Efficacy: the belief that a task or behaviour change is do-able, and that carrying out that task or behaviour will achieve the desired result.

Egocentrism: the tendency to see the world only from one's own point of view, which Piaget believed was an essential feature of early childhood.

Electra complex: the Freudian notion that at a certain stage a girl becomes aware that she lacks a penis. She is said to feel 'penis envy' and blame her mother for her feelings of castration. A girl then rejects her mother and turns to her father. The complex is named after the Greek myth in which Electra connives at the death of her mother who had murdered her father.

Electroencephalography (EEG): a method of recording electrical signals generated by the brain, from the surface of the scalp.

Emotional leakage: occurs when the facial expressions commonly associated with an emotion are suppressed and the emotion is shown, or 'leaks' out, elsewhere in other parts of the body below the head (such as feet and hands). Also known as *leakage*.

Encoding: the transformation of a sensory input into a form (code) for storage in memory.

Episodic: relating to events or episodes.

Episodic memory: the part of the memory that holds details of people, places and events.

Ethologist: one who researches the behaviour of animals, and who works primarily in their natural habitats rather than in the laboratory.

Experimental control: the version of the independent variable that differs from the experimental condition only in the way that the experimenter wishes to investigate.

Experimental group: a group in an experiment that is given the treatment whose effect is being studied (see *Control group*).

Extinction: the gradual fading of behaviour when it fails to produce a reinforcing consequence.

Extravert: a psychological type who is more concerned with social life and the external world than with inner experience.

Facial primacy: this refers to the fact that the face is viewed by people as the most important part of the body for conveying information about emotions.

Factor analysis: a statistical technique that reduces a large number of test interrelationships to a small number of factors.

False memory syndrome: apparent memories for events usually of a disturbing nature, which did not actually occur.

Family therapy: treatments taking the whole family, rather than the individual, as a focus.

Fissure: particularly large sulci are called fissures.

Focal theory: John Coleman's view that different issues come in and out of focus at different parts of adolescents' lives.

Free association: a form of word association in which a subject reports any word that comes to mind in response to a stimulus. Also the reporting of anything that comes to mind, without modification.

Functional magnetic resonance imaging (fMRI): MRI that reflects activity in the brain while a patient or research participant performs a task.

Gender identity: the concept of oneself as either feminine or masculine.

Gene: transmission of individual hereditary traits contained in a chromosome.

Generalization: the production of a response by a stimulus similar, but not identical, to the original stimulus when learning took place.

Generalized anxiety disorder: chronic long-term high anxiety. The individual is continually anxious and frightened.

Gestalt: a German school of psychologists who in the early twentieth century argued that the whole is more than the sum of the parts.

Glia: cells in the nervous system that provide support for neurons.

Grey matter: parts of the brain that consist mainly of cell bodies and have a greyish appearance.

Gyrus/gyri: the well known ridges in the cerebral cortex are called gyri (singular is gyrus).

Hallucinations: a perception of an external stimulus that does not exist, often in the form of hearing a voice.

Hermaphrodite: an individual who has both male and female reproductive organs, also applied to individuals in whom there is a contradiction between their external genitals and/or secondary sexual characteristics and various internal structures; for example, gonads.

Hippocampus: part of the brain, its shape has been likened to a seahorse, important in memory.

Hypothalamus: a part of the brain situated below the thalamus that includes several clusters of cells important for the control of behaviour. It is concerned with particular emotions, motivation and sleep.

Iconic memory: the sensory memory system for vision.

Identification: a process of personality development involving taking on the characteristics of other people.

Identity crisis: the notion that adolescence is defined by a transition between the identities of the child and the adult, and that this creates stress and tension.

Imprinting: learning that occurs within a limited period early in life (usually in relation to the mother and likened by Lorenz to a pathological fixation), and that is relatively unmodifiable.

Independent variable: the conditions in an experiment that the experimenter varies.

Insight: the discovery of the solution to a problem.

Instrumental conditioning: a type of conditioning described by Edward Thorndike, in which gaining reinforcement depends on some action by the experimental animal.

Intelligence: a general ability whose definition remains elusive.

Interactionism: the view that both person and situation are important in determining behaviour.

Intersubjectivity: the shared experience and meaning that is built up in interactions between parent and infant.

Interthinking: Neil Mercer's term that summarizes how language enables joint co-ordinated intellectual activity to occur between people.

Intrinsic motive pulse: Colwyn Trevarthen's proposed mechanism within babies that enables them to display 'communicative musicality' in their interactions.

Introvert: a psychological type who is more concerned with the inner life and reflection than with social life and the external world.

IQ tests: tests designed to measure the 'intelligence quotient'; that is, intelligence defined in some operational manner.

Lateral geniculate body: a part of the brain that acts as a relay for visual information from the eye to the visual cortex (area striata).

Levels of processing theory: the theory that memories for items that are deeply processed (usually in the form of words and meanings) are stronger than those for items processed only superficially.

Limbic system: several interconnected brain structures that all seem to be involved in emotion.

Linguistic relativity hypothesis: the suggestion that the way we think is determined by the way we use language.

Lobes (occipital, temporal, parietal, frontal): the way we divide up the cerebrum into different areas, based on the position of the main sulci.

Longitudinal approach: investigation of development that follows one or more groups of people over time.

Long-term memory: the relatively permanent part of the memory system.

Magnetic resonance imaging: a non-invasive form of brain imaging.

Meninges: three protective layers that cover the brain and spinal cord.

Method of loci: a mnemonic device that involves attributing items to be remembered to places.

Mnemonist: a person specializing in the use of memory.

Moderator variable (use of): using a second measure in conjunction with a particular score to make a better prediction; for example, the prediction of school achievement from an intelligence test might be improved if a measure of motivation were also used.

Monotropism: an idea put forward by John Bowlby that an infant has an innate tendency to become attached to one particular individual with the implication that this attachment is different in kind from any other subsequent attachments formed.

Motivation: the readiness to act to achieve certain goals and outcomes.

Motor reproduction: the physical carrying out of behaviours learned through observation.

Mutual gaze: when two people look at each other simultaneously.

Neglect: a rare condition where sufferers ignore part of their sensory input.

Neurons: nerve cells.

Neurotransmitter: a chemical substance that passes on information between neurons, either exciting or inhibiting the receiving cell.

Nucleus/nuclei: the part of a cell that contains the chromosomes. Also used to refer to clusters of cells.

Object permanence: the concept that objects still exist when they are out of sight, and that Piaget proposed was acquired in infancy.

Oedipus complex: the Freudian notion that at a certain stage boys experience a conflict between sexual desire for the mother and punishment (castration) by the father, and that derives from a famous Greek myth.

Oestrogen: a sex hormone produced by the ovaries and responsible for the development and maintenance of many female characteristics.

Operant behaviour: any behaviour that, following the established setting conditions, leads to reinforcement.

Operant conditioning: a form of conditioning explored by Burrhus F. Skinner, in which an experimental participant obtains reinforcement when it performs the desired behaviour.

Optic chiasma: the point in the brain that is a cross-over junction for the optic nerves.

Ovary: the sex gland in the female that produces ova and sex hormones.

Panic disorder: a disorder in which severe fear escalates to a full-blown panic, typically 'out of the blue', rather than in response to any specific feared object or situation.

Paranormal: any psychological phenomenon that cannot be explained by current psychological theories, including telepathy, psychokinesis, poltergeists, clairvoyance and many others.

Parasympathetic nervous system: the cranial and sacral parts of the autonomic nervous system. Active in relaxed or quiescent states of the body.

Peer tutoring: joint activity in which a more experienced child works with a less experienced one.

Perceptual defence: the apparent refusal to see words that might be upsetting or taboo.

Perceptual hypotheses: testable predictions based on pervious experience about the identity of an object or situation.

Personal Construct theory: a theory of the mind put forward by George Kelly.

Personal construct: an important way in which an individual views his or her world. A pattern or template that the individual uses to make sense of his or her experience (from George Kelly's Personal Construct Theory).

PET scanning: Position Emission Tomography scanning is a computer-aided scanning technique that can be used to show which area(s) of the brain is active under different stimulus and response conditions.

Phenomenological consciousness: the feeling that we all have that we are conscious.

Pituitary gland: the 'master gland' of the body, situated just below the hypothalamus, this gland controls the production of many of our hormones.

Placebo: an inert substance used in place of an active drug, given to a control group in an experiment.

Plastic: malleable, can be changed.

Pluralistic ignorance: the phenomenon in which everybody in a group looks to others to define a situation resulting in delayed action or no action. Often occurring when an emergency is viewed as an ambiguous situation and thus no one reacts to it.

Positive psychology: a new approach to psychology, emphasizing strengths and positive emotions rather than weaknesses and negative emotions.

Positivity bias: the bias towards viewing a situation in such a way as to enhance self-esteem.

Post-mortem: after death.

Posture mimicry: the adoption, often without the person being aware of it, of a posture shown by someone she or he likes or loves; thus two friends may be seen to display the same posture.

Prejudice: negative or hostile attitudes towards groups of people that are based on over-generalized stereotypes (see *Stereotypes*).

Presumed central tendency: the expectation that others will respond with the average or 'normal' response.

Preventative health behaviours: health related behaviours that can promote good health and actions that can lead to the early detection of disease or disease risk factors.

Primacy effect: the finding that when information is learned in a sequence, the information learned first is better remembered than information presented later in the same sequence.

Primary prevention: attempts by individuals to reduce or eliminate risks to health.

Proactive interference: the interference of items stored in memory with the learning and recall of new items.

Progesterone: a sex hormone produced by the ovaries and responsible for preparing the uterus for pregnancy and the breasts for lactation.

Projective tests: open-ended personality tests whose results rely on the subjective interpretation of the tester.

Psychoanalysis: a method developed by Freud and his followers concerning the treatment of mental and nervous disorders in which the role of the unconscious is emphasized.

Psychodynamics: the psychological approach that Freud began. This approach is based on the idea that the unconscious is a source of drive or motivation.

Psychometrics: the theory and practice of psychological testing.

Psychoses: severe mental disorders, typically characterized by a loss of contact with reality.

Qualitative research: research methods that contrast with the quantitative approach and are concerned with subjective data. This research might include verbal or written reports, use of open-ended questions (that have not been converted into points on numerical scales) and case studies.

Quantitative research: analysing data as numerical values. This approach is used in traditional psychology, with the emphasis on objectivity and 'the scientific method'.

Rational non-adherence: rational decisions made by patients that may affect their decision to adhere to medical treatment or advice.

Readiness potential: the electrical activity in the brain that occurs even before we know that we intend to do something.

Reflex: a physiological reaction, such as an eye-blink to a bright light, over which we have no control.

Reinforcement: an outcome of a behaviour that increases the likelihood that the behaviour will be performed again.

Reliability: a statistical index of the degree to which a test provides consistent measurements.

REM sleep: a phase of the sleep cycle characterized by the eyes making rapid movements that can be seen through the eyelids.

Repertory grid: a technique devised by George Kelly to assess personal constructs.

Respondent behaviour: a type of behaviour that, unlike operant behaviour, corresponds to a reflex action.

Retention: the storage of information.

Reticular activating system: (also known as the reticular formation) a network of cells running up through the brain stem. It receives inputs from all sensory pathways and is closely connected to the spinal cord, thalamus and cortex. Thought to play an important role in arousal.

Retina: the part of the eye that is sensitive to light and contains the rods and cones.

Retrieval: recovery of information from storage.

Retroactive interference: the interference in memory of items memorized earlier, by items subsequently learned.

Rods: elements of the retina for black-and-white vision.

Role conflicts: the possible clashes between the different social roles that people take on: includes role discontinuity (sudden breaks or changes), and role incongruence (conflicting sets of values).

Role-taking: the process of imitating and identifying with the behaviour of other people or role models.

Scaffolding: the process by which a more experienced person guides children's participation in learning activities.

Schedules of reinforcement: the rate at which behaviour produces the reward – the weekly pay packet, for example.

Schema (plural schemata): cognitive structures that are abstract representations of events, people and relationships from the real physical world.

Schizophrenia: one of the most severe forms of mental disorder often accompanied by hallucinations and disordered thinking.

Secondary prevention: interventions designed to detect and treat illness at an early stage in its development. Aims to slow down or stop disease.

Self-concepts: our views of different aspects of ourselves, which include self-identities (how these are combined), self-esteem (our view of our own worth) and self-efficacy (how effective we feel we are).

Semantic: involving words and word meanings.

Semantic memory: the part of memory that holds knowledge.

Sensory threshold: the level at which low levels of stimulation are first perceived.

Shaping: the gradual teaching of a complex behaviour by reinforcement of closer and closer approximations to it.

Shaping-up: the gradual production of a complex behaviour by initially rewarding more and more accurate approximations to it.

Short-term memory: the part of the memory system taken to be of limited capacity and only able to hold material for relatively short periods of time.

Single channel theory: the theory that only one channel of information can be processed at a time.

Size constancy: the phenomenon whereby items look the same size even when they are different distances away and so stimulate different numbers of the visual cells on the retina.

Social cognition: term used in social psychology to describe the ways in which people make sense of social situations.

Social comparison: people's constant need to validate their opinions by comparing them with those of others.

Social co-operation: the idea that children's learning is based on their interactions with the more experienced members of their culture, central to Vygotsky's theory.

Social facilitation: the increase in speed of a response as a result of social stimuli from others.

Socialization: the process whereby newborns gradually become fully fledged members of society.

Socio-cultural approach: theoretical approach to human development which stresses that thinking and learning can only be investigated within a social and cultural context.

Soma: body: the body of a cell.

Speciesism: a term used to describe the view that one species is more important than any other. Usually used in relation to humans versus other animals.

Spreading activation model: the idea that information in long term memory is organized according to a series of links between related items.

S-R Psychology: the branch of psychology concerned with scientific study of the relationship between what is done to an organism (**s**timulus) and what the organism does (**r**esponse).

Stages of development (Piaget's theory): Piaget proposed that children develop through four stages of cognitive development, the sensori-motor, pre-operational, concrete operational and formal operational stages.

State dependent learning: the well-documented phenomenon whereby information is easier to recall when in circumstances similar to those in which it was learned.

State-dependent memory: memory that is formed in a particular biological state, such as when a person is drunk, and so is best recalled when the person is in a similar state.

Stereotypes: generalized sets of beliefs or attitudes about groups of people that are usually inaccurate.

Story linkage: a mnemonic device that involves building a story around items to be remembered.

Strange Situation: Mary Ainsworth's standardized method for assessing infant attachment.

Sulcus/sulci: the grooves on the surface of the cerebral cortex.

Symbolism: a major developmental acquisition of the second year of life that enables the child to represent objects internally that are not immediately present.

Sympathetic nervous system: the part of the autonomic nervous system made up of the ganglionic chain lying outside, and parallel to, the spinal cord. Active in emotional excitement.

Synapse: the region where one neuron communicates with another.

Synaptic transmission: passage of messages from one neuron to another by chemical means.

Temporal contiguity: the requirement for two events to occur close together in time in order for them to be associated with each other.

Tertiary prevention: treatments or actions to slow down the effects of serious disease or injury. Aims to rehabilitate the patient.

Thalamus: a sub-cortical area of the cerebrum that functions as a particularly important relay-station to and from other areas of the nervous system.

Theory of mind: concept that summarizes current thinking about how children perceive themselves in relation to other people, and how they perceive others' mental states.

Top down: the influence of information from 'higher up' the processing chain.

Transparencies: non-realistic aspects of young children's drawings where some parts of the scene or objects portrayed are visible through other parts.

Transsexual: a person with a disorder of sexual identity. For example, a transsexual man typically feels himself to be a female trapped in a male body and may want to live as a woman and to have surgery to feminize the body.

Unconditional response: a behaviour, such as a reflex, that naturally occurs following a given stimulus.

Validity: a statistical index of the degree to which a test measures that which it is supposed to measure.

Ventricles: four linked fluid-filled spaces within the brain.

Wernicke's area: brain area concerned with language comprehension named after Carl Wernicke, who in the nineteenth century first described the effects of damage in this area.

White matter: parts of the brain that consist mainly of bundles of nerve processes, which appear white in colour.

Within participants or repeated measures: an experimental design where the same participants undergo all conditions of the independent variable and each one's results are compared with him/herself on the different conditions.

References

1: INTRODUCTION: BEGINNING TO UNDERSTAND YOU

Cutler, W.B., Preti, G., Krieger, A., Huggins, G.R., Garcia, G.R. and Lawley, H.J. (1986). Human axillary secretions influence women's menstrual cycles: The role of donor extract from men. *Hormones and Behaviour, 20,* 463–473. [The experiment using male axillary secretions.]

2: BODY LANGUAGE

Abel, M.H. and Hester, R. (2002). The therapeutic effects of smiling. In M.H. Abel (ed.), *An Empirical Reflection on the Smile*. Lewiston, N.Y.: Edwin Mellen. [Facial feedback hypothesis.]

Argyle, M. (1975). *Bodily Communication*. London: Methuen. [Body language figures taken from here.]

Argyle, M. (1990). *Bodily Communication, 2nd edn*. London: Routledge. [A detailed study of body language.]

Balogh, R.D. and Porter, R.H. (1986). Olfactory preferences resulting from mere exposure in human neonates. *Infant Behaviour and Development, 9(4),* 395–401. [Recognition of babies by odour.]

Brody, L.R. (2000). The socialization of gender differences in emotional expression: Display rules, infant temperament, and differentiation. In A.H. Fischer (ed.), *Gender and Emotion: Social psychological perspectives*. Cambridge: Cambridge University Press. [Gender and cultural differences in smiling.]

Collett, P. (2004). *The Book of Tells: How to read peoples' minds from their actions*. Bantam Books: London. [Arm pronation.]

Cutler, W.B., Preti, G., Krieger, A., Higgins, G.R., Garcia, C.R. and Lawley, H.J. (1986). Human axillary secretions influence women's menstrual cycles: The role of donor extract from men. *Hormones and Behaviour, 20,* 463–473. [Male secretions and the menstrual cycle.]

Doherty-Sneddon, G. (2004). Don't look now . . . I'm trying to think. *Psychologist, 17(2),* 82–85. [Children thinking.]

Eibl-Eibesfeldt, I. (1970). *Ethology: The biology of behaviour*. New York: Holt, Rinehart and Winston. [Facial expressions of deaf-blind children; odours and Mediterranean people.]

Ekman, P. (1992). *Telling Lies: Clues to Deceit in the Market Place, Politics and Marriage*. London: W.W. Norton. [All about lies, quotation on page 80.]

Ekman, P. (2004). Happy, sad, angry, disgusted. *New Scientist, 184(2467)*, 2 October, 4–5. Retrieved 11 October 2004 from www.newscientist.com. [Facial expressions: quotation on page 4.]

Ekman, P. and Friesen, W.V. (1969). The repetoire of nonverbal behaviour: Categories, origins, usage and coding. *Semiotica, 1*, 49–98. [Four types of display rules for facial expressions.]

Ekman. P. and Friesen, W.V. (1974). Detecting deception from the body or face. *Journal of Personality and Social Psychology, 29*, 288–294. [Experiment on deception.]

Ekman. P. and Friesen, W.V. (1975). *Unmasking the Face.* Englewood Cliffs, N.J.: Prentice Hall. [Facial expressions.]

Fisher, J.D., Rytting, M. and Heslin, R. (1976). Hands touching hands: Affective and evaluative effects of an interpersonal touch. *Sociometry, 39*, 416–421. [Purdue University study.]

Fridlund, A.J. (1994). *Human Facial Expression: An evolutionary perspective.* San Diego: Academic. [Emotions expressed in the face.]

Hall, E.T. (1969). *The Hidden Dimension.* New York: Anchor Books. [Body language in Arabs, Japanese and Americans.]

Hall, J.A., Carter, J.D. and Horgan, T.G. (2000). Gender differences in nonverbal communication. In A.H. Fischer (ed.), *Gender and Emotion: Social psychological perspectives.* Cambridge: Cambridge University Press. [Gender and differences in smiling and emotional expression.]

Henley, N.M. (1977). *Body Politics: Power, sex and nonverbal communication.* Eaglewood Cliffs, N.J.: Prentice Hall. [Gaze behaviour: quotation on page 179.]

Hess, E.H. (1965). Attitudes and pupil size. *Scientific American, 212*, 46–54. [Pupil size.]

Jourard, S.M. (1966). An exploratory study of body accessibility. *British Journal of Social and Clinical Psychology, 26*, 235–242. [Contact between couples.]

Kaitz, M., Lapidot, P., Bronner, R. and Eidelman, A. (1992). Parturient women can recognize their infants by touch. *Developmental Psychology, 28*, 35–39. [Recognition by touch of an infant's hands.]

Kendon, A. (1967). Some functions of gaze-direction in social interaction. *Acta Psychologica, 26*, 22–63. [Four functions of gaze behaviour.]

Knapp, M.L. (1992). *Non-verbal Communication in Human Interaction.* New York: Harcourt Brace Jovanovich. [Relevant to many topics and includes Morris and Montagu references to touch and foetal responses to touch.]

Krout, M.H. (1954). An experimental attempt to determine the significance of unconscious manual symbolic movements. *Journal of General Psychology, 51*, 121–152. [A study of blocked emotions.]

Russell, M.J., Switz, G.M. and Thompson, K. (1980). Olfactory influence on the human menstrual cycle. *Pharmacology, Biochemistry & Behaviour, 13*, 737–738. [Odours and the human menstrual cycle.]

Sheldrake, R. (2003). *The Sense of Being Stared at and Other Aspects of the Extended Mind.* New York: Crown. [Studies on being stared at.]

Vrij, A. (2000). *Detecting Lies and Deceit: The psychology of lying and the implications for professional practice.* Chichester: John Wiley. [Studies on lying: quotation on page 54.]

Wolpe, J. (1958). *Psychotherapy by Reciprocal Inhibition.* Stanford, Calif.: Stanford University Press. [The beginnings of assertion training.]

3: YOUR PERSONALITY

Block, J. (1971). *Lives Through Time.* Berkeley, Calif.: Barcroft Books. [A longitudinal study of stability of personality over time.]

Block, J. (1995). A contrarian view of the five-factor approach to personality description. *Psychological Bulletin, 117*, 187–215. [Gives you a summary of the Big 5 approach, plus a detailed critique of it.]

Bowers, K. (1973). Situationism in psychology: An analysis and critique. *Psychological Review, 80*, 307–336. [An influential critique of the extreme situationist position.]

Costa, P.T. and McCrae, R.R. (1992). *Revised NEO Personality Inventory (NEO P1-12) and NEO Five-Factor Inventory (NEO-FFI): Professional manual.* Odessa, Fla.: Psychological Assessment Resources. [The test derived from the five factor theory of personality organization.]

Eysenck, H.J. and Eysenck, M.W. (1981). *Personality and Individual Differences: A natural science approach.* New York: Plenum. [Explains Eysenck's theory and also his attempt to update his thinking in the light of research.]

Jankowitz, D. (2003). *The Easy Guide to Repertory Grids.* Chichester: Jossey/Bass/Wiley. [As the title suggests, an introduction to how to construct and analyse a repertory grid.]

Kelly, G. (1955). *The Psychology of Personal Constructs, Vols. 1 and 2.* New York: W.W. Norton. [The 'classic' and original book on personal construct theory.]

Mischel, W. (1968). *Personality Assessment.* New York: Wiley. [A classic in personality theory.]

Mischel, W. (2003). *Introduction to Personality, 7th edn.* Chichester: Wiley. [A comprehensive overview of more recent developments.]

Peterson, C. and Seligman, M.E.P. (1984). Causal explanation as a risk factor in depression: Theory and evidence. *Psychological Review, 91*, 347–374. [The original theory on links between attributional style and depression.]

Weiner, B. and Graham, S. (1999). Attribution in personality psychology. In L. Pervin and O. John (eds.), *Handbook of Personality Theory and Research.* New York: Guilford. [Bernard Weiner is a major attribution theorist and this chapter provides a good overview of the field.]

4: YOUR SEX: ON BEING MALE OR FEMALE

Archer, J. (1984). Gender roles as developmental pathways. *British Journal of Social Psychology, 23*, 245–256. [Archer's analysis of masculine and feminine 'pathways' in development.]

Baron-Cohen, S. (2003). *The Essential Difference: Men, women and the extreme male brain.* London: Allen Lane, Penguin. [Biological explanations for gender differences in ability.]

BBC News (UK) (2004). UK's pay gap 'wider than thought'. Retrieved 20 October 2004 from http://bbc.co.uk/1/hi/business/37548472.stm [The pay of women and men.]

Carter, C. and Åström, K. (2004). A cross-sectional study of UK academics suggests Santa Claus might be a professor. *Pharmaceutical Journal, 273*, 897–899. [Beards and professors.]

Colapinto, J. (2004). Gender gap: What were the real reasons behind David Reimer's suicide? Retrieved 2 November 2004 from http://slate.msn.com/toolbar.aspx?action=print&id=2101678 [David Reimer's life and death.]

Coleman, J.C. and Hendry, L. (1999). *The Nature of Adolescence.* London: Routledge. [A broad-ranging account of adolescence that highlights the issue of gender differences.]

Davison, G.C., Neale, M.N. and Kring, A.M. (2003). *Abnormal Psychology.* New York: John Wiley. [See sexual disorders including transsexualism.]

Department of Education and Skills (2004a). GCE/VCE A/AS examination results for young people in England, 2003/04 (provisional). Retrieved 21 October 2004 from http://dfes.gov.uk/rsgateway/DB/SFR/s000529/index.shtml. [A-level results.]

Department of Education and Skills (2004b). GCSE and equivalent results for young people in England, 2003/04 (provisional). Retrieved 21 October 2004 from http://dfes.gov.uk/rsgateway/DB/SFR/s000528/index.shtml. [GCSE results: quotation on page 2.]

Dershowitz, A. (2005). After Larry, who dares speak out? *Sunday Times, News Review*, 27 February, 4. [Larry Summers' views on aptitudes of women and men at the high end of the scale.]

Education Correspondent (1996). Women kept out of professorships. *The Times*, Friday 26 July, 7. [Very few women professors.]

Freud, S. (1933). 'Femininity' (lecture 33), in *New Introductory Lectures on Psycho-analysis* (1973). Harmondsworth: Penguin. [Freud's views concerning gender identity development.]

Gray, J. (1992). *Men Are from Mars, Women Are from Venus*. London: Element, HarperCollins. [Quotations are from pages 19 and 17 respectively.]

Hampson, J.L. (1965). Determinants of psychosexual orientation. In F.A. Beach (ed.), *Sex and Behaviour*. New York: Wiley. [Research on hermaphrodites.]

Heim, A. (1970). *Intelligence and Personality*. Harmondsworth: Penguin. [The mediocrity of women.]

Imperato-McGinley, J., Peterson, R.E., Gautier, T. and Sturla, E. (1979). Androgens and the evolution of male-gender identity among male pseudohermaphrodites with 5 ∝-reductase deficiencies. *New England Journal of Medicine, 300(22)*, 1233–1237. [Studies of 'girls' who change to boys, quotes on pages 1236 and 1234 respectively.]

Katcher, A. (1955). The discrimination of sex differences by young children. *Journal of Genetic Psychology, 87*, 131–143. [Children's understanding of sex differences.]

Kohlberg, L. (1966). A cognitive developmental analysis of children's sex-role concepts and attitudes. In E.E. Maccoby (ed.), *The Development of Sex Differences*. London: Tavistock. [Cognitive developmental theory.]

Lynn, D.B. (1966). The problem of learning parental and sex-role identification. *Journal of Marriage and the Family, 28*, 466–470. [Social learning theory.]

Maccoby, E.E. and Jacklin, C.N. (1974). *The Psychology of Sex Differences*. Stanford: Stanford University Press. [The authoritative review of the 1970s.]

McGillicuddy-De-Lisi, A. and De-Lisi, R. (2002). *Biology, Society and Behavior: The development of sex differences in cognition*. London: Ablex. [A detailed text on gender differences in cognition.]

Mischel, W. (1966). A social learning view of sex differences in behaviour. In E.E. Maccoby (ed.), *The Development of Sex Differences*. London: Tavistock. [Social learning theory.]

Morris, J. (1974). *Conundrum*. New York: Harcourt Brace Jovanovich. [A transsexual's story.]

National Statistics Online (2004). *The UK Time Use Survey*. Retrieved 14 December 2004 from http://www.statistics.gov.uk/timeuse/summary_results/housework_work.asp. [Childcare and housework.]

Pook, S. (2004). Hewitt launches drive against 'career sexism'. *News. Telegraph*. Retrieved 28 October 2004 from http://www.telegraph.co.uk/news/main.jhtml?xml=/news/2004/10/27/nism27.xml&sSheet=/news/2004/10/27/ixhome.html. [Career sexism.]

Rubin, J., Provenanzo, F.J. and Luria, Z. (1974). The eye of the beholder: Parents' views on sex of newborns. *American Journal of Orthopsychiatry, 43*, 720–731. [Fathers' initial reactions to their newborns.]

Rutter, M., Caspi, A., Fergusson, D., Horwood, L.J., Goodman, R., Maughan, B., Miffitt, T.E., Meltzer, H. and Carroll, J. (2004). Sex differences in developmental reading disability: New findings from 4 epidemiological studies. *Journal of the American Medical Association, 291(16)*, 2007–2012. [Reading disability in boys.]

227

Shields, S. (1978). Sex and the biased scientist. *New Scientist, 80(11321)*, 752–754. [Early research on sex differences and Darwin's quote on page 752.]

Smith, P.K. (1986). Exploration, play and social development in boys and girls. In D.J. Hargreaves and A.M. Colley (eds.), *The Psychology of Sex Roles*. Milton Keynes: Open University Press. [Gender constancy and gender stability.]

5: YOU AND OTHERS

Argyle, M. and Colman, A. (eds.) (1994). *Social Psychology*. Harlow: Longman. [Cross-cultural studies of the Milgram obedience experiment.]

Aronson, E., Wilson, T.D. and Akert, R.M. (2002). *Social Psychology*. Upper Saddle River, N.J.: Prentice Hall. [Includes discussion of conformity and body image and of Zimbardo's prison experiment.]

Asch, S.E. (1955). Opinions and social pressure. *Scientific American, 193*, 31–35. [Studies of conformity.]

Brickner, M.A., Ostrom, T.M. and Harkins, S.G. (1986). Effects of personal involvement: Thought-provoking implications for social loafing. *Journal of Personality and Social Psychology, 51*, 763–769. [Social loafing and social facilitation.]

Brown, R. (1986). *Social Psychology, 2nd edn*. New York: Free. [Many aspects of the topic of social loafing.]

Cohn, L.D. and Adler, N.E. (1992). Female and male perceptions of ideal body shape. *Psychology of Women Quarterly, 16*, 69–79. [Women view themselves as heavier than they are.]

Cumberbatch, G. (1997). Media violence: Science and common sense. *Psychology Review, 3*, 2–7. [The effects of TV violence.]

Donnerstein, E. and Smith, S.L. (1997). Impact of media violence on children, adolescents, and adults. In S. Kirschner and D.A. Kirschner (eds.), *Perspectives on Psychology and the Media*. Washington, D.C.: American Psychological Association. [The impact of media violence: quotation on page 35.]

Eysenck, H.J. (1996). Personality theory and the problem of criminality. In J. Muncie and E. McLaughlin (eds.), *Criminological Perspectives: A reader*. Thousand Oaks, Calif.: Sage. [Contains details of the Eysenck Criminality Scale.]

Eysenck, H.J. (1997). Addiction, personality, and motivation. *Human Psychopharmacology: Clinical and experimental, 12*, S79–S87. [Contains details of the Eysenck Addiction Scale.]

Feshbach, S. (1961). The stimulating versus cathartic effects of a vicarious aggressive activity. *Journal of Abnormal and Social Psychology, 63(2)*, 381–385. [The effects of viewing violence.]

Festinger, L. (1957). *A Theory of Cognitive Dissonance*. Stanford: Stanford University Press. [Festinger's original statement of his theory.]

Gilbert, G.M. (1951). Stereotype persistence and changes among college students. *Journal of Abnormal and Social Psychology, 46*, 245–254. [A follow-up to the Katz and Braly study.]

Gross, R. (2001). *Psychology: The science of mind and behaviour*. London: Hodder and Stoughton. [Kitty Genovese case and quotation page 434.]

Hansen, C.H. and Hansen, R.D. (2000). Music and music videos. In D. Zillmann and P. Vorderer (eds.), *Media Entertainment: The psychology of its appeal*. London: Lawrence Erlbaum Associates. [Review of research showing that fans of 'problem music' tend to commit more criminal acts and are more likely to use illegal drugs than are non-fans.]

Haslam, S. and Reicher, S. (2003). Beyond Stanford: Questioning a role-based tyranny. *Dialogue* (Bulletin of the Society for Personality and Social Psychology), *18*, 22–25. Retrieved

6 January 2005 from http://www.ex.ac.uk/Psychology/seorg/exp/02%20Experiment %20Dialogue.pdf. [Prison simulation study.]

Karlins, M., Coffman, T.L. and Walters, G. (1969). On the fading of social stereotypes: Studies in three generations of college students. *Journal of Personality and Social Psychology, 13*, 1–16. [The latest of three studies of stereotyping.]

Katz, D. and Braly, K.W. (1933). Racial stereotypes of one hundred college students. *Journal of Abnormal and Social Psychology, 13*, 1–16. [The first attempt to identify ethnic stereotypes.]

Kravitz, D.A. and Martin, B. (1986). Ringelmann rediscovered: The original article. *Journal of Personality and Social Psychology, 50*, 936–941. [The tug-of-war study.]

Kenrick, D.T., Neuberg, S.L. and Cialdini, R.B. (2002). *Social Psychology: Unravelling the mystery, 2nd edn.* Boston: Allyn and Bacon. [Conformity and watching violent films etc.]

Latane, B., Williams, K. and Harkins, S.G. (1979). Many hands make light work: The causes and consequences of social loafing. *Journal of Social Psychology, 27*, 822, 832. [Social loafing.]

Lippman, W. (1922). *Public Opinion.* New York: Harcourt, Brace. [Original discussion of the term *stereotype*.]

Milgram, S. (1963). Behavioural study of obedience. *Journal of Abnormal and Social Psychology, 67(4)*, 371–378. [Experiment on obedience to authority.]

Milgram, S. (1974). Conversation. *Psychology Today*, June, 71–80. [TV and its influence on violence.]

Moscovici, S. (1980). Cited in M. Argyle and A.M. Colman (eds.), *Social Psychology.* Harlow: Longman. [Conformity and consistency in the confederates.]

North, A.C. and Sheridan, L.P. (2004). Criminality, addiction, and liking for problem music. Manuscript submitted for publication. [Research showing links between these.]

Stoner, J.A.F. (1961). Cited in M. Argyle and A.M. Colman (eds.), *Social Psychology.* Harlow: Longman. [The risky shift.]

Zajonc, R.B. (1965). Social facilitation. *Science, 142*, 269–274. [Social facilitation.]

6: YOUR EMOTIONS

Ainsworth, M.D.S. (1982). Attachment: Retrospective and prospect. In C.M. Parkes and J. Stevenson-Hinde (eds.), *The Place of Attachment in Human Behaviour.* New York. Basic Books. [The *Strange Situation*.]

Averill, J.R. (1982). *Anger and Aggression: An essay on emotion.* New York: Springer-Verlag. [A stimulating book, covering many social, psychological and cultural aspects of anger.]

Berkowitz, L. (1999). Anger. In T. Dalgleish and M. Power (eds.), *Handbook of Cognition and Emotion.* Chichester: Wiley. [Discusses his theory of anger and the role of various factors in anger reactions.]

Berryman, J.C., Smythe, P.K., Taylor, A., Lamont, A. and Joiner, R. (2002). *Developmental Psychology and You.* Oxford: Blackwell. [Measurement of attachment and love in infants is discussed in chapter 3.]

Bowlby, J. (1971). *Attachment and Loss. Vol. 1: Attachment.* Harmondsworth: Penguin. [Attachment in infants and monotropism.]

Dutton, D.G. and Aron, A.P. (1974). Some evidence for heightened sexual attraction under conditions of high anxiety. *Journal of Personality and Social Psychology, 30*, 510–517. [Men on swaying bridge experiment.]

Freud, A. and Dann, S. (1951). An experiment in group upbringing. *Psychoanalytic Study of the Child, 6*, 127–168. [Orphan Holocaust survivers.]

Groth, A.N. (1979). *Men Who Rape.* New York: Plenum. [A clinical account of sexual aggression.]

Hatfield, E. and Rapson, R.L. (1995). *Love and Sex: Cross-cultural perspectives.* New York: Allyn and Bacon. [*Passionate Love Scale.*]

Hazebroek, J., Howells, K. and Day, A. (2001). Cognitive appraisals associated with high trait anger. *Personality and Individual Differences, 30,* 31–45. [Describes the study on high/low trait anger discussed in the text.]

Howells, K. and Day, A. (2003). Readiness for anger management: Clinical and theoretical issues. *Clinical Psychology Review, 23,* 319–337. [An extended analysis of angry people being unready to be treated.]

Howells, K., Day, A. and Wright, S. (2004). Affect, emotions and sex offending. *Psychology, Crime and Law, 10,* 179–195. [Reviews the evidence that emotional states are important antecedents for sexual offending.]

Lee, J.A. (1988). Love styles. In R.J. Sternberg and M.L. Barnes (eds.), *The Psychology of Love.* New Haven: Yale University Press. [Style/colours of love.]

Murstein, B.I. (1988). A taxonomy of love. In R.J. Sternberg and M.L. Barnes. (eds.), *The Psychology of Love.* New Haven: Yale University Press. [Love classified; includes comment on Casler, Erikson and Walter.]

Novaco, R.W. (1994). Clinicians ought to view anger contextually. *Behaviour Change, 10,* 208–218. [Demonstrates the social embeddedness of triggers for anger.]

Ortony, A., Clore, G.L. and Collins, A. (1988). *The Cognitive Structure of Emotions.* Cambridge: Cambridge University Press. [An influential example of the cognitive approach to understanding emotions.]

Schaffer, R. (1977). *Mothering.* London: Fontana. [Mother–infant attachment: includes comment on Freud and Emerson.]

Sluckin, W. (1972). *Imprinting and Early Learning.* London: Methuen. [Imprinting: includes comment on Lorenz.]

Spielberger, C.D. For a summary of Spielberger's work see the BBC www.bbc.co.uk/health/conditions/mental_healthy/coping_anger1/shtml.

Steele, H. and Steele, M. (2003). Psychotherapeutic applications of the adult attachment theory. In M. Marrone and M. Cortina (eds.), *Attachment Theory and the Psychoanalytic Process.* London: Whurr. [Adult attachment.]

Sternberg, R.J. and Barnes, M.L. (1988). *The Psychology of Love.* New Haven: Yale University Press. [Discusses adult love; includes comment on Casler, Erikson and Walster.]

Wyer, R.S. and Srull, T.K. (eds.) (1993). *Perspectives on Anger and Emotion: Advances in social cognition, Vol. 6.* Hillsdale, N.J.: Lawrence Erlbaum Associates. [A series of papers focusing on the work of Leonard Berkowitz, but also illustrating contemporary theories. See also the chapter 'Where does anger dwell?' by Clore and others.]

7: YOUR BRAIN

Cherney, L.R. (2002). Unilateral neglect: A disorder of attention. *Seminars in Speech and Language, 23,* 117–128. [A review of this unusual phenomenon.]

Damasio, A.R. (1999). *The Feeling of what Happens: Body and emotion in the making of consciousness.* London: Heinemann. [Theories of consciousness.]

James, W. (1890/1984). *The Principles of Psychology.* New York: Harvard University Press. [One of the classics.]

Libet, B. (2004). *Mind Time: The temporal factor in consciousness.* Cambridge, Mass.: Harvard University Press. [An experimental approach to the nature of consciousness.]

Maguire, E.A., Spiers, H.J. and Good, C.D. (2003). Navigation expertise and the human hippocampus. *Hippocampus, 13,* 250–259. [Taxi-drivers' brains.]

Schachter, S. and Singer, J.E. (1962). Cognitive, social and physiological determinants of emotional state. *Psychological Review, 69,* 379–399. [Exploration of emotion.]

Sperry, R.W. (1969). Hemisphere deconnection and unity in conscious awareness. *American Psychologist, 23,* 723–733. [Pioneering work on split-brain preparations.]

Weiskrantz, L., Warrington, E.K., Saunders, M.D. and Marshall, J. (1974). Visual capacity in the hemianopic field following a restricted occipital ablation. *Brain, 97,* 709–728. [The discovery of blindsight.]

8: YOUR HEALTH

Chapple, A., Ziebland, S. and McPherson, A. (2004). Stigma, shame and blame experienced by patients with lung cancer: A qualitative study. *British Medical Journal, 328,* 1470–1473. [Experiences of patients with lung cancer.]

Department of Health (1998). *Report of the Scientific Committee on Tobacco and Health.* London: HMSO. [Public Health document outlining the dangers of tobacco.]

Department of Health (1999). *Saving Lives: Our healthier nation.* London: HMSO. [Key strategy for Public Health, UK.]

DiMatteo, M.R. and DiNicola, D.D. (1982). *Achieving Patient Compliance.* Elmsford, N.Y.: Pergamon. [Factors influencing adherence to medical treatment and advice.]

Janis, I. and Feshbach, S. (1953). Effects of fear-arousing communications. *Journal of Abnormal and Social Psychology, 48,* 78–92. [Fear appeals.]

Jebb, S. (2004). *Why the UK Must Stop Overeating.* Retrieved 25 January 2005 from http://news.bbc.co.uk. [Commentary on the dangers of obesity.]

Harari, P. and Legge, K. (2001). *Psychology and Health.* Oxford: Heineman. [See chapter here on using medical services.]

Kent, G. and Dalgleish, M. (1996). *Psychology and Medical Care.* London: Saunders. [Relationship between psychology and medicine.]

Kindelan, K. and Kent, G. (1987). Concordance between patients' information preferences and general practitioners' perceptions. *Psychology and Health, 1,* 339–409. [Differences in what information doctors and patients think is important.]

Langley, S. Doctor's Know Best? People's Knowledge Regarding Definitions of Medical Terms and Lay Satisfaction with Information Provided by Doctors. Unpublished dissertation, Coventry University, UK. [Ratings of patient knowledge.]

Ley, P. (1989). Improving patients' understanding, recall, satisfaction and compliance. In A. Broome (ed.). *Health Psychology.* London: Chapman and Hall. [Explores role of clear verbal information.]

Ley, P. and Morris, L.A. (1984). Psychological aspects of written information for patients. In S. Rachman (ed.), *Contributions to Medical Psychology.* Oxford: Pergamon. [Explores role of clearly presented written information.]

Locker, D. (1981). *Symptoms and Illness: The cognitive organization of disorder.* London: Tavistock. [Factors triggering medical consultations.]

Pitts, M. and Phillips, K. (1998). *The Psychology of Health: An introduction.* London: Routledge. [See introductory chapter.]

Richards, H., Reid, M. and Watt, G. (2003). Victim-blaming revisited: A qualitative study of beliefs about illness causation, and responses to chest pain. *Family Practice, 20,* 711–716. [Experiences of patients with heart disease.]

Roter, D., Lipkin, M. and Korsgaard, A. (1991). Sex differences in patients' and physicians' communication during primary care medical visits. *Medical Care, 29*, 1083–1093. [Female patients prefer female doctors.]

Rothman, A., Martino, S.C., Bedell, B.T., Detweiler, J.B. and Salovey, P. (1999). The systematic influence of gain- and loss-framed messages on interest in and use of different types of health behaviour. *Personality & Social Psychology Bulletin, 25*, 1355–1369. [Presents a framework for evaluating messages about health.]

Taylor, S.E. (1995). *Health Psychology.* Singapore: McGraw Hill. [See chapter on patient–practitioner interaction.]

Toynbee, P. (1977). *Patients.* New York: Harcourt Brace. [A broad perspective of the patient experience.]

Wanless, D. (2004). *Securing Good Health for the Whole Population.* HMSO. [Strategy for Public Health, UK. Quotation on page 183.]

Witte, K. and Allen. M. (2000). A meta-analysis of fear appeals: Implications for effective public health campaigns. *Health Education Behaviour, 27*, 591–615. [Evaluation of the 'fear appeal' literature.]

Zhang, M., Lee, A. and Binns, C.W. (2003). Physical activity and epithelial ovarian cancer risk: A case-control study in China. *International Journal of Cancer, 105*, 838–843 [Exercise and reduced cancer risk.]

9: YOUR DEVELOPMENT ACROSS THE LIFESPAN

Coleman, J.C. and Hendry, L. (1990). *The Nature of Adolescence, 2nd edn.* London: Routledge. [Includes the 'focal theory'.]

Collis, G.M. and Schaffer, H.R. (1975). Synchronisation of visual attention in mother–infant pairs. *Journal of Child Psychology and Psychiatry, 16*, 315–320. [Research on mothers and babies looking at things together.]

Frith, U. (1989). *Autism: Explaining the enigma.* Oxford: Blackwell. [Includes the false belief task used in Exercise 9.1.]

Gibson, E.J. and Walk, R.D. (1960). The 'visual cliff'. *Scientific American, 202*, 64–71.

Hargreaves, D.J., Purves, R.M., Welch, G.F. and Marshall, N. (2005). Developing identities and attitudes in musicians and music teachers. (Manuscript submitted for publication.) [The TIME project.]

Harris, P.L. (1989). *Children and Emotion.* Oxford: Blackwell. [Includes Harris's account of 'theory of mind'.]

Leslie, A.M. (1990). Pretence, autism, and bases of 'theory of mind'. *The Psychologist, 3*, 120–123. [Work on pretence.]

Lewis, M. and Brooks-Gunn, J. (1979). *Social Cognition and the Acquisition of Self.* New York: Plenum. [Includes research on the infant's acquisition of self.]

McGarrigle, J. and Donaldson, M. (1974). Conservation accidents. *Cognition, 3*, 341–350. [The social setting affects children's conservation abilities.]

Mercer, N. (2000). *Words and Minds: How we use language to think together.* London: Routledge. [Different uses of language in different settings, and the idea of 'interthinking'.]

Piaget, J. and Inhelder. B. (1967). *The Psychology of the Child.* London: Routledge. [Piaget's own introductory account of his theory.]

Tizard, B. and Hughes, M. (1984). *Young Children Learning: Talking and thinking at home and school.* London: Fontana. [Different characteristics of talk at home and at school.]

Topping, K. (1992). Co-operative learning and peer tutoring: An overview. *Psychologist, 5*, 151–162. [Broad-ranging review.]

Trehub, S., Schellenberg, E. and Hill, D. (1997). The origins of music perception and cognition: A developmental perspective, in I. DeLiège and J.A. Sloboda (eds.), *Perception and Cognition of Music*. Hove: Psychology Press. [A review of Trehub's work showing that infants can respond to musical features of sounds.]

Trevarthen, C. (1999). Musicality and the intrinsic motive pulse: Evidence from human psychobiology and infant communication. *Musicae Scientiae, Special Issue*, 155–215. [Trevarthen's theory of the 'intrinsic motive pulse'.]

Vygotsky, L. (1961). *Thought and Language*. Boston, Mass.: MIT Press. [Vygotsky's increasingly influential theory of teaching and learning.]

Wimmer, H. and Perner, J. (1983). Beliefs about beliefs: Representations and constraining function of wrong beliefs in young children's understanding of deception. *Cognition, 13*, 103–128. [False belief task about a boy called Maxi.]

10: PSYCHOLOGICAL PROBLEMS

American Psychiatric Association (2000). *Diagnostic and Statistical Manual of Mental Disorders, 4th edn. Text Revision. (DSM-IV-TR)*. Philadelphia: American Psychiatric Association. [The most widely used description of the major mental disorders and their diagnostic criteria.]

American Psychological Association. *Monitor on Psychology*. Retrieved March 2004 from www.apa.org/monitor/maro4/persontoc.html. [An overview of personality disorders and their treatability.]

Beck, A.T. and Freedman, A. (1990). *Cognitive Therapy of Personality Disorders*. New York: Guilford. [An important book outlining the cognitive approach to treating personality disorders.]

Chadwick, P. and Birchwood, M. (1994). The omnipotence of voices: A cognitive approach to auditory hallucinations. *British Journal of Psychiatry, 164*, 190–201. [Demonstrates how a symptom of schizophrenia can be subjected to a psychological analysis.]

Chadwick, P., Birchwood, M. and Trower, P. (1996). *Cognitive Therapy for Delusions, Voices and Paranoia*. Chichester: Wiley. [An excellent and influential example of how cognitive behavioural therapy has been applied in a creative way to some of the problems associated with schizophrenia.]

Mathews, A. (2002). Emotional processing biases: Nature and modification. In L. Blackman and C. von Hofstein (eds.), *Psychology at the Turn of the Millennium. Vol. 1: Cognitive, Biological and Health Perspectives*. Hove: Psychology Press. [An account of some of the cognitive biases associated with emotional disorders such as anxiety.]

Seligman, M.E.P. (1971). Phobias and preparedness. *Behavior Therapy, 2*, 307–320. [The main source relating to the idea that phobias have an evolutionary function.]

Seligman, M.E.P. (2003). *Authentic Happiness*. New York: Random House. [A popular book outlining the basis for positive psychology.]

Wells, A. (2002). Brief cognitive therapy for social phobia. In W. Dryden and F. Bond (eds.), *Brief Cognitive Behaviour Therapy*. Chichester: Wiley. [Illustrates some of the work being conducted in the treatment of social phobia, by an influential researcher and theorist.]

11: YOUR VIEW OF THE WORLD: PERCEPTION AND THINKING

Broadbent, D.E. (1954). The role of auditory localisation and attention in memory span. *Journal of Experimental Psychology, 47*, 191–196. [Single channel theory of attention.]

Carmichael, L., Hogan, H.P. and Walter, A.A. (1932). An experimental study of the effect of language on the reproduction of visually perceived form. *Journal of Experimental Psychology, 15,* 73–86. [Experiment on the influence language has on thought.]

Carroll, J.B. (1956). *Language, Thought and Reality: Selected writings of Benjamin Lee Whorf.* New York: MIT Press and Wiley. [Linguistic relativity hypothesis.]

El-Murad, J. and West, D.C. (2004). The definition and measurement of creativity: What do we know? *Journal of Advertising Research, 44,* 188–201. [A review of trends in creativity research with an emphasis on creativity in advertising.]

Gregory, R.L. (1966). *Eye and Brain.* London: Weidenfeld and Nicolson. [Perceptual hypotheses theory.]

Hobson, P. (2002). The Cradle of Thought. London: Macmillan. [The development of thought.]

Hubel, D.H. and Wiesel, T.N. (1959). Receptive fields of single neurons in the cat's striate cortex. *Journal of Physiology (London), 148,* 574–591. [Discovery of feature detection cells.]

Jancke, L., Specht, K., Nadim Shah, J. and Hugdahl, K. (2002). Focused attention in a simple dichotic listening task: An fMRI experiment. *Cognitive Brain Research, 16,* 257–266. [A twenty-first century experiment on attention.]

Langham, M., Hole, G., Edwards, J. and O'Neill, C. (2002). An analysis of 'looked but failed to see' accidents involving parked police vehicles. *Ergonomics, 45,* 167–185. [Psychology applied to a real-life problem.]

Piaget, J. (1967). Language and thought from a genetic point of view. In J. Piaget, *Six Psychological Studies.* New York: Random House. [Piaget's view on the place of language in the development of thought.]

Sabey, B. and Staughton, G.C. (1975). Interacting roles of road environment, vehicle and road user, 5th International Conference of the International Association for Accident Traffic Medicine, London, TRRL, Crowthorne, Berkshire. [Early work on this practical situation.]

Shiffrin, R.M. and Schneider, W. (1977). Controlled and automatic human information processing: II. Perceptual learning, automatic attending and a general theory. *Psychological Review, 84,* 127–190. [The circumstances under which we can 'multi-task'.]

Treisman, A.M. (1960). Contextual cues in selective listening. *Quarterly Journal of Experimental Psychology, 12,* 242–248. [Some features are more important than others in the selection process.]

Vygotsky, L.S. (1962). *Thought and Language.* Cambridge, Mass.: MIT Press. (Original Russian edition published in 1934.) [The relationship between thought and language.]

Wallas, G. (1926). *The Art of Thought.* New York: Harcourt Brace Jovanovich. [Four stages of creative thinking.]

12: LEARNING ABOUT YOUR WORLD

Bandura, D.A., Ross, D. and Ross, S.A. (1961). Transmission of aggression through imitation of aggressive models. *Journal of Abnormal and Social Psychology, 63,* 575–582. ['Bobo' doll experiments.]

Block, N. (1991). Evidence against epiphenomenalism. *Behavioral and Brain Science, 14,* 760–762. [Phenomenal and other types of consciousness.]

Breland, K. and Breland, M. (1961). The misbehaviour of organisms. *American Psychologist, 16,* 681–684. [What animals won't learn and why.]

Craik, F.I.M. and Lockhart, R.S. (1972). Levels of processing: A framework for memory research. *Journal of Verbal Learning and Verbal Behaviour, 11,* 671–684.

Garcia, J. and Koelling, R.A. (1966). Relation of cue to consequence in avoidance learning. *Psychonomic Science*, 4, 123–124. [Experiment with rats and saccharine solution, the results of which dismissed several rules of classical conditioning.]

Haier, R.J. (2003). Brain imaging studies of intelligence: Individual differences and neurobiology. In R.J. Sternberg, J. Lautrey and T.I. Lubart (eds.), *Models of Intelligence: International perspectives*. Washington D.C.: American Psychological Association. [Research on the relationship between brain activity and intelligence.]

Horn, J.L. and Cattell, R.B. (1967). Age differences in fluid and crystallized intelligence. *Acta Psychologica*, 26, 107–129. [Intelligence that affects or is affected by learning.]

Macfarlane, D.A. (1930). The role of kinesthesis in maze learning. *University of California Publications in Psychology*, 4, 277–305. [Rats can run a maze previously learnt by swimming.]

Neisser, U., Boodoo, G., Bouchard, T.J., Jr., Boykin, A.W., Brody, N., Ceci, S.J., Halpern, D.F., Loehlin, J.C., Perloff, R., Sternberg, R.J. and Urbina, S. (1996). Intelligence: Knowns and unknowns. *American Psychologist*, 51, 77–101. [Report of the task force report on intelligence.]

O'Donohue, W. and Ferguson, K.E. (2001). *The Psychology of B. F. Skinner*. Thousand Oaks, Calif., US: Sage Publications. [Skinner's life and work.]

Pavlov, I.P. (1927). *Conditioned Reflexes*. London: Oxford University Press. [Original English language version of classical conditioning experiments.]

Skinner, B.F. (1974). *About Behaviourism*. London: Jonathan Cape. [A review by the famous American behavourist.]

Thorndike, E.L. (1911). *Animal Intelligence*. New York: Macmillan. [Cats and puzzle boxes.]

Tolman, E.C., Ritchie, B.F. and Kalish, D. (1946). Studies in spatial learning: II. Place learning versus response learning. *Journal of Experimental Psychology*, 36, 221–229. [Cognitive maps.]

Watson, J.B. and Rayner, R. (1920). Conditioned emotional reactions. *Journal of Experimental Psychology*, 3, 1–14. [Classical conditioning of the baby Albert.]

13: YOU AND OTHER ANIMALS

Beninger, R.J., Kendall, S.B. and Vanderwoof, C.H. (1974). The ability of rats to discriminate their own behaviour. *Canadian Journal of Psychology*, 28, 79–91. [Self-awareness in rats.]

Berryman, J.C., Howells, K. and Lloyd-Evans, M. (1985). Pet owner attitudes to pets and people: A psychological study. *Veterinary Record*, 117, 659–661. [Relationships between people and pets.]

Bitterman, M.E. (1965). The evolution of intelligence. *Scientific American*. London: W.H. Freeman. [Intelligence compared in a variety of animals.]

Boysen, S.T., Berntson, G.G., Shreyer, T.A. and Hannan, M.B. (1995). Indicating acts during counting by a chimpanzee (Pan troglodytes). *Journal of Comparative Psychology*, 109(1), 47–51. [Chimpanzee counting.]

Crocker, J. (1985). Respect of feathered friends. *New Scientist*, 1477, 47–50. [Tool use in crows and the 'talking' parrot are discussed.]

Darwin, C. (1871). *The Descent of Man and Selection in Relation to Sex*. John Murray: London. [Discusses human evolution.]

Davis, H. and Memmott, J. (1982). Counting behaviour in animals: A critical evaluation. *Psychological Bulletin*, 92(3), 547–571. [Counting behaviour; quotation on page 547.]

Dawkins, M.S. (1980). *Animal Suffering: The science of animal welfare.* London: Chapman and Hall. [Research on hens' preferences.]

Eaton, G.C. (1976). Social order of Japanese macaques. *Scientific American, 235(4),* 96–106. [Cultural transmission in macaques.]

Gallup, G.G., Jr. (1979). Self-awareness in primates. *American Scientist, 67,* 417–421. [Use of mirrors by chimpanzees.]

Griffin, D.R. (1976). *A Question of Animal Awareness.* New York: Rockefeller University Press. [Discussion of mental experiences.]

Herman, L.M. (2002). Exploring the world of the bottlenosed dolphin. In M. Bekoff, C. Allen and G.M. Burghardt (eds.), *The Cognitive Animal.* London: MIT Press. [Cognition in dolphins.]

Holland, V.D. and Delius, J.D. (1983). Rotational invariance in visual pattern recognition by pigeons and humans. *Science, 218,* 804–806. [Pigeons and pattern recognition.]

McFarland, D. (1993). *Animal Behaviour: Ethology and evolution.* London: Pitman. [Wide-ranging coverage; McFarland quotation on page 506.]

Reiss, D. and Marino, L. (2001). Mirror self-recognition in the bottlenose dolphin: A case of cognitive convergence. Proceedings of the National Academy of Sciences USA, *98,* 5937–5942.

Riddell, W.I. (1979). Cerebral indices and behavioural differences. In M.E. Hahn, C. Jensen and B.C. Dudek (eds.), *Development and Evolution of Brain Size: Behavioural Implications.* London: Academic. [An index of brain development.]

Rohles, F.H. and Devine, J.V. (1966). Chimpanzee performance on a problem involving the concept of middleness. *Animal Behaviour, 14,* 159–162. [Chimpanzees and the concept of middleness.]

Ryder, R.D. (1975). *Victims of Science.* London: Davis-Poynter. [Speciesism and animal experimentation considered.]

Shelldrake, R. (1999). *Dogs who Know their Owners Are Coming Home and Other Unexplained Powers of Animals.* Hutchinson: London. [Telepathy in dogs.]

Snowden, C.T. (2001). From primate communication to human language. In F.B.M. de Waal (ed.), *Tree of Origin: What Primate Behavior can Tell Us about Human Social Evolution.* London: Harvard University Press. [Hockett and language in non-human animals.]

14: WHAT PSYCHOLOGISTS CAN DO – FOR YOU?

British Psychological Society (2004). *Careers in Psychology.* Leicester: British Psychological Society. [Free leaflet.]

Index

Note: page numbers in italics denote figures, boxes or tables

abilities   58–9, 60, 214
ability tests   58–9, 214
abnormality   155
academic subject preferences   59–60
accidents, looked but failed to see   162, 166
acoustic code   166–7, 169, 184, 214
action potentials   104, 214
adaptation, species   192, 193–4
addiction   66, 67
adherence to medication   123–4, 125
adolescence   56, 140–1
adrenal gland   214
adrenaline   14, 214
Adult Attachment Interview   83, 214
adults   83; attachment   83–4; life transitions   141–3; love   83–8
age factors   187, 214
aggregation   214
aggression: anger   88–96; attribution theory   92; behaviour   88–9, 91; cognitive   89; gender differences   56; indirect   77; instrumental   89–90; intent   93; personality disorder   153; posture/gesture   22; violence   74–5, 90
agoraphobia   146, 148–9, 150, 214
Ainsworth, Mary   82
alcohol use   34, 105
Allen, Mike   118

ambivalence   22
American Psychiatric Association   153; see also DSM (Diagnostic and Statistical Manual)
American Psychological Association   75, 185, 187
American Sign Language   195
amphetamine   106
amygdala   100, 214
androgens   49–51, 214
androgyny   214
anger   80, 90–1; aggression   88–96; analysing your own   93; arousal   88; attribution theory   92; cognitive appraisal   95; contrary reactions   95; expression   14–15, 18, 19; features of   92–5; frustration   91; high trait   90, 94; interpersonal events   92; physical symptoms   95; preventative measures   96; trigger for   91–2; violence   90
Anger Diaries   92, 93
anger management   95–6, 208
Anger Management film   96
animal behaviour research   190; ethics   102, 198, 200
animals: counting   191; and humans   191, 198–201; language   194, 195; therapeutic use   200
anorexia nervosa   72

anthropomorphism 197–8
antismoking campaign 118
antisocial act experiments 77
antisocial personality disorder 154
anxiety 145–6; arousal 80;
cognitive-anxiety loop 149; four
systems 147; generalized 146,
217; genetics 148; separation
81, 82; social 150–1; sources of
147–9; time limited 155; treatment
149–50
apes 195
aphrodisiacs 10
applied psychology 114, 145, 157–8,
214
appraisal, cognitive 93, 95
Arabs 14, 17, 20, 24–5
Archer, John 56
Argyle, Michael 14, 28
arm pronation 24
Aron, Arthur 80
Aronson, Elliot 64
arousal: anger 88; anxiety 80;
cortico-reticular loop 33–4; sexual
25
ascending reticular activation system
34, 110–11, 214, 221
Asch, Solomon 70–1
assertiveness training 74
assistance animals 200
association cortex 99, 104, 214
Association for the Study of Obesity
116
associations: learning 175; love 80;
stimulus–response 177–8
Åström, Kristina 60
attachment behaviour 81–4, 214
attachment tests 214
attention 164–6
attitudes 64, 65, 116–17, 169
attribution theory 43–5, 80, 92, 215
audience effects 70, 215
auditory cortex 98, 165
authoritarian personality 215
authority/obedience 73–4
autism 171–2
autonomic nervous system 14, 88,
215
Averill, James 92, 95

aversion 91
avoidant personality disorder 154
awareness 196–8; see also
self-awareness
axillary secretions 8–9, 24, 25
axon 104, 105, 215

babbling 131, 133
babies: babbling 131, 133;
communication 131–2, 133, 135;
development 128–32; Japanese
25; love 80, 81–3; mirrors 198;
perception 128–31; sexually
differentiated treatment 55; smell
24; smiles 81–2; social development
131–2; touch 25; visual cliff
130–1
Badcock, Richard 203
Bandura, Albert 182–3
Banyard, Philip 114
Baron-Cohen, Simon 59
bats 196
BBC Prison Experiment 75
Beattie, Geoff 203
Beckham, David 63, 72
Beckham, Victoria 72
bees 194, 195–6
behaviour 2; bias 44; biological
perspective 30, 49; changes
116–17; crowds 77; dynamics 33;
gaze 20; health 115, 116–17;
hormones 49–51; influences
69–70; introspection 4;
observations 7, 47; personality
30, 56–8; predictions 180–2;
problems/solutions 30–1; regression
140; reinforcement 30; shaping
178, 180, 222; taxonomy 33
behaviour, types of: aggressive 88–9,
91; attachment 81–4, 214;
inhibited 69; loving 85; operant
219; problematic 151; respondent
221; sex-appropriate 51, 55, 56,
57–8; sexual 50–1; social 28, 34,
92, 128; socially learned 28, 89–90
behaviour genetics 186, 187, 215
behaviour modification 178, 180, 215
Behaviourism 175, 176–8, 215
beliefs 116–17; false 133, 134

Berkowitz, Leonard 91
Berryman, Julia 201
bias 44, 47, 220
bicycle accident example 92–3
bicycle-riding example 101
Big Brother TV programme 203
biological differences *60*
biological factors 10, 51–4, *60*
biological perspective 30, 49
bipolar constructs 39
Birchwood, Max 152
Bitterman, Morton *193*
blame 43–4, 119
blind area, visual cortex 106
blindness 5–6, 11–12, 160, 173
blindsight 106, 185, 215
Block, Jack 37
Bluesky, Annabella *207*
Bobo doll experiment 182–3
Bocking, Nat *136*
bodily changes: *see* physiology
body image 72, *73*
body language 11; improvements
 27–8; learned/innate 14; lying
 26; odours 24–5
Boon, Julian 203
borderline personality disorder *154*
bottom up theory 163, 215
Bowers, Kenneth 37
Bowlby, John 83
Boysen, Sarah 191
brain: cerebral hemispheres 98,
 107–8, 215; consciousness 99,
 109–11; emotion 109; functional
 specialization 108; lateralization
 59; memory 101; mind 109–10;
 oxygen consumption 104;
 post-mortem examination 102;
 structure 98–101; white/grey
 matter 98, 218, 223
brain damage: children 108–9; effects
 102; larger scale 106–7; studies of
 204; treatment 112
brain development index 192–3
brain scans 102, *103*, 104, 167, 187
brain surgery 102
brain waves 111
brainstem 110–11, 215
Braly, Kenneth 66

breast feeding 3
breath contact 24–5
Breland, Keller 182
Breland, Margaret 182
Brickner, Mary 70
British people 14
British Psychological Society 203
Broadbent, Donald *165*
Broca's area 108, 215
Brody, Leslie 17
Brooks-Gunn, Jeanne 132
Brown, Roger 66
bulimia 72
Bush, George W. 24
business organizations 212–13
bystander apathy 69–70

cancers 116, 118, 119
cardiovascular disease 90
career sexism 60–1
caregivers 127
Carlson, N. 112
Carmichael, L. *171*
Carter, Sarah *60*
castration fears 51, 54
categorical approach 156, 157
catharsis 3, 215
Cattell, Raymond 35
causality 44–5, 215
cells: central nervous system 104–5,
 106; communication 105–6
central nervous system 98, 104–5,
 106, 215
cerebellum 101, 215
cerebral cortex 59, 98–9, 100, 111,
 215
cerebral hemispheres 98, 107–9,
 215
cerebrospinal fluid 98, 215
Chadwick, Paul 152
chaffinches 194–5
Chapple, Alison 119
charity relief appeals 77–8
Cherney, Leora 106
childcare 61, 114
children: brain damage 108–9;
 caregivers 127; development 127;
 female role-models 55–6; orphans
 83, *84*

chimpanzees: American Sign Language 195; middleness 191; mirror test 197; termite fishing 183; tool-use 193–4

Chinese people 80

Christianity 199

chromosomes 49, 215

cissies 56

Clark, D.M. *156*

classical conditioning: *see* conditioning, classical

clinical psychology 114, 204–6; offenders *209–10*; sexual problem case studies *205–6*; treatment methods 4, 145

Clore, Gerald 93–4

coaction effects 70

cocaine 105, 106

codes, acoustic 166–7

Coffman, Thomas 66

cognition 215; aggression 88–9; emotion 80; process 216; situated 128; social 137–40; *see also* social cognition models

cognitive behavioural therapies 47, 96, 150–1, 152, *156*, 215

cognitive consistency theories 65

cognitive developmental theory 54

cognitive dissonance theories 65, 215

cognitive map 180, *181*, 215

cognitive perspectives, personality 38

cognitive psychology *166, 172*, 204

cognitive-anxiety loop 149

Colapinto, John 53

Coleman, John 140

Collett, Peter 24, 203

Collis, Glyn 131

Colman, A.M. 11, 12

colours 195–6

commissures 108, 216

commitment 85, 87, 88

communication: babies 131–2, 133, 135; cells 105–6; displacement 194; doctor–patient 120, 122, 123, 125; gender differences 58; health information 118; honeybees 194, 195–6; intersubjectivity 131–2, 218; non-verbal 14; signals 22–4; smell 24–5; teaching *142*;

technology 78; *see also* body language; conversation

comparative psychology 190, *193*, 204

computer use 59

concordance, degree of *186*

concrete operational stage 137

conditioning 30; appetitive 34; aversive 34; classical 175, *176, 177*, 180, 215; instrumental 178, 218; learning 175, *176*; operant 179, 180, 219; phobias 147, 148

cones: *see* rods and cones

conformity 70–3, 74

Confucius 17

conscientiousness *36*

consciousness 216; awareness 196–8; brain 99, 110–12; experience 185; Freud 110, 170; learning 183–5; phenomenological 185, 220; zombies *109*

conservation 137, 138, 216

constructive alternativism 38, 216

context 15–16, 36–7, 169

control, perceived 117

control groups 8, *9*, 216

conversation 17–18, 135, 163–4; *see also* communication

coping techniques 152

copulation 50–1

corpus callosum 59

correlational study 216

cortex 216; *see also* cerebral cortex

cortico-reticular loop 33–4

counselling psychology 114, 145, 206

counting 191

Cox, Tracey 203

Coyne, Sarah 77

Cracker 203

Craik, Fergus 184

creativity 172–3

criminality 34, 66, *67*, 90

cross-sectional approach 216

crowds 77

crows 193

cultural differences: conformity 71–2; conversation 17–18; display rules 15–16; eye contact 17–18; gender 60; social loafing 70; Strange

Situation   82; touch   14, 25; violence   90
Cumberbach, Guy   75
Cutler, Winnifred   8–9

Dalgleish, Mary   124–5
Damasio, Antonio   110
Dann, Sophie   *84*
Darwin, Charles   15, 58
data driven theory   163
Davis, Hank   191
Dawkins, Marion   199
Day, A.   96
deafness   160, 173
deceit   26–7
decision making   70
delusions   151, 216
dendrites   104, 216
Department of Health   115
dependent personality disorder   *154,* 156
depression   44–5, 155
deprivation, parental   *84*
depth perception   *131*
Dershowitz, Alan   60
desensitization effect   75, 149–50, 216
development: babies   128–32; children 127; ecological approach   127, 216; perceptual   128–31; physical 55–6; Piagetian stages   137, 171, 222; psychological   140–1; social 131–2
developmental psychology   127–8, 204
Devine, James   191
Di Matteo, Robin   123
Diagnostic and Statistical Manual: see DSM (*Diagnostic and Statistical Manual*)
Diana, Princess   72, *73*
diffusion   69
dimensional approach   156
DiNicola, Dante   123
discourse analysis   *172*
discrimination   60–1, 175, 216
disease   90, 119
disgust   14, *19*, 80
displacement, communication   194
display rules   15–17
distinctiveness information   43–4
DNA   *188*

doctors   120, 122, 123, 125
Doherty-Sneddon, Gwyneth   20
dolphins   195, 197, 198
dominance   20, 21, 24, 32
Dominican Republic   51
Donaldson, Margaret   138
Donnerstein, Edward   75
dopamine   106, 112, 216
double dissociation   *108,* 216
double-blind studies   9
dreams   3, 4–5, 11
drives   80
drop-in centre example   64
drugs, recreational   105
DSM (*Diagnostic and Statistical Manual*) 153, 154, 155, 156, 216
dual tasking   164–5
Dutton, Donald   80
dyslexia   173, 207–8

eating disorders   72
echolocate   196, 216
ecological approach, development   127, 216
educational psychology   114, 204, 207–8, *208*
EEG (electroencephalography)   111, 217
Effect, Law of   178
efficacy   216
egocentrism   137, 217
Eibl-Eiberfeldt, Iranaus   25
Einstein, Albert   6
Ekman, Paul   15, 18, *19*, 26, 80
elderly people   114, 125
Electra complex   54, 217
electricity, sensing   196
electroencephalography (EEG)   111, 217
elephants   193
El-Murad, Jaafar   173
embarrassment   122
Emerson, Peggy   83
emotion: brain   109; Chinese   80; cognition   80; Ekman   80; facial expression   14–15; feelings   109; gender   15–16; gestures   21–4; hippocampus   100–1; perception 132–3; physiological changes   7, 80,

emotion: brain (*cont'd*) 109; postures 21–4; state dependent learning 169

emotional leakage 21–2, *23*, 217

empathy *103*, 197–8

empty nest syndrome 143

encoding 166, 169, 217

endocrine system 8–9

environment 33, 54, 148, 187, 197

Epictetus 38

epilepsy 108

ergonomics 208, 211

Erikson, Erik 83–4, 140

Eros *85*, 87–8

errors, memory 166–7

Eskimo culture 24

ethical factors 8, 74, 102, 112, 198, 200

ethologist 217

evolution *191*, 193

examination results 59–60

excitation, residual 92

exercise 116

Exercise on Prescription 116

exercise psychology 211, *212*

experiences: consciousness 185; early life 3, 54; learning 181–2, 183; mental 190; self-reporting 7; sight 5–6, 11–12

experimental psychology *166*, *172*, 204

experiments: control 217; group 217; natural *53*, 83, *84*; participants 8–9; power structure 73–4; touch *26*; validity *166*

Expert Patients Programme 125

expressions: *see* eyes, expressions; facial expression

extinction, stimulus-response 176–7, 217

Extraversion 32, 33–4, 35, *36*, 217

eye contact 17–18, 20

eyes: dilation of pupils 19–20; expressions 18–19; pupil size 19–20; retina *161*, *162*; rods and cones 104, 160–1, 216, 221; vision 160–1

Eysenck, Hans 32, 33, 34

Eysenck Addiction Scale 66, *67*

Eysenck Criminality Scale 66, *67*

face-saving 65

face-to-face contact 17

facial expression 217; emotions 14–15; innate 16–17; micro 16, 27; universality 15

facial feedback hypothesis 17

factor analysis 32, 35, 217

faking-good/-bad 47

false memory syndrome 217

family environment 148

family interventions 152, 217

fathers 54

fatty acid levels 71

fear 14, *19*; Chinese 80; health information 118; phobias 146; social modelling 147–8; treatment 149–50; victim 75

fear appeals 118

feature detection cells 161, 163

feelings 2, 80, 109; *see also* emotions

femininity 49, 56

Ferguson, Kyle 178–9

Feshbach, Seymour 118

Festinger, Leon 64–5

fissures 98, 100, 217

flight or fight reaction 14, *22*

fMRI (functional magnetic resonance imaging) 102, *103*, 167, 217

focal theory 140, 217

foetal cells 112

football hooliganism study 77

forensic psychology 114, 145, 203, 209

free association 3, 217

French, Chris 203

Freud, Anna *84*

Freud, Sigmund 3, 54, 83, 110, 170

Friesen, Wallace 15, 18, *19*, 26

Frith, U. *134*

frontal lobe 98, *99*, 108, 218

frustration-aggression theory 91

functional magnetic resonance imaging: *see* fMRI

functional specialization 108

Gallup, Gordon   197
Garcia, John   181
gaze   20, 21, 219
gaze aversion   20, 26
gender differences   56–9; abilities
   58–9, 60; aggression   56;
   communication   58; cultural
   differences   60; display rules
   16–17; doctors   120; emotional
   display   15–16; gaze   21;
   intelligence   58–9; lifespan
   transitions   142–3; media   57;
   power   58; problem-solving   58;
   relationships   57; school   59–61;
   stereotypes   49, 55, 56, 59; verbal
   abilities   58; workplace   60, 61
gender identity   217; biology   51–4;
   Freud   54; hormones   52; learned
   52, 53; sex   51–5; social learning
   theory   55; twin boy experiment
   53
gender roles   61, 142–3
General Practice Assessment
   Questionnaire   124
generalization   175, 217
genes   188, 217
genetic disorders   51
genetics   217; anxiety   148; individual
   differences   33; tool-use   193–4;
   traits   186, 188
genomics   188
Genovese, Kitty   69
Gestalt psychology   161–2, 217
gestures   21–4, 131
Gibson, Eleanor   129, 130–1
glia   104, 217
gonads   49
gorillas   198
gossiping example   64
Gray, John   57–8
greetings   14
Gregory, Richard   162–3
grey matter   98, 218
Griffin, Donald   190, 192
group polarization phenomenon   70
group pressures   71–2
group work   139–40
growth spurt   56

guide dogs   200
gyri   98, 218

habit reversal task   193
Haier, Richard   187
Hall, Edward   14, 17, 24
Halliwell, Geri   72
hallucinations   151, 152, 218
Hampson, Joan   52
Hampson, John   52, 53
happiness   14, 19, 80
Harai, Philippe   125
Hargreaves, David   142
Harris, Paul   132
Hatfield, E.   86
head injuries   102
health   6, 12, 114, 118
health behaviour   116–17
Health Belief Model   117, 124
health campaigns   115, 118
health psychology   114, 145, 206–7
Health Trusts, UK   125
healthcare   120, 122
hearing dogs   200
Heidenreich, T.   156
Heim, Alice   58
Henley, Nancy   21, 25
Henry VIII   49
hens   183, 199
heredity/intelligence   187; see also
   genetics
hermaphrodite   52, 218
Hess, Eckhard   19–20
Hewitt, Patricia   60–1
hippocampus   100–1, 218
histrionic personality disorder   154
HIV/AIDS   114, 205–6
Hobson, P.   173
Hochbaum, Godfrey   117
Hockett, Charles   194
Hogan, H.P.   171
home environment   187; see also family
   environment
homicide   90
honeybees   194, 195–6
Hopi Indians   170
hormones   14, 49–51, 52, 100
housework   61

Howells, Kevin   96, 201
Hubel, David   161
Hughes, Martin   135
human genome   *188*
human problems   157–8
human resource management   212
human sense   137–8
humans and animals   *191*, 198–201
humour/racism   68
hunger   80
Hyde, Janet   58
hypothalamus   100, 218

iconic memory   218
identification   54, 55, 218
identities   140–1, 143, 218; *see also*
   gender identity
ignorance, pluralistic   69, 220
illness: chronic   123, 215; prevention
   116–19; smoking-related   115, 116,
   118; susceptibility   117; time-limited
   155
illusion, visual   162
imitation   55, 183, 194; *see also*
   mimicry
Imperato-McGinley, Julianne   51
imprinting   81, 218
Impulse Control   33
industrial psychology   208, 210
infants: *see* babies
information processing   164
information retrieval   166–7
information storage   168
Inhelder, Barbel   137
inhibition   34
insight   218
instincts   3, 80
intelligence   218; fluid/crystallized
   187, 216; gender differences
   58–9; health   6, 12; heredity
   187; learning   185, 187; reasoning
   192; species   193
intention   93, 190, 192
interactionism   37–8, 218
interference, retroactive/proactive
   220, 221
Internet   78, 122, *123*, 127
interpersonal events   92
intersubjectivity   131–2, 218

interthinking   135, 218
interviews   47
intimacy   *85*, 87
intrinsic motive pulse (IMP)   132,
   218
introspection   4
Introversion   32, 33–5, 218
Inuit people   170
IQ   187, 218
Ireland, Northern   69
Islam   199

Jacklin, Carol   56, 58
James, William   109
Jancke, Lutz   *165*
Janis, Irving   118
Japanese people   14, 17, 25
Jebb, Susan   116
Jones-Griffiths, Philip   *16*
Jourard, Marc   25
Judaism   199

Karlins, Marvin   66
Katz, David   66
Kegels, Stephen   117
Kelly, George   38, 39, 43
Kendon, Adam   20
Kent, Gerry   124–5
Kindelan, Kevin   120
knowledge base   132
knowledge/power   116
Koelling, Robert   181
Kohlberg, Lawrence   54
Krout, Maurice   22–4

labelling, diagnostic   157
labelling, memory technique   170–1
Lange, Carl   109
Langham, Martin   *166*
Langley, Sue   120, *121–2*
language   133, 135; animals   194,
   195; discourse analysis   *172*;
   functions   107–8; learned   194–5;
   left-handed people   109; medical
   professionals   120; openness   195;
   thought   *167*, 170–1, 190
Lapps   14
lateral geniculate body   *161*, 218
lateralization of brain   59

Lauterbach, W.   *156*

learning: associations   175;
   conditioning   175, *176*;
   consciousness   183–5; by
   consequences   178–80; co-operative
   138, 139; experiences   181–2, 183;
   intelligence   185, 187; peers   138,
   139–40, 219; punishment   179–80;
   reinforcement   182–3; social context
   135, 138, 182–3; state dependent
   169, 222

Lee, John Alan   *85*, 87

left-handedness   109

Legge, Karen   125

Leslie, Alan   132

levels of processing theory   184, 218

Lewis, Michael   132

Ley, Philip   124, 125

Libet, Benjamin   110

lie detectors   7

lies   26–7

life changes   38, 141–3

lifespan approach   128, 142–3

lifestyle change   115, 119, 123

light patterns   161

limbic system   100, 218

linguistic relativity hypothesis   170,
   218

Lippman, Walter   66

listening: dichotic   *165–6*; reflective
   76

lobes   218

loci, method of   167, 219

Locker, David   119–20

Lockhart, Robert   184

longitudinal approach   141, *142*,
   219

Lorenz, Konrad   81, 83

love: adults   83–8; attachment   81–8;
   babies   80, 81–3, 82–3; colours of
   85, 87–8; parenthood   84; signs of
   84–5; triangular theory   *85*, 87;
   types and styles   80, 85, *86*, 87–8

Loza, Wagdy   *46*

Loza-Fanous, Amel   *46*

Ludus   *85*, 87–8

lung cancer   119

Lynn, David   54–5

Lynn, Marcia   58

macaques   194

Maccoby, Eleanor   56, 58

McFarland, David   195, 196–7

Macfarlane, Donald   180

McGarrigle, James   138

McPherson, Ann   119

magnetic resonance imaging: *see* MRI

Maguire, Eleanor   101

Mania   88

Mann, Samantha   26

Marino, Lori   197

marriage   88

Marshall, Nigel   *142*

masculinity   49, 51, 56

Mathews, Andrew   149

maze learning tests   192

media: gender portrayals   57; health
   information   118; psychology   203;
   violence   74–7, 182–3

medical advice   120, 124–5; *see also*
   healthcare

medical terms   *121–2*

medication: adherence to   123–5, 221;
   elderly   125

Memmott, John   191

memory: brain   101; codes   166–8;
   context   169; declarative   101,
   216; encoding   166, 168; episodic
   167, 217; errors   166–7; false
   217; iconic   218; improvements
   167, 168; labelling   170–1;
   long-term   *107*, 167, 168–9, 219;
   meaning/rhyme   *184*; mechanisms
   166–9; mnemonic devices   183–4;
   processing, levels of   184; retention
   166, 168, 184, 221; retrieval   166,
   168, 221; semantic   167, 221;
   short-term   *107*, 166–7, 168–9,
   222; spreading activation model
   167; stages   166–8; state dependent
   168, 222

Mencken, H.L.   84–5

meninges   98, 219

menstrual cycle   8, 9, 24, 50

mental health problems   105

mental images   191–2

Mercer, Neil   135

meta-analysis   118

middleness concept   191

Milgram, Stanley   73–4, *77*
mimicry   *23; see also* imitation
mind, theory of   132–3, 223
mind/brain   109–10
Minnesota Multiphasic Personality
   Inventory   47
mirrors   132–3, 197, 198
Mischel, Walter   37–8, 54–5
mnemonic devices   183–4, 219
modesty   18
Molloy, Cordelia   *18, 23*
monitoring feedback   20
monotropism   83
mothers   80, 127, 131
motivation   219
motor cortex   98
motor reproduction   219
mounting behaviour   50–1
MRI (magnetic resonance imaging)
   102, *103*, 219
Murstein, Bernard   84–5
music, problem styles   66–7
multiethnic classes   140

narcissistic personality disorder
   154
National Crime and Operations Faculty
   210
national differences   14
National Health Service   115
natural experiments   *53*, 83, *84*
nature/nurture debate   52, 185
neglect, visual   106, 185, 219
NEO Personality Inventory   47
neural activity   110
neurons   104, 105, 219
Neuroticism/Stability   33
neurotransmitters   104–5, 219
Nicholson, Jack   96
Nietzsche, Friedrich   6
non-adherence, rational   123–4
non-conservation   138
non-smokers   116
North, Adrian   66, *67*
Novaco, Raymond   92
nuclei   99, 100
number test, conservation   138
nurses   26, 145–6

obedience experiments   73–4
obesity   116
object permanence   129, 137, 219
observations: behaviour   7, 47;
   imitation   183, 194
obsessive-compulsive personality
   disorder   *154*
occipital lobe   98, *99*, 218
occupational psychology   114, 204,
   211
O'Donohue, William   178–9
odours   8–9, 24–5; *see also* smell
Oedipus complex   54, 219
oestrogens   50, 219
offenders   *46*, 96, *209–10*
Ogden, Jane   115, 123
openness   *36*, 195
opportunity, equality of   61
optic chiasma   219
oral hygiene   118
orphaned children   83, *84*
Ortony, Andrew   94
ovarian cancer   116
ovaries   49, 50, 51, 219

pain   89, *103*
panic disorder   146, 148–9, 150, 219
paranoid personality disorder   *154*,
   155–6
paranormal phenomena   203, 219
parapsychology   196
parasympathetic nervous system   219
parenthood   84, 147–8; *see also*
   fathers; mothers
parietal lobe   98, *99*, 106
Parkinson's disease   112
passion   *85*, 87
patients: and doctors   120, 122, 123,
   125; expert knowledge   122, *123*;
   perceptions   124; split-brain   108;
   support groups   125
patterning, duality of   195
Pavlov, Ivan   175, *176*
peace campaigning example   64–5
peer groups   140
peer learning   138, 139–40, 219
penile erection   11
penis envy   54

perception: attention   164–6;
   awareness   196–8; babies   128–31;
   emotions   132–3; feature detection
   cells   161, 163; organization laws
   161–2; patients   124; sensation
   160–3; single channel theory   164;
   theories   162–3
perceptual defence   219
perceptual hypothesis   162–3, 219
perfumes   25
Perner, Josef   133
personal construct theory   31, 38–42,
   220; repertory grid   39–42
personality: assessment   46–7, 204;
   behaviour   30, 56–8; cognitive
   perspectives   38; consistency
   36–8; dimensions   35–6, 47;
   interactionism   37–8, 218; offenders
   46; situationism   37; traits   31–2,
   155–6
personality development theory   63
personality disorders   150, 152–5;
   labelling   157; prevalence   154,
   155; traits   153–4, 155; types   154
perspective   162, 163
Pervin, Lawrence   36
pet animals   199–201
PET (positron emission tomography)
   167, 220
Peterson, Christopher   44
phallic stage   54
Phillips, Keith   115
phobias   146, 147–50
physiological psychology   109, 204
physiology: emotion   7, 80, 109;
   pressure to conform   71; sensory
   160
Piaget, Jean   54, 128–9; stages of
   development   137, 171, 222
pigeons   191–2
pigs   25, 182
Pitts, Marion   115
pituitary gland   100, 220
placebo   8, 220
plastic   220
playing   131, 136
pleasure   18
polygraph   7

Polynesians   14
Ponzo illusion   162, 163
positive psychology   158, 220
positron emission tomography (PET)
   167, 220
post-mortem   102, 220
postures   21–4
power: experimenter   73–4; gender
   differences   58; knowledge   116;
   social influence   77–8; touch   25;
   tyranny   75
predictions   46, 133, 134, 180–2
pregnancy   50
prejudice   65–6, 67, 68, 220
pre-operational stage   137
presumed central tendency   220
pretence   132
preventive measures: anger   96; health
   115, 116–19, 220; primary   115,
   220; screening   119; secondary
   115, 221; tertiary   115, 223
primacy effect   220
primary auditory cortex   98, 165
primary somatosensory cortex   98
primary visual cortex   98, 106–7, 161
prison psychology   204, 209
prisons   46, 75; see also offenders
proactive interference   220
problem music styles   66–7
problem-solving techniques   58, 96,
   192
processing, levels of   184, 218
progesterone   50, 220
projective tests   220
proteomics   188
provocation   91–2, 94
pseudohermaphrodites   52
psychiatry   4, 145, 157–8
psychoanalysis   3, 4, 54, 220
psychodynamic perspective   30, 220
psychological perspective   151–2
psychology   2–6, 140–1; as career
   203–4; media   203; psychiatry   4,
   145, 157–8; as study of behaviour
   2, 120
psychometric tests   47, 220
psychoses   220
Psychoticism   33

puberty   52, 56
Public Health Service, US   117
punishment   179–80
Purdue University   26
Purves, Ross   142

qualitative research   220
quantitative research   220
questions   135

racism   68
rape   206
rapid eye movement (REM)   11, 111,
   221
Rapson, R.L.   86
rational non-adherence   123–4, 221
rats: cognitive map   180, 181;
   self-awareness   197; sex hormones
   51; Skinner box   179–80; temporal
   contiguity   181–2
reaction times   192
readiness potential   110, 221
reading, teaching of   139–40
reading disability   58
The Real Cracker   203
reasoning   192
reconditioning   177
referees   211
reflex   221
refusals   76
regression   140
rehabilitation of offenders   96
Reimer, Bruce   53
reinforcement   30, 179–80, 182–3,
   221
Reiss, Diana   197
rejection   44–5
relationships   30, 57, 83, 92, 155,
   201, 203
relaxation, deep muscle   149
reliability   221
reoffending risk   46
repeated measures ANOVA   165–6
repertory grid   39–42, 201, 221
representations, internal   129
reproduction, female   8–9
responses: conditional   175, 176;
   elicited/emitted   180; involuntary

14; unconditional   175, 176, 223;
   see also stimulus–response
responsibility, diffusion of   69, 216
retention, memory   166, 169, 184,
   221
reticular activation system: see
   ascending reticular activation system
retina   161, 162
retirement   142–3
retrieval, memory   166, 169, 221
retroactive interference   221
rewards   178–9
Richards, Helen   119
Riddell, William   192–3
Riedl, Martin   138
risks   6, 116, 118
risky shift   12, 70
rodents: see rats
rods and cones   160–1, 216, 221
rods and cones of eye   104, 160–1
Rohles, Fredrick   191
role conflict   63, 140, 221
role discontinuities   140
role incongruence   140
role models   55–6, 63
role play   27–8, 63, 76, 96
Rorschach Inkblot Test   47
Rosenstock, Irwin   117
Roter, Debra   120
Russell, Michael   24
Rutter, Michael   58
Ryder, Richard   199

Sabey, Barbara   162
saccharine flavouring experiment
   181–2
sadness   14, 19, 80
Sally-Anne task   134
salmon   196
Santa Domingo community   51, 52, 53
Sapir, Edward   170
satiety centre   102
Saving Lives: Our Healthier Nation (DoH)
   115
scaffolding   139, 221
scanning of brain   102, 103, 104, 167,
   187
Schachter, Stanley   109

Schaffer, Rudolph   81, 83, 131
schedules of reinforcement   221
schema, negative   68, 221
schizoid personality disorder   *154*
schizophrenia   151–2, 221
schizotypal personality disorder   *154*
school environment   59–61
Scientific Committee on Tobacco and
    Health   116
screening   115, 119
sea otters   193
*Securing Good Health for the Whole
    Population* (Wanless)   115
self-anaesthetization   95
Self-Appraisal Questionnaire   *46*
self-awareness   31, 132–3, 196–7, *200*
self-blame   119
self-concepts   141, 221
self-esteem   44
self-harm   155
Seligman, Martin   44, 45, 148, 158
semantic   167, 221
Senior Investigation Officer   *209–10*
sensation   160–3, 195–6
sensitive period, attachment   81–2
sensitivity   34–5, 195–6, 197
sensori-motor stage   137
sensory cortex   104
sensory receptor cells   104, 163
sensory threshold   221
separation, baby/mother   81, 82
serotonergic synapses   105
serotonin   105
service animals   200–1
sex: assigned   52, 53; gender identity
    10, 51–5; hormones   49–51
sex differences   10, 49, 55–6, 59
sexism   60–1
sex-typing   51
sexual attraction   84
sexual offences   90
sexual problem case studies   *205–6*
shaping of behaviour   178, 180, 222
shaping-up   222
Sheldrake, Rupert   *21*, 196
Sheridan, Lorraine   66, *67*
shopping lists example   183
side effects   123

sight experience   5–6, 11–12
signals, gestural   22–4
silk moths   196
Singer, Jerome   109
single channel theory   164, 222
situationism   36–7
size constancy   162, 222
Skinner, Burrhus F.   178
Skinner box   178–80
sleep   111–12; REM   112, 221
smell   24–5, 196; *see also* odour
smiles   14, 16–17, 81–2
Smith, Stacey   75
smoking-related illness   115, 116, 118
Snowden, Charles   194
social behaviour   28, 34, 92, 128
social categorization   68–9
social cognition models   116–17, 128,
    222
social comparison   64–5, 222
social context, learning   135, 138,
    182–3
social co-operation   139, 141, 222
social facilitation   70, 222
social influences   33, 70, 77–8, 131–2,
    147–8
social learning theory   54–5, 69
social loafing   69–70
social phobia   *156*
social psychology   64, 204
social roles   63, *75*
social skills   27–8
socialization   222
socio-cultural approach   128, 222
soma   104, 222
somatosensory cortex   98
sorrow   80
spatial abilities   58, 59
species   192, 193–4
speciesism   198, 199, 222
speech patterns   26
speech production   58, 108
Sperry, Roger   108
Spielberger, Charles   90
spinal cord   98
split-brain patients   108
split-span procedure   *165–6*
sport psychology   211, *212*

spreading activation model   167, 222

S-R: *see* stimulus–response

SRRIs (specific serotonin re-uptake inhibitors)   105

Stability   33, *36*

Stanford Prison Experiment   *75*

Stangier, U.   *156*

stared-at sensation   *21*

stem cells   112

stereotypes   222; consistency   37; femininity/masculinity   49, 56; gender   55, 59; HIV/AIDS   114; prejudice   65–6; racial   66, 140; sex difference   49, 55

Sternberg, Robert   *85*, 87

stigma   157

stimulation   34–5

stimulus-response   222; associations 177–8; Behaviourism   175, 176–8; classical conditioning   175; discrimination   175; temporal contiguity principle   181–2

Stoner, James   70

Storge   *85*, 87–8

story linkage   167, 222

Strange Situation procedure   82, 222

stress   148, 211

stress management   *206*

stroke patients   59, 102, 108

submissiveness   32, 39

subordination   20, 21

substance abuse   155

substantia nigra   112

succession rules   61

suffering   198

sulci   98, 222

Summers, Larry   60

supermarkets   212

support groups   125

surprise   14, 18, *19*, 80

sweat, male   8–9, 24, 25

symbolism   129, 222

sympathetic nervous system   14, 222

synapse   105, 222

synaptic gap   *106*

synaptic transmission   105, 223

synchronization   131

Tarrier, Nicholas   152

taxi drivers example   101

Taylor, Shelley   120

Teacher Identities in Music Education (TIME) project   141, *142*

teaching   *142*

team coaches   211

technology   78

telepathy   196

television violence   74, *77*

temperamental dimensions   35–6

temporal contiguity principle   175, 181–2, 223

temporal lobe   98, *99*, 100, 108, 218

tennis   *212*

Terman, Lewis   12

termite fishing   183

testes   49

testosterone   49–51, 59

thalamus   99, 111, 223

Thematic Apperception Test   47

thinking   169–72; convergent   216; creativity   172–3; divergent   216; social behaviour   128; *see also* thought

thinness conformity   72, *73*

Thorndike, Edward   178, 179

thought: and behaviour   2, 7, 169–72; disorder   151; language   *167*, 170–1, 190; *see also* thinking

thought experiment   *106, 107*

tidiness trait   36–7

time concepts   170

TIME project   141, *142*

Tizard, Barbara   135

Tolman, Edward   180, *181*

tomboys   56

tool-use   193–4

tooth decay talks   118

top down theory   163, 223

TopFoto   *130*

Topping, Keith   140

touch   14, 25–6

touch experiment   *26*

Toynbee, Polly   120

traits   155–6, 157; anger   90, *94*; environmental factors   *186*; genetics *186, 188*; personality   31–2, 155–6;

personality disorders 153–4, 155; situationism 36–7; temperamental dimensions 35–6; testing for 32

transparencies 223

transsexualism 53–4, 223

Trehub, Sandra 132

Treisman, Anne 164

Trevarthen, Colwyn 131–2

tumours 102

Turner's syndrome 49

turn-taking 131

twins studies 53, 186, 187

unconscious mind 3, 30

underarm secretion: see axillary secretions

uterus 50

vaginismus 205

validity 166, 223

variables 9; dependent 9, 165, 216; experimental 165; independent 9, 165, 218; moderator 219

ventricles 98, 223

verbal abilities 58

victims 75

vigilance 34

violence: aggression 74–5, 90; anger 90; cultural differences 90; desensitization effect 75; media 74–7, 182–3; television 74, 77

vision 160–1; see also neglect, visual; sight experiences

visual cliff device 129, 130–1

visual cortex 98, 106, 107

visual field 108

visual imagery 173

visual perception experiment 70–1

Vrij, Aldert 26, 27

Vygotsky, Lev 139, 171

Walk, Richard 129, 130–1

Wallas, Graham 173

Walter, A.A. 171

Walters, Gary 66

Wanless, Derek 115

Warmth 36

Watson, John B. 176–7

weight loss 117

weight/size relationship 5, 11

Weisel, Torsten 161

Weiskrantz, Larry 106, 107

Welch, Graham 142

Wells, Adrian 151

Wernicke's area 108, 223

West, Douglas 173

white matter 98, 223

Whorf, Benjamin Lee 170

Williams, Robbie 63

Wimmer, Hans 133

within participants/repeated measures experiments 165, 223

Witte, Kim 118

Wolpe, Joseph 27–8, 149

womb 50

woodpecker finches 193–4

workplace gender differences 60, 61

youth unemployment 141

Zajonc, Robert 70

Zhang, M. 116

Ziebland, Sue 119

Zimbardo, Philip 75

zombies 109